Charles Jennings was born in London and was educated there and at Oxford University. He is married with two children, and lives in London where he works as a writer and journalist. His new book, *People Like Us*, will be published in 1997.

'A perfect dilettante tourist for our times ... a very funny creation'
Laurie Taylor, *The Times*

'A comic tour de force'

Independent

'Scabrously funny ... very readable, fast moving and full of delightful vignettes. So much travel-writing has a veneer of sentimentality that it is exhilarating to find something more astringent'
Daily Telegraph

'Sharply funny, well-researched ... it rings uncomfortably true'
The Times

'Made me laugh out loud ... for that, almost anything can be forgiven'

Spectator

'Well written, rigorously researched and scrupulously honest, *Up North* is that rarity, a travel book that succeeds on local turf'
Scotland on Sunday

'A Rib-tickling, fall-off-your-stool laughing, hilarious, can't-put-down voyage of discovery that could easily cause the North-South divide to be consolidated by the construction of our own Berlin Wall ... wickedly funny'
Huddersfield Daily Examiner

'Disgusting'

Cllr Alec Bovill, Mayor of Grimsby

UP NORTH

Charles Jennings

An *Abacus* Book

First published in Great Britain by Little, Brown 1995
This edition published by Abacus 1995
Reprinted 1995, 1996 (twice), 1997

A CIP catalogue record for this book
is available from the British Library.

ISBN 0 349 10685 1

Typeset by Hewer Text Composition Services, Edinburgh
Printed in England by Clays Ltd, St Ives plc

Abacus
A Division of
Little, Brown and Company (UK)
Brettenham House
Lancaster Place
London WC2E 7EN

Acknowledgements

I would like to thank the following people and institutions for their help in writing this book: Chris Hirst, Ivan Hill, Andrew Morrall, Paul Keers, the library service of the London Borough of Richmond Upon Thames, Sarah Menguç, Richard Beswick; and my wife and my two sons, who cheered me on.

ONE

I t all started when I went to Birmingham, walked and drove around for hours and only felt justified once I'd left the nice parts and found a deeply depressing restaurant just off the Bull Ring. Here, a man at the next table spent five minutes hawking into a handkerchief before sitting back, candidly examining the contents and announcing, 'That's got rid of *that* one.'

The decor at this place had last been attended to in the early 1970s: melamine dado, begrimed ultramarine wallpaper, teak-finish wood-effects. There was a four-ale bar at one end of the room, run by a madwoman in flyaway glasses whose pleasure was to tell you that you couldn't have anything. The handle came off the tap when she was pulling my pint. She squinted at me with clear satisfaction and said, 'You'll have to have something else, now. That one's off.' A middle-aged man with an extended family scuffling around him like a basketball team made up of mixed Social Security fraudsters then came up and asked for 'A nice packet of cheese and hunion crips [sic], har, har.' She just said no.

Outside the restaurant, the underprivileged of Birmingham milled around the open-air market, haggling over dross – PVC dolls, bruised apples, rolls of unemployable wrapping paper. I struggled to eat a piece of beef which had the texture of boiled suede. It was so tough it bent my knife. The gravy had a good deal of vinegar in it, which helped to break the tissues down, but it did cross my mind that I might have to start fraying at it with my bare hands.

The family of fraudsters sat down in the lounge area and started to fight each other. A girl who ought to have been at school shouted at her child, 'Eddie. You come back here or I'll belt yow. Come 'ere, y'little bastard!'

Her man, a twenty-year-old in a grimy shell suit, leant across to the middle-aged man who hadn't bought any crisps.

'Lend us a fiver, Dave,' he said. 'I can git it back to yow on Thursday. Now sweat, Dave.'

'Fook off,' said the middle-aged man, sipping his pint.

This was what I had travelled a hundred and twenty miles to see. It was here, all around the Bull Ring and Birmingham New Street Station in the city centre's south-eastern corner – a scrapheap of thirty-year-old dreams and ambitions, a soiled and damaged vision of the future. It had taken me hours to find it, trudging blindly around Navigation Street and Stephenson Street, hunting for what I believed Birmingham to be: the graveyard of the 1960s; England's ugliest city. Now I had found it I felt oddly complacent. I had reached the Birmingham which I had dreamed about.

One reason it took me hours to find it is that New Street and the Bull Ring are now so compromising to Birmingham's *amour-propre* that the city has done its best to hide them. There are precious few street signs pointing the way. At the same time New Street Station has actually been buried under a 1990s shopping centre called Pallasades. This is a temple to consumerism which combines the style of an American brothel with the insides of a microwave and expects you, once trapped inside, to spend your way out. The thing about Pallasades which makes it different from all the other shopping arcades in Britain is that every now and then you glimpse a tiny British Rail sign and an arrow pointing into the ground.

These mark the way to the main-line station below, which was rebuilt in the first half of the 1960s – at around the same time as Euston Station in London. The sense of period you get when you follow the arrows out of Pallasades and drop, via an escalator, through a gap in the space–time continuum is overwhelming. You find yourself wearing Terylene slacks and humming 'You've Lost That Loving Feeling' under your breath. You look around at New Street and see a yawning, timeless underground cavern filled with thirty-year-old formica, bare concrete and the pervasive smell of people with indigestion waiting for delayed trains.

I struggled through the New Street concourse, taking a wrong turn out to the cab rank (a black hole filled with understandably dour-looking cabbies and Modern Movement san-serif noticeboards covered in dirt). I then doubled back into the Bull Ring development. This is partly a covered market, partly a windswept open-air marketplace, partly home to the Rotunda, designed and built at the same time as New Street Station and now a defunct symbol of past hopes, like a kind of pyramid. Somehow humbled, I gazed up at the Rotunda's twenty-four *Stingray*-style circular storeys, designed by James A. Roberts and placed boldly at the junction of New Street and High Street.

The whole area has, of course, been deemed a failure and is now up for redevelopment. Indeed, for a long time a question mark has hung over the future of the Rotunda itself, which 1960s fetishists prize almost as much as the E-Type Jag and the pink Pifco hairdryer. The latest news, though, is that it's been made a listed building. So it should be able to continue justifying its existence, both as one of the few memorable landmarks of the city and as something for people like me to come and laugh at in a sentimental, supercilious way. Whether the inhabitants of the building – Lloyd's Bank, Egyptair and the Legal & General – want to stay there, surrounded by graffiti and cement, is another matter. I bought a postcard of the Rotunda and was interested to see that the photographer had managed to include an authentically bold smear of orange-coloured puke some passer-by had left in the foreground.

Wandering back into the covered market, I found a very jaunty butcher holding up slabs of raw flesh, shouting, 'Look at that. What a little beauty! Reminds me of the wife, that does.' There were shops with names like ERIC WUNDLE and WOT-U-WANT, and there were hot pork sandwiches for sale near the shouting butcher. There was also a curious, smelly, determinedly morose atmosphere about the place. It was as if Bull Ring people had all, at some time, turned down the opportunity to sign up the Beatles and were resigned to kicking themselves every day for the rest of their lives.

And outside, round a corner from the flapping open-air market stalls, written on a buttress of the roaring, four-lane Queensway Ring Road under which the market strives for existence, I discovered a bit of forlorn optimism, put up in tall brass letters by the council, thirty years ago: 'Probably in no other age or country was there ever such an astonishing display of human ingenuity as may be found in Birmingham.'

The author was Robert Southey and the date of writing was 1807, well before the City of Birmingham had even been incorporated. Southey, of course, died of softening of the brain.

I don't think I met a northerner until I was nineteen and even then I didn't really believe in him. I was at college with him and he wore a denim stetson hat with a matching denim waistcoat and a pair of ludicrous ten-league cowboy boots. He smoked slim panatella cigars, drank his ale with practised ease and used to say things like, 'Well, that's me done,' or, 'You great daft fairy.' He looked like something from a Sergio Leone western and he came from Tyne and Wear.

What got to me was that, to my suburban London eyes, he looked and sounded ridiculous. But so far as he was concerned, so far as his northern sensibilities were concerned, he was absolutely right on the money. At the time, I used to sport rather a nice dark-blue velvet jacket and did my best to talk like a hybrid of David Bowie and Sir Anthony Blunt: London style, as it were, but with all the angles covered. To be frank, I was trying to impress upon any ingenuous provincial girls I could find the notion that I was a little bit metropolitan, a little bit raffish, a little bit Big Time. And yet here was this caricature out of *The Likely Lads*, a fellow countryman of mine whose manners and customs were so alien to me he might as well have come from Alabama. He was working class, he made his own bread, he sucked the air in between his teeth while pondering a question and he actually once said to me, 'Work? You don't know the meaning of the word.' That was my first real taste of the North. This is how attitudes become fixed.

I am a southerner, a London southerner. I've lived in London almost all my life. I grew up in north London, around Finchley, but that has since proved a bit bleak and windswept, so I now live in the more Mediterranean suburbs of south London. From this vantage point, everywhere from Cambridge southwards is tolerable, being more or less part of Greater London. I find the same values, the same snobberies, the same London-centredness. Things simply don't change that much from Bristol to Dover or from Worcester to Chelmsford. In this half of England I feel safe (not from physical attack, you understand; just safe) because there are south London cockney voices wherever I turn. There are dodgy, wideboy consultants driving Range Rovers. There are restaurants serving little things in piquant sauces and charging fifty quid a head for it. There are public schools and there are commuter belts overrun by desperate self-employed businessmen who made a load in the 1980s and saw it evaporate in the 1990s.

There are also far too many cars, the railways are toilets, there are periodic droughts and there are millions of tourists disgorging themselves from sooty buses in order to squint at Nelson's Column and whatever's left of the Royal Family. Indeed, the tentacles of London stretch so far that for practical purposes, it's unnecessary – even impossible – to leave it. I feel at home wherever I go.

What's more, like all capital city dwellers (especially those living in the suburbs), I am relentlessly condescending and parochial. I have no idea what's going on outside my patch (loosely defined by a curry-house, some schools and a couple of supermarkets), but I candidly assume that however rotten the metropolis becomes, it and all its related works are still superior to anywhere else.

Of course, defining myself as a Londoner has necessarily entailed finding something to define myself against. And over the years, I've had plenty of time to work up a small armoury of prejudices against the North of England. Could have been the French, could have been Irish immigrants, it turned out to be northerners. What's more, these prejudices have not been shaken by my occasional trips up there or by friendships with non-southerners. My bigotry is a clear but baseless mixture of clichés and reach-me-down cultural misassumptions, ignoring all those specific personal experiences which argue that at least I might wish to alter my views and at most I might be slightly mad.

I know what I think, and I think that northerners start roughly where the A1 joins the M25 around Potters Bar. I also believe that northerners think that we in the South are idle, conceited and immoral and that we all vote Conservative. I think I believe, too, that northernness is grounded in a world of back-to-back terraced housing, towering Victorian factories, violence, extreme urban bleakness, civic pride, poor weather, moorland, radicalism, comical regional accents, dreadful architecture, widescale deprivation and an inferiority complex towards the South manifesting itself in unthinking hostility towards Londoners.

Well, wouldn't you feel the same after three decades Down South, having been fed an indiscriminate diet of *Coronation Street* and Bernard Manning? If you'd been steeped in Slade, Jimmy Nail, the Tetley tea-bag men (when I hear anyone use the word 'nowt' I reach for my gun), anyone who appears in an advertisement for any kind of bitter beer which has a northern provenance, Alan Bennett, *Viz* magazine, The Great Morrissey, D.H. Lawrence, Geoff Boycott, Victoria Wood, Arthur Scargill, Arnold Bennett and Sir Marcus Fox, Chairman of the Tory Backbenchers' 1922 Committee? If all you'd ever learned about a place was gleaned from Michael Parkinson's wearisome Yorkshire canniness ('Can they really make up my glasses in one hour? We'll see.') or Victoria Wood saying, 'I've had a clip round the ear with a wrestler's braces and there's nowt to it'? Would you want to go there? How tolerant would you be?

It's a kind of bigotry that otherwise guilt-ridden white middle-classers like myself can sustain and nurture, because it is, to a great extent, a two-way street. For years, I've been happy to run down the North because there is no easy division between oppressor and oppressed, between the bigot and the object of bigotry. We both do it. No country is too small to contain idiotic north/south, francophone/anglophone, Flemish/Walloon, urban/rural factionalisms and England has a long and vulgar tradition of northerners despising southerners and southerners deriding northerners. Generations come and go, and southerners and northerners still feel the same way about each other. It's just a fact of English life, like the Pennines, supermarket chains and television.

In the end, of course, knowing that you have these wholly unfeasible views can be a bit of a burden. And if someone gives you the opportunity to explore your prejudices freely and frankly, to confront the object of your mistrust and bafflement, you take it. Or you make an excuse and hang the phone up. In fact, it was a mixture of opportunity and embarrassment that made me seize the chance to go north. This isn't the same embarrassment or shame one might feel about holding some sort of vile prejudice against racial or sexual minorities, nothing like that. I just felt that for a man in his mid-thirties, I was blatantly ignorant. I know how to find my way around my bit of south London pretty well by now and I can blunder around foreign countries without being killed or arrested, but how much mileage can a supposedly educated, theoretically mature human being get from saying, 'Where *is* Pontefract exactly?' or 'Does Salford really exist?' and simpering massively. I was starting to feel like a fool.

Naturally I had the hope, in the back of my mind, that the North would turn out to be even worse than I had imagined. I hoped that I would be able to come back with that look of pompous, concerned sagacity on my face, the look which all serious travellers wear when they're telling you about something really dreadful, like conditions in Calcutta or what it's like to take the bus out of Los Angeles. Better still, I thought I might even be able to harden my prejudices into certainties. No one, I told myself, will ever again have to make allowances for the fact that I haven't the first idea what I'm talking about. I would be sounding off from a position of almost unique strength. The southerner who saw it with his own eyes.

But you always get problems when you plan your itinerary from a basis of complete ignorance. Left to my own devices, I would have argued that the North begins somewhere around Hemel Hempstead. Others told me it was nearer Stoke-on-Trent. I compromised. I chose Birmingham. It seemed right: well north of where I was, strong tradition of metal-bashing (that thing that northerners do, along with coal-mining and sheep-farming), reputation for large-scale ugliness, full of Hard Men, victim of industrial decline, risible regional accent. I know that no northerner would consider Birmingham anything other than mere Midlands, even a morose adjunct of London; but don't forget that this was my perspective – me, an invertebrate southerner, calling the shots.

I even had witnesses. I told a close friend of mine who was born and brought up there – Erdington, to be specific – that I was off to Birmingham. He's the nearest thing I know to a northern Hard Man and he said, 'You're even stupider than I thought you were. The place is a shit hole.'

He then told me how his enormously tough Birmingham grammar school had been in a pitched battle with the neighbouring comprehensive school. Nothing unusual in that, you might think. But this being Birmingham (the legendary Birmingham I was looking for), the grammar school masters, far from trying to stop the fighting, had actually orchestrated it. Apparently, they tricked the comprehensive boys into believing that the grammar boys were all spavined midgets by sending in a wave of very small children to have the crap beaten out of them by the comprehensives, who then lapsed into overconfidence, dropped their guard and found themselves immediately being set upon by the grammar school's own Hard Men, who wiped them all over the Warwickshire countryside. ('Didn't fook around again with us after that.')

At about the same time, he took up running as a sporting activity, so that he could get home after closing time without being attacked by the city's maniacs. 'Always walk down the middle of a street at night,' he told me. 'Then you can see them coming. Gives you ten seconds to get into your stride.'

One of the lecturers I had at college was a Brummie. His party piece after the end-of-term exams was to take the smallest member of our undergraduate group, sit on his chest and bang his head on the ground. I remember the victim in our year was called Dave. Dave wore pink Doc Marten's and was an Anarcho-Syndicalist from, inevitably, London. There you go: the Birmingham way.

More recently, I had to appear on a talk'n'music radio show on BBC Radio Birmingham. This was presented by a spiritual cousin of these people, an extremely belligerent man who shouted at me on air nonstop for half an hour, before silencing me in the middle of the word 'inevitably' and putting on a record by T. Rex. I suppose I was meagre fare at eleven in the morning and needed spicing up, but even so. I was bundled out of the building, my ears ringing.

'He's a real character, isn't he?' they said.

It sounded like just the place to start. How could I have known that it wouldn't be what I'd thought? How can you know before you get there? I didn't, so I snatched up my car keys and at once got lost on the South Circular.

TWO

B ut Birmingham was difficult and wrong. As I swished into town on the A34, through the unreconstructed parts of Birmingham – Sparkhill and Sparkbrook – I caught sight of the city centre gleaming distantly on its Warwickshire upland in the way I imagine Las Vegas gleams distantly in its Nevada desert. Without realising what I was doing, I found myself admiring the boxes of municipal yellow flowers hung out on the central reservation. I saluted a fancy-looking mosque, covered in green and silver tinsel. Cunning road signs directed me infallibly round to the International Convention Centre, leaving me in a landscape bordered by the National Indoor Arena, Central TV and the ICC itself.

And what did I find as I swept into a clean, well-ordered car park round the back of the ICC and Symphony Hall? I found myself (and I mean this as a profound compliment) in what appeared to be a kind of tolerable Milton Keynes. I was open-mouthed with amazement in a canyon of steel, glass, light, space, shifting reflections and air. Not only that, but there were other, abundant, unfilled car parks to my left and right which (unlike the ones I'd left behind in London) were not also sixty-foot urinals.

I stopped the car, got out and walked uneasily round the corner to Centenary Square. This is an extremely large stone-flagged open space which the council clearly has yet to find a use for, except possibly to dramatise the perspectives leading to the ICC and the Birmingham Repertory Theatre. It is also somewhere to put a huge neo-Stalinist statue in apricot fibreglass. This made rather an impression on me at the time and I later discovered that I was right to have been impressed. The piece – at £250,000 – is the single most expensive work of art commissioned by the council as part of their £800,000 scheme to transform Birmingham into an international centre of artistic creativity.

Was it worth it? It is a startling object portraying a mob of young Stakhanovite service industry professionals striding immensely towards the front door of the Symphony Hall, a Birmingham Symphony Orchestra tuba player dogging their footsteps. They epitomise a new generation of Brummies, the clean, white-collar types who *are* today's Birmingham. A large, well-bulked turd rising up from a factory chimney behind them symbolises the industrial past from which they are escaping. The bloke who designed it turned out to be a nice old boy in a cravat. 'I wanted to evoke,' he explained in an interview, 'the Birmingham that had just been knocked down.'

Even as I stood in the shadow of the apricot monster, the director of the Birmingham Museum and Art Gallery was investing a further £130,000 in an exhibition of customised motorbikes. A six-ton piece of steel designed by sculptor Antony Gormley had been cast in the form of a mummy's coffin and implanted at an angle in one of the city centre's pavements. A real artist had even designed the brickwork laid on the ground of Centenary Square. Clearly, something was present in Birmingham which, according to my scheme of things, should not have been. Instead of nothing but ugliness, there was a groping towards style. There was some kind of aesthetic sensibility.

Queen Victoria had the curtains of her train window drawn when passing through the Birmingham/Black Country region, lest the sight offend her eyes. Nobody told me that things had changed since then. Have other writers extolled the pleasures of the city centre? No. Have they ever given it a good write-up? No. By and large, they treat Birmingham like the fat boy in the playground and poke it with sharp sticks.

Charles Dickens, for instance, gives the region a terrible panning in *The Old Curiosity Shop*, when he describes the passage of Nell and her grandfather through the marginally fictionalised wasteland between Birmingham and Wolverhampton. This is, according to Dickens, 'A cheerless region, where not a blade of grass was seen to grow; where not a bud put forth its promise in the spring; where nothing green could live but on the surface of the stagnant pools, which here and there lay idly sweltering by the black roadside . . .' and so on.

George Melly, in his autobiographical *Owning-Up*, puts it more succinctly. Writing about the Birmingham of the 1950s, he poses the question, 'Why is Birmingham, the town we christened "The Arsehole of England", so horrible a place?' There were various reasons, among them, 'Sundays are deader. The accent more hideous. The pubs more reluctant to sell proprietary brands . . .' Searching for an image to epitomise the city, he turns to (seems unlikely now) Birmingham's indigenous whisky industry: 'A bottle of the local whisky once rattled about undrunk in the bottom of the bandwagon *for over a month* and it is not that we were given to Scotch advert chichi. It was simply undrinkable even when we were drunk.' Curiously enough, some decades later, George popped up in a newspaper advertising campaign extolling the virtues of Birmingham on behalf of the local tourist authority. Just shows how a place can change.

Meanwhile, nearly a hundred and fifty years after Dickens, David Lodge provides us with a typically snotty update of Little Nell's journey in his novel *Nice Work*. In a conscious reprise of Dickens' text, he goes on about 'A familiar landscape . . . an expanse of houses and factories, warehouses and sheds, railway lines and canals, piles of scrap metal and heaps of damaged cars, container ports and lorry parks, cooling towers and gasometers. A monochrome landscape, grey under a low grey sky, its horizons blurred by a grey haze.' This is what the book's Brummie protagonist, Vic Wilcox, drives through every morning, being condescended to all the while by Lodge's authorial voice. Lodge actually has powerful Birmingham connections – a PhD at the University of Birmingham and subequently a Chair there – but is clearly racked with embarrassment at this association and is busy belittling it under the guise of contemporary literature.

Big, boring and ugly: what better reasons for visiting a northern town? But the plan unravelled minute by minute as I crossed the road from Centenary Square to Victoria Square. I wandered into an amphitheatral space in front of the Birmingham Central Library ('The Biggest In Europe' it says on a biro I bought there) and the Museum and Art Gallery. This was bathed in brilliant sunshine and was scattered – I'm not making this up – with young people reading poetry. Not aloud, but clearly reading it. The Town Hall (1834, modelled on the temple of Castor and Pollux) smiled down on this endeavour, while the Museum and Art Gallery (1885), backing onto the Council House (1879), lent an air of pleasant, subdued pomposity to the scene.

On from there, through the commodious thoroughfare which is Colmore Row, past the mercantile splendour of Newhall Street and Edmund Street, to St Philip's Cathedral, and even that was in the middle of a face-lift. A man was tuning freshly gilded organ pipes as rays of sunlight beat through the windows. Round Temple Row and the heart of downtown Birmingham's financial district, through crowds of purposeful, healthy-looking people (night starvation? Not us!) and back west I went towards Gas Street Basin.

Now what does the name Gas Street Basin suggest to you?

A sanitary fitting? The title of a Bessie Smith song? At the very least, something like a waste outflow from a coking plant? Of course not. It's a bit of Birmingham's priceless industrial heritage, the confluence of several murky canals on the south-western edge of the city centre. Actually, Birmingham got one of its principal leg-ups from canals: once the canal boats began to arrive in the eighteenth century, they helped to transform the entire region into the heartland of the Industrial Revolution. By the mid-1800s, however, the trains had come and the canals were on their way out. By the 1970s (I am told), Gas Street Basin was no more than a sump of neglect, a place to bunk off school/smoke reefers/get your head kicked in by skinheads. To be honest, the atmosphere hasn't exactly been transformed, but there are clear signs that the council which gave us the ICC and the pedestrianisation around Temple Row and Corporation Street will not rest until this part of town (which might also bring in some extra revenue) has been tarted up.

To this end, they have been re-laying the canal footpaths, refurbishing the bridges and persuading small, unnecessary shops to start up on the quaysides and sell pomanders and jars of costly English honey: ideal for strolling middle-class shoppers and visiting Taiwanese businessmen with three-quarters of an hour to kill. Neat herringboned brickwork lies beneath your feet and there are brightly painted canal boats inhabited by hippies parked promiscuously around Bridge Street. The only thing missing is a wrought-iron public convenience, and I only wanted one of those because I'd read that nineteenth-century Birmingham had been famed for its outside toilets: the Home of the Iron Convenience, as it was known. A bog by the canal would have been apt. Still, Gas Street Basin is, or will be, a Covent Garden of the North with stagnant waters in which to admire your own reflection, as well as that of the Hyatt Regency Hotel which strikes a paradoxically futuristic note as it looms over the Basin's black waters.

To be honest, I was a bit unnerved by the Hyatt, as I stood on the shores of Gas Street Basin, catching a light tan in the Midlands sun. Not only is it extremely large, sinister and shiny in the I.M. Pei/Hong Kong International style, it also featured prominently on the front page of my tourist hand-out, 'Birmingham: The Big Heart Of Britain', and was apparently depicted on the council's non-denominational Christmas card for 1993. Why?

Still, having braced myself for George Melly's 'Arsehole of England', as it were, I was, increasingly, gloomily admiring of the way Birmingham seemed to be *making an effort*. I was even more cynically admiring of the way that this generation of planners has managed to camouflage the legacy of the previous generation of planners and get everything down into one sector of the city, specifically to impress the pants off the American, Japanese and Korean businessmen who come into town with a view to contributing to the region's economy.

Once out of the clutches of New Street (or better still, coming in from the airport in a chauffeured car) all your money-packing foreigner will see of Birmingham is that south-western corner of the city centre which has been nipped and tucked to the last brick. The rest can go hang: the immediate impression is exemplary. And the effect is as arresting to a Londoner like me as it must be to the boss of a foreign machine-tool company. We sad metropolitans now take it as an article of faith that there is no such thing as planning or foresight or responsibility in the way cities are run. We assume that all big places are like London: chaotic, beggar-infested and terminally incapable of self-improvement. The word 'civic' has ceased to have any meaning down here, except as the name of a Japanese car. To come from London to a place where there appears to be some sort of confident civic design at work (however expedient or piecemeal it might actually be) is at the same time intoxicating and envy-provoking.

* * *

Oddly, this is not how Birmingham got started. Birmingham began as a kind of refuge for highly industrious cranks. Back in 1538, John Leland, author of *The Laboryouse Journey and Serche of J. Leylande for Englandes Antiquities*, described the emergent Birmingham as 'A good market towne . . . with many smithies . . . that use to make knives and all manner of cuttynge tooles and many lorimers that make byts and a great many naylors.' To this ant-hill was added the vital ingredient which turns a town of a few thousand into a city of one million: libertarian anarchism. During the seventeenth and eighteenth centuries, Birmingham's manufacturing concerns grew at an amazing rate, not least because all kinds of freebooters, inventors and adventurers arrived there. And why did they arrive there? Because, as one commentator put it, 'It awarded almost perfect freedom to all who chose to come. Dissenters and Quakers and heretics of all sorts were welcomed . . . no trade unions, no trade gilds, no companies existed, and every man was free to come and go.' The result was that Birmingham became *the* free trade town, a place where business went on almost completely unhampered by any kind of commercial or municipal restraint.

If this sounds strange in comparison with the stodgy collectivism with which Birmingham is so often associated today (the biggest local authority in Britain, sitting on a £1 billion budget; the great Longbridge walk-outs of the 1970s), well then, think of Warwickshire as a kind of Georgian Ohio. In this climate of unbridled self-expression, such figures as James Watt (inventor of the steam engine), Matthew Boulton (more steam engines), Joseph Priestley (chemist) and John Baskerville (printer and type founder) all throve.

Actually, Joseph Priestley didn't thrive. In 1791, a mob crying 'Church and King for ever' burned down Priestley's house and laboratory, as a consequence of which the doctor fled to America and never returned. John Baskerville, on the

other hand, took non-conformism to new lengths by being
an atheist (in the mid-eighteenth century) and having his
corpse interred in the bottom of a windmill.

At any rate, Birmingham became the Toy Shop of
Europe: the railways came in 1837; Birmingham Small
Arms became the largest private arms manufacturer in
Europe; Birmingham University, England's prototypical
redbrick, was founded in 1900, and forty years ago the
place was turning out BSA motorbikes and Rovers in
prodigious quantities. My guess is that Birmingham offi-
cially became lacklustre with the arrival of the Chamberlain
family: Joseph, who took over local politics in the last
century, and Neville, who went on to become the sad old
booby on the steps of the aeroplane waving Hitler's signature in the air.

And I blame them generally for turning Birmingham
from a rather glamorous-sounding rioter's paradise (the
mobs were busy from 1643 – robbing the King's baggage
train – to 1901, when they attacked the Town Hall with a
battering ram on account of Lloyd George) into the sort of
city that pioneers town-planning schemes (1911), one-way
traffic (1933) and municipal airports (1933). Which leads
us aptly to modern Brum, with its schemes and its
materialism and its clumsy rationalities. Only the Proof
House really seems to keep the old anarchic freedoms alive.
The Proof House is where Brummies test guns. They do
this by the simple, even engagingly moronic, practice of
overloading the suggested charge for each firearm and
seeing if the whole thing blows up when they fire it. If
it doesn't explode, it passes. Can you imagine the Germans
doing that?

I stood and stared at the Hyatt Regency and realised that
this was not what I had come here for. I took a deep breath
and made myself find New Street Station and the Bull Ring.
I was not going to be thwarted, even it meant forcing myself

to see the city through a veil of ordure. That's how I really got started.

Then I went to see a couple of doctor friends who live in Sutton Coldfield, a little way beyond the city limits. I was feeling guilty and foolish by this time. Far from presenting itself as a nicely risible victim, Brum (interesting metathesis, by the way) was turning the tables on me. The New Street/ Bull Ring experience had given me something to cheer about, but not enough. I knew I had got off on the wrong foot. So I compensated for this by shamelessly jettisoning my original plan and arguing for a completely new way to view the place. It became my mission to tell people what a tremendous town Birmingham was, even if they were already living there and had had plenty of time to make up their own minds. For me, the city was bathed in a golden glow.

To give you an idea of the state I was in, I drove through Spaghetti Junction on the way to Sutton Coldfield and was so busy gawping at it in wonder, I nearly crashed the car into a concrete pier. What a masterpiece Spaghetti Junction is! (I thought.) What a testament to human ingenuity! I don't know why I only drove round it once. I could have spent a day on Spaghetti Junction, with only vertigo and nausea to slow me down. It was a cathedral in the air, a game of Möbius strips covered in thundering buses, cars and lorries driven by apprehensive-looking individuals who strongly suspect they've missed their turn.

Sutton Coldfield was another shock. It looked like London without actually being London. It didn't have the awful, invisible brooding presence of the capital waiting massively somewhere over its horizon of roofs and chimneys. It was quiet, it was middle class, there were plenty of places with a nice bit of lawn front and back. There were off-licences selling Australian Chardonnay. There were road junctions where unnaturally well-preserved middle-aged women sat tensely in Mini Metros waiting for the lights to change. It was like London but it was better than London. It was like London before it had let itself go.

But my friends are southerners and all they could talk about was moving. Despite the fact that neither had lived in London for years and consequently had little idea of what a midden the place now is, their dream was to shackle themselves at awesome expense to somewhere like Ealing or Highbury.

'But this is really nice,' I cried, pointing out their plot of garden and their agreeable Edwardian interior features. 'You couldn't get anything like this for the same price in London.'

'Birmingham's okay,' they said, 'but's it's a bit . . . dull.'

'*Dull?* With the ICC and all those wonderful car parks and the big statue made out of fibreglass?'

'Dull and dirty. And the way the people talk.'

'Whereas London is clean? And everyone sounds like Nigel Havers? Are you insane?'

There was the greenery of Warwickshire half a mile from their doorstep. There was the throbbing cultural power-house that is today's Birmingham a couple of miles in the other direction. It was reasonably priced. There was even an authentic whiff of community in the form of a scrawny old boy, maybe seventy years old, whom I observed to come out of his house a couple of doors up the road shortly after the dustmen had been, to pick up scraps of paper dropped from the bins. At the end of his mission he stopped at the bottom of the road, compacted his hoard of litter and sat on a low garden wall to get his breath back. When offered a cup of tea, he said pleasantly, 'No thanks, I've got one waiting for me at 'ome.' In London, this kind of behaviour would have labelled him as either bats or working for the Drug Squad. But up here, such things were still allowed to happen.

'He always does it,' said the wife with a perplexed look on her face. 'So what's happening in London then? Nick's hoping for a job there. Or Cambridge. Or Bristol at a pinch. Preferably London.'

The capital had them in its deadly, pretentious thrall. If that's where your ambitions lie, then nothing can change you, least of all another city. I have known Londoners who've moved to smaller towns and even to the countryside and they make a big song and dance about how much their lives are improved by not being in the Smoke. But most of the time all they really want to do is go back to the dirt, expense, unpleasantness and inefficiency they secretly love. How on earth is Birmingham supposed to overcome this?

A bit later on, the husband took me round to his local pub, which was full of robust men drinking beer and telling each other jokes about penises and what have you; the sort of thing robust men like to do in a drinking situation. It was all perfectly friendly. I was going to explain to him how refreshing it was that there was none of that unease you experience in London pubs after about nine in the evening, when you have to keep a corner of your eye open for drooling tramps or lagered-up psychos in stolen Next bomber jackets, but I couldn't be bothered. It was just tolerable and sweaty and crowded and fairly malodorous, the way a crowded pub ought to be. I sucked on my drink gratefully and he contented himself with telling me, the way off-duty doctors do, about tuberculosis.

The nightmare continued. Dudley, Wolverhampton and Walsall, Birmingham's Black Country neighbours, were more of the same. I sailed out of Birmingham by some strange northern route (it felt worryingly like the outskirts of Guildford) and set my sights on the Black Country. I was entertaining the same feelings in my breast that I'd entertained before getting to Birmingham: now, at least, I was in for some real muck, now I was going to see some true grime and ugliness, real degradation. J.B. Priestley (of whose

English Journey I was, believe me, acutely aware) noted that 'The Black Country unrolled before you like a smouldering carpet.' What else could you expect from Dudley, Walsall and Wolverhampton? These places were no-hopers. I felt it in my bones.

I was strengthened in my faith by a poster I saw promoting the Black Country Development Corporation. This depicted a black, shiny apple, apparently made of obsidian or polished jet, out of which a bite had been taken. The flesh revealed by the bite was gold-coloured. You get the message? Bite deep into the unpromising exterior of the Black Country and you find the riches of Croesus. It looked revolting. It looked like an apple so old and corrupted that it had turned black, while its insides had undergone some sort of weird chemical mutation into a substance that resembled a precious metal, but which would in fact initiate a chronic, lingering degeneration if swallowed, rather like Bailey's Irish Cream. If this is the best the Black Country can do to sell itself, I tittered, it must be even worse than I thought.

I had also been given a pointer by another friend, who told me that in the days when he was young and free, he and his flatmates would amuse themselves by listening to a double LP of the Reverend Ian Paisley's speeches. This is a pretty perverse kind of fun, as you might imagine, and took a certain frame of mind to make it worth indulging in. But there was a kind of fun that was even stranger and more perverse than that. When they tired of the Reverend Paisley and were really abjectly, hopelessly in need of some sort of freakish mental stimulation, they would put on an LP called *Off The Cuff*, by the Black Country comedian, Harry Harrison. Harry Harrison was, from all accounts, so awful, so uniquely rotten that he only began to be palatable after they'd had a good session with Doctor Paisley first. That, in a microcosm, was the Black Country.

* * *

I shan't go into the details of Walsall and Dudley, except to remark that as towns which grew fattish on the back of Birmingham's expansion, they ought, with the passing of time and money, to have looked sad.

The way it turned out, unfortunately, Dudley, Walsall and, subsequently, Wolverhampton left me feeling like an escapee from a Martin Amis novel. Over a period of several hours, I turned into one of those moral cripples who inhabit books like *Money* and *Success*, sweating up and down the seamier reaches of town, morbidly obsessed with dirt, decay and human failure. It was the same problem as Birmingham, made worse by the fact that Birmingham had already cheated on me. However desperately I searched for Black Country grime, disease, or at a pinch, graffiti, I couldn't see any.

At one point I did find some litter blowing down a street in Dudley which I fell upon with a cry of recognition, reminding me as it did of my own home town. At another point I came upon a road-drill compressor with a broken exhaust and the fumes made me think of London's Cromwell Road. At another, I saw a fading advertisement, painted on the side of a house, which said 'Medically Approved Bile Beans'. That wasn't bad, it had the savour of an old Bert Hardy *Picture Post* snap of Britain struggling to pull itself together after the war, the smell of age-old ineptitude.

But to be honest, that was an aberration. The Black Country is actually about as black as my back garden. Less black, in fact. What foundries and ore smelters and smithies there were have largely been cleared away by long uninterrupted years of recession and Conservatism. Metal-processing of one sort or another has been going on in the Black Country since the fourteenth century and until recently the area turned out vast quantities of metal components, electrical machinery, locks and, literally, nuts and bolts. Like the ruined hulk of Fort Dunlop on the verges of the M6, most of this is now of historical interest only. The

end product is, at worst, some interesting piles of heterogeneous crud and, at best, some pleasant red-brick buildings
dotted around verdant business parks and other such
investment opportunities. The Black Country is now the
emerald and brick-red country, which to a man used to
travelling on the London Underground is disorientating.

So I toiled around Dudley and Walsall, dogged by a sense of
gathering futility, before drifting in on the A41 to Wolverhampton. Several hours later, I had gazed on the serene
fifteenth-century charms of St Peter's, the town's principal
church, had admired the Art Gallery (a bit like Oxford's
Ashmolean only less preposterous), approved of the French
Empire-style law courts, attracted an incredulous glance
from the assistant in a bookshop by actually tendering
money in exchange for *Aynuk & Ayli's Black Country Joke
Book* (complete with an advert at the back for Harry
Harrison's *Off The Cuff*), winked at the endearing hanging
baskets of flowers that adorned the street lamps, nodded a
good day at a small crowd of unemployed young persons
who were sitting soberly and politely, eating Chinese take-
aways under an equestrian statue of Prince Albert, given full
marks to the comfortable mixture of old and new architecture which Wolverhampton displayed, smiled all around me
at the alert, well-fed, racially integrated population, found
no fault whatsoever with the pedestrianisation and the
excellent new bus shelters and then finally returned to my
parked car and had something along the lines of a nervous
breakdown.

I think the turning point, the moment at which I really
thought I might as well give up the whole thing, came when
I found a pub with the sign 'Motorcyclists By Appointment
Only' by its entrance and nearby another one bearing the
legend 'Dress Code Applicable'. And this in Wolverhampton. The *Black Country*. Attitudes like that belong in *Hove*.
What with all the town-centre smartness and the injunctions

concerning dress code, I seriously began to wonder if I hadn't crossed the Channel (in my sleep, perhaps) to some provincial French town. The place had the same clean, handsome, prosperous air about it that you find once you get south of Boulogne. I tried to imagine the place in thick drizzle, with armies of heavy metal fans drinking and vomiting in the streets, Ozzy Osbourne trading Aynuk & Ayli jokes with Slade (local boys, all); anything to get the taste of decency out of my mouth, but I couldn't.

The only thing that perked up my spirits was a poster advertising 'An Evening With Jethro (Slightly Naughty!)' at the Dudley Town Hall, to remind me that I had indeed come a long way from the dangerous and beguiling suavity of London. Perhaps somewhere in the Wulfrun Shopping Centre (Wolverhampton's well-preserved 1960s retail development) late at night, when all the clean-limbed Wolverhamptonians had gone off to Dudley to watch slightly naughty Jethro, I might have caught a hint of existential decay, somewhere among the unsold dustpans and bendy action toys, but somehow I doubted it.

One of the great sleights-of-hand of clever places like Wolverhampton and Birmingham is to give the impression that the munificence which gives us clean town halls, pedestrianisation and art galleries is general and endless. Imagine my surprise, then, when I read in the papers a few weeks later that Birmingham City Council was being reprimanded for diverting money that should have been spent on schools and colleges into new prestige projects to boost the city's image. That the spanking new international Birmingham had been paid for by raiding the school cashbox. This, at least, was the view expressed by a special commission – set up, somewhat bafflingly, by the council itself – chaired by Professor Ted Wragg. The way he saw it, the city council had, over five years, spent £250 million less on education than the Government thought it should and that it should spend an extra £300 million on education over the next five years with two-thirds of that sum going towards repairing Birmingham's disintegrating school buildings.

Not only that, but the day after I read about the school funds, there was an old girl on the *Today* programme, complaining that the council had spent twenty years failing to put inside toilets into people's council houses. She, for one, was sick to the back teeth with having to go out at midnight in February for a pee. Apparently, there were still 12,000 houses in Birmingham without inside lavatories. And why had they failed to put in the toilets? Because the money had gone on raising the city's international profile instead. Someone else then advanced the argument that by raising the city's international profile, so much money would be attracted into Birmingham that pretty soon anyone who wanted a lavatory inside their house, rather than outside in the pouring rain, could have one, but he didn't sound convincing.

And then there was the City of Birmingham Symphony Orchestra. Now, if there is one single thing which has done Birmingham a power of incontrovertible good, then it is the CBSO under the leadership of Simon Rattle (a Merseysider by upbringing). Nothing else says so clearly to sceptical nancy Londoners that Birmingham is a place with a soul, with a future, with a sense of fitness of things.

Well, at the time of writing, the CBSO had gone £250,000 into the red and Rattle was chewing the carpet about Arts Council funding and the general sinking feeling he was experiencing about the future of his orchestra. And this from within the confines of the magnificent new Symphony Hall, with its twenty-four-inch-thick granite walls, its shock-absorbed floor, its Adam red decor, its impossible flying walkways (Piranesi style, if you ever go there), its irreproachable acoustics (I let myself in there one afternoon and spent a very happy time coughing, belching and farting to myself from all over the auditorium. I have never sounded so mellow, my *timbre* so golden) and its overwhelming sense of prosperity and lushness. The Symphony Hall alone is enough to persuade you that you've wound up in somewhere really dynamic, like Munich, or Atlanta, Georgia.

And yet there was a cloud hanging over it and just about everything else I clapped eyes on. A cloud in the biggest council in the kingdom, the place where people and politicians had banded together to build The Big Heart Of England, where local councillors are supposed to come round at election time and say, 'Remember me, Mrs Rix? I got the light put up your back passage, ha, ha.' The whole tenor of the council's activities in the 1980s, it seemed, had been predicated on the economic principle of Trickledown, which, as we now all know, is about as effective in the real world as filling the petrol tank of your car with horse manure. And this from a Labour council who, in normal circumstances (you would have imagined), would have run screaming from such Adam Smith Institute insanities.

Who would have thought it? Who would have thought that there was a bottom line somewhere? The new Labour council leader, Theresa Stewart, has pledged (does anyone else around here pledge, by the way? Or is it only something that politicians and discount electrical goods stores do?) to change the emphasis of expenditure and put the people's money into more sensible things from now on: schools, pavements, libraries, hospitals. An ex-Brummie, writing in *The Guardian*, noted that 'Maybe the sneering journalists who slate the pretentious Brummies are right. How dare this cultural dust bowl twin itself with Barcelona, Frankfurt or Lyons? For the hacks from the Smoke, the best thing in Birmingham was the road out of Spaghetti Junction.' But I am a hack from the Smoke and I thought it was great. An ingenuous hack, maybe, but a Londoner. And I fervently hope that this doesn't mean the end of Centenary Square and the apricot statue. But do the international capitalist swashbucklers, arriving at Birmingham airport and scuttling down to the Hyatt Regency, know this?

I went and had a Balti. Baltis are basically a midlands variation on the theme of curry but without the rice, cutlery, or plates. More than that, a Balti is a rough-hewn, primitive thing, self-consciously unkempt, like Bruce Willis. A Balti arrives in a kind of army surplus stores wok made of tin; you have a nan bread to scoop it up with. You may be given a spoon, or you may be left to suffer. In my limited experience of these things, the Balti is (a) hot as hell (b) distinctly liquid, to afford the Balti house owner the satisfaction of seeing you cover yourself in gravy (c) served in conditions of wondrous austerity.

I found my Balti in the Sparkbrook region of Brum, to the south-east of the city. This, after the nightmare of the enchanted Black Country, was comfortingly flyblown, run-down and neglected. Rows of drab nineteenth-century workers' terraces stretch away to either side of the main road which itself boasts an assortment of dead or crazy shops. If you want to repair a very old motorcycle, buy a complete but unreconditioned suite of office reception furniture from 1981, invest in seventy yards of factory-second buff carpeting, or simply splash out on a gunny sack of garbanzo beans, then this is your place.

It is also the underside of the civic dream, the proof that the council's flash ambitions had a fairly small ambit in which to make an effect. The municipal money evidently ran out well within the ring road and Sparkbrook and Sparkhill have been left free of indoor toilets, doubtless with some lousy schools and with some especially tangy litter drifting up and down the streets. As a rule, Londoners generally notice these things in an abstract, impersonal way. Nowadays we only really bother about decay when it gets stuck to our clothing or tries to get into our homes. Here, of course, it is part of a larger argument about social and economic theory as applied to a city of one million people; but that's Birmingham's problem.

Sparkhill and Sparkbrook are also the parts of town where the Asian population seems to be obliged to hunker down until it can work its way out to somewhere nicer, such as Sutton Coldfield. Birmingham, like most big industrial cities, has plenty of black and Asian inhabitants – largely the result of the boom years of the late 1950s and early 1960s, when the old Empire was called upon to provide tens of thousands of bus conductors, hospital orderlies and labourers to service the bustling white man. To the north-west of town, Handsworth is rather more famously home to the black ruffneck yout', who every now and then like to have a bit of a riot to keep everyone on their toes. And who can blame them? If you had had to spend years putting up with Enoch Powell as MP for Wolverhampton, a twenty-minute bus ride away, wouldn't it get on your nerves?

Back in Sparkbrook, I wanted to try the I Am The King Balti ('Sets the tastebuds wildly out of control' according to my Essential Balti Guide) or, failing that, the Punjabi Paradise ('Neatly decorated in pink with a potted palm in the window to justify the "Paradise" part of the name'), but they were both shut. So I settled for a cramped and strikingly unsophisticated restaurant in Ladypool Road. Not only was I the only person there, I also found that the lavatory washbasin had been placed in the restaurant itself (PLEASE WASH YOUR HANDS said a notice above it, clearly legible even to those in the window seats) and that there was a picture of someone – the proprietor? – shaking hands with the Prime Minister of Pakistan. A waiter, or possibly the chef – at any rate, a fat guy in an apron that had clearly done duty in a busy abattoir – came up to me and asked, 'Eat?' So I agreed and he placed a steaming potty of chicken and spinach in front of me.

I dipped into my lunchtime copy of *The Birmingham Post*. In it, there was an article about a man called John Main-

waring, whose claim to fame was that he was 'The manifestation of Ziggy Stardust'. This was good news. It was nice
to know that, even while the rest of the world came apart
around us, Birmingham was still throwing up England's
most risible pop acts. Who could forget Slade, Black
Sabbath, The Moody Blues, Robert Plant and John Bon-
ham (the two most visibly *tonto* members of Led Zeppelin),
or Roy Wood: loud, absurd and all of them from Birmingham or somewhere near it? Of all these, perhaps the most
hopeless were the most durable – The Moody Blues, who
appear every now and again, still looking like five geography
teachers on a night out in Selly Oak.

John Mainwaring, it turned out, was born in Bloxwich,
near Walsall, and now lived in Wolverhampton. He was
nine hundred years old and had a close encounter with a
UFO when he was a child. He wore oriental satin robes,
electrocuted hair and plenty of slap in the manner of David
Bowie *circa* 1972, and had a number one hit in the Lebanon.

'There are,' he said, 'many strong parallels between Bowie
and myself.' Judging by the pictures, he was a great big lad
with strapping thighs and a chunky Midlander's chin. 'I've
been a fat Ziggy, a thin Ziggy – all different types of Ziggy.
But always Ziggy.' Had he been born thirty years earlier,
however, I've no doubt that this mooncalf would have been
riding around on a BSA, claiming to be the manifestation of
Gene Vincent.

After twenty minutes, I was beginning to feel the first
surges of blissful discomfort that a large curry will always
bring, when a bearded tramp came in and settled himself at
a table near mine. He looked like an Afghani refugee. He
barked at the waiter in a strange tongue and smoked a
cigarette the way I used to try and smoke a joint, that is,
holding the fag close to his knuckles, cupping his hand
around the filter end and inhaling deeply through the O
formed by his thumb and forefinger.

Shortly after that, a large golden Mercedes drew up

outside and the man who was in the picture shaking hands
with the Prime Minister of Pakistan got out and swept into
the restaurant. Several associates rushed through the door
after him. From being virtually empty, the place was
suddenly full of swarthy men, shouting at each other. The
waiter burst out of the kitchen in his bloodstained apron and
declaimed loudly at the man who shook the Prime Minister
of Pakistan's hand. I thought they were going to attack each
other with curved knives, when the man who shook the
Prime Minister of Pakistan's hand did a sort of balletic
swivel and rushed out of the restaurant, dragging his
accomplices with him and sucking the smoking tramp along
in his slipstream.

I finished my Balti. I was ready to leave, to look for
somewhere a lot worse. And what should I find, on the
edge of a verdant municipal park with multi-ethnic children
playing happily in it, but an iron convenience, a genuine
rococo Victorian *pissoir*, handsomely preserved and in full
working order? The Home of the Iron Convenience. I gazed
at it, inside and out. It was free of messages, freshly tiled, as
clean and inviting as the day it had been erected. A whole-
some breeze blew through it. Perhaps it was the advance
guard of an army of rejuvenated *pissoirs*, destined to fill the
newly Victorianised streets of the greater city of Birmingham, arm-in-arm with the canals, the Museum and Art
Gallery, the Town Hall, the Council House. Perhaps it was
Sparkbrook's own version of the Chamberlain Square
Memorial Fountain. Or perhaps it was the last gasp of
Birmingham's straining to re-invent itself for the international business community, the last gasp of the Trickledown
theory. Whatever it was, it was a great bog.

THREE

To be utterly frank, it had never occurred to me that A.J.P. Taylor and I had that much in common; until I found an essay he wrote for *Encounter* magazine back in the 1950s. In this, among other things, Manchester's best-known historian observed that 'Manchester will soon offer offices, warehouses and vast stretches of desolation. You can already stand in the districts cleared of slums and feel as solitary as in the Sahara; only the rows of street-lamps remind you that human beings once lived here.'

Forty years on, this is exactly how it struck me as I toiled out of the Piccadilly railway station. I sweated along Piccadilly, past Mangle Street and into what purports to be the centre of town. It was as if the war had only just ended. I generally find that stepping off a train and carrying an overnight bag stuffed with unnecessary socks and pull-overs is a sure way to bump heavily and persistently into strangers as I struggle past them on the street. But not this time. However much I hefted my bag around and swung it at the calves and shins of passers-by, there just weren't enough people to hit. Moreover, there was more derelict and flattened land around me than I could ever remember seeing in a big English city. So even if I'd come close with my burden of sweaters and smalls, the brighter Mancunians could simply have stepped off the pavement and onto a block's worth of waste ground.

The centre, according to my map, was Piccadilly Gardens. This turned out to be an irregular polygon filled with tarmac, paving slabs, weather-beaten trees, a clutch of winos, a bus depot and some lugubrious trams. The scene was framed by a mixture of expansive, under-used roads and terminal-looking shops. After Birmingham, where everyone steams across town in a fug of enterprise and where the air is filled with the clicking of ball-point pens as council executives sit together in frantic plenary sessions, this torpid desolation unnerved me. Was it plague, perhaps?

And yet this, like Birmingham, was supposed to be England's Second City. This too used to be the Workshop of the World. I don't know how Birmingham and Manchester settled their competing claims to these titles, but I suppose claims were like that in the nineteenth century ('I used your soap two years ago; since then I have used no other'). But Birmingham was never Cottonopolis. And I had this idea that whatever else might have happened to Manchester in the last hundred years, the riches that had come from turning raw cotton into cloth would have been enough to keep the city busy until I got to it.

In fact its wealth is standing all over the place in the guise of many extremely large buildings: but the ready cash has run out.

The ready cash started rolling *in* during the sixteenth century, when the young Manchester had started to make a name for itself as a centre for wool and flax processing. By the seventeenth century, this had changed to the manufacture of fustians and smallwares (ribbons and edgings and what have you) and – significantly – to the weaving of cotton, imported from the Levant. In the eighteenth century, things really took off: the spinning jenny was invented, the power-loom appeared, the price of coal came down and new canals allowed Manchester to get cotton in large quantities from the port at Liverpool. In 1781, we imported 5,000,000 pounds of raw cotton. By 1801, this had risen to 56,000,000 pounds. Basically, Manchester and the towns around it were clothing India, the Far East and (curiously) Latin America in their finished products.

Throughout the nineteenth century, Manchester just throve. The coal came out of the ground in immense quantities; the cotton poured in and the finished goods poured out. The Manchester Ship Canal (completed 1894) oiled the wheels of commerce. The vast buildings kept on being put up. Rich from cotton, Manchester became the regional centre of the financial and service industries, while the engineers who had started life working on power-mills and looms went on to make all kinds of manly equipment – trains; machine tools, even cars at one time. The *Manchester Guardian* (founded 1821) went from strength to strength. Manchester University, one of Britain's great seats of learning, flourished (founded 1851; reorganised 1903). I once met someone who had taken her degree at this great institution. I got terrifically excited and said, well, what was it like? And all she could say was, 'It really did rain an awful lot and . . . I didn't go into town very much.'

Then, as with so much of British Industry, it all went wrong this century. The trouble started when those countries which had been exporting cotton to Manchester and re-importing it in finished form, or just buying the stuff ready-made, found out how to perform the whole process themselves. China and Japan developed their own cotton industries in the early 1900s, and by the 1930s India was making most of its cotton products itself and even banning imports of the British variety. Then the Second World War came along, the trading patterns of the nineteenth century finally disintegrated completely and, from 1950 onwards, the textile industry lost, on average, 12,000 workers a year. Coal followed an equally precipitate decline and now has ceased to mean anything at all (particularly when you think that at the time of writing, only sixteen British Coal pits are left operating in the UK as a whole).

The *Manchester Guardian* slunk off to London and became

the *Guardian*, Published in London and Manchester. The city
put in a bid to host the Olympic Games and failed. The
Hacienda nightclub opened, closed and then reopened.
Manchester put in another bid to host the Olympics and
failed again. It became notorious for containing a fantasti-
cally violent, crime-ridden area called Moss Side, where
even drug barons locked the car doors and told their wives
what time to expect them home. Manchester became
Gunchester. And there are these *holes* in the scenery, as
spotted by A.J.P. Taylor and still there when C.A. Jennings
wandered out of Piccadilly Station. The last time I saw so
many grasses, bushes and saplings growing out of abandoned or semi-derelict buildings was in southern Turkey.

This is not mere suburban prissiness. I know what a
degraded urban environment looks like. I once lived near
the M40 flyover in North Kensington, a part of London which
was so urban-alienated and street-smart I had difficulty (on
account of stylelessness and nerves) ever getting out of the front
door, dressed as I normally was in a tweed jacket and
spectacles and blinking constantly in the haze of puke,
marijuana exhalations and road mender's tar which filled
the streets. I know what a run-down town looks like, but
Manchester gave me the creeps. My first really northern town.

Let me take you, as it says in the tourist hand-out 'Celebrity
Walks in Great British Cities', around Manchester. Actually, Bobby Charlton has the unenviable task of walking
around Manchester for 'Celebrity Walks' (Sooty, as in Sooty
and Sweep, a celebrity without legs, does Bradford; while
Gary Lineker gets – poor sap – Leicester), but Bobby plays it
with a typically clear head. His strategy is simply to miss out
just about everything as he follows a top-hat-shaped itinerary from the Granada TV Studios Tour, past some shops,
past some more shops, past the Art Gallery and finally to
Chinatown, 'Through the splendid Chinese Arch.'

The way I did it was to wander about haphazardly

describing a series of Zs, Xs and Qs, constantly passing and repassing places such as the Free Trade Hall and the Arndale Centre without actually realising they were there. At the same time I allowed myself to descend into deeper and deeper abysms of gloom.

First of all, I blundered into the area in front of the almost too famous Town Hall (finished in 1877, Alfred Waterhouse's best-known work after the Natural History Museum in London). Here, true to the form first shown around Picca-dilly Gardens, it was about as bustling as Dartmoor. Known as Albert Square, this space boasts a rather nice monument to the Prince Consort and used to have traffic all over it. Apparently, one of Manchester's mayors, Leslie Lever (also Labour MP for Ardwick), used to proceed around Albert Square, bowing and waving to the people. But the council pedestrianised it in the vain hope, I suppose, that world-class tumblers and mime artists would be encouraged to do their tricks there and bring life to the scene, in the same tiresome way they do to the equally barren cement patch in front of the Beaubourg Centre in Paris.

Well, the mime artists weren't there when I was there. Nor was anyone else, which may be why Bobby describes Piccadilly Gardens as 'The heart of the city', on account of the relatively welcoming presence of its argumentative derelicts and morose-looking Lancastrians heading for the bus station.

Still, hungry for excitement, I marched over to an enormous notice board in front of the Town Hall. It was crowned with the legend 'Manchester – Making it Happen' and had one notice on it, printed on a sheet of A4 paper. This read, 'Greater Manchester Campaign against domestic violence. Singer Claire Mooney followed by a disco.' About a hundred yards away, an office worker sat on a bench and picked at a McDonald's in a Styrofoam clam. A further hundred yards away from him, some secretaries hurried across the concrete plain into the shelter of a pub.

The only real signs of life were coming from inside the Town Hall itself, where a BBC film team was shooting scenes from a drama in which Ian Richardson played a psychopathic Prime Minister and Michael Kitchen played the future King of England in a pair of athletic shorts. There were costumes hanging up on racks and many highly strung BBC film people wandering around the corridors with clipboards. Apparently, Manchester Town Hall is what film makers use in lieu of the Palace of Westminster. So I tucked my daily newspaper, my notebook and my banana snack firmly under my arm and walked blatantly into some of the rooms. But if the Palace of Westminster really looks like the Manchester Town Hall inside, then we are in worse trouble than I thought.

It was wonderful, in a way, to see these immense Victorian municipal furnishings, with their leather tops and their beefy, turned legs, sprawling in high, untenanted rooms. It was equally agreeable to look out through Waterhouse's chilly stone windows while a washed-out sun lit up the tonnage of wooden panelling covering the walls behind me. I enjoyed going up and down the insanely elaborate staircases and stairwells. I almost took pleasure in a sort of bust they keep on the ground floor, of Sir John Barbirolli – conductor of Manchester's Hallé Orchestra from 1943 to 1970 – which looks like a spider with three heads and which clearly is the product of a drugged but intermittently lucid mind. And I liked the civic touch of a set of double doors with 'The Lord Mayor, Private' written on their frosted glass (the burden of civic duty in Manchester is such that the Mayor actually lives in his Town Hall).

At the same time, the whole place looked as though it had been last cleaned in 1960. There was a patina of grime over everything. It was like being in a fish tank whose water had been left to evaporate. Although there were occasional council apparatchiks wandering about ('Have you found those reports yet, Mandy? Not to worry'), the life seemed to have left the building. If it had been someone's ancestral home, you'd have said, I give this family another two generations before they either fall apart through inanition and madness or are evicted by the mortgage company. Who cares for this place? Apart from the BBC?

Later on I bumped into a Mancunian undertaker, the way one does, so I asked him what was special about his home town. He said, 'Manchester's all about community.'

Oh, yes?

'Warmth and community. It's the sort of place where people go out of their way to help each other.'

He had a brass fish on his lapel to indicate that he was a born-again Christian, so that may have had something to do with it. He also warned me in a community-minded way about visiting the notorious Hacienda nightclub ('Oh no, you don't want to go there. They get a lot of trouble there.' How did *he* know?). He went on to say how sad it was that they didn't get the Olympics.

'It would have given a lot of hope to the young people. Too many of them are stuck without jobs.'

But what about the emptiness? What about the wide open spaces? What about all the buildings that are falling down or have fallen down? What about the Town Hall?

'Yes,' he said after a pause, 'I think the council's let us down, rather.'

He was a nice fellow and he certainly caused me to think of undertakers in a new light, but it wasn't much of an explanation. Teach me to ask the locals direct questions, I thought. You only get nonsense in reply.

Outside, in a street round the back of the Town Hall, I found the Mayor. It couldn't have been anyone else. He was sitting in a stretched Ford Granada, wearing formal clothes and a chain of office and had a woman with him whom I took to be his wife. He had evidently come out of his home, got into his car and been abandoned. There was no driver,

no policeman, no one for hundreds of yards in any direction
to take an interest in him. Even he'd been left to rot. I peered
at him through the smoked glass and mouthed, 'Manchester
– Making it Happen,' and he twitched a faint, apprehensive
smile in reply.

I pressed on from there to Deansgate, one of the ugliest
streets in the world. The northern end of this three-quarter-
mile-long, dead-straight drag is home to the Cathedral
(basically fifteenth century, but knackered about by the
Victorians). In practical terms, this means that Manchester's principal Anglican church is right next to the A56 dual
carriageway and, beyond that, overlooks an NCP car park
about the size of Wembley Stadium. Its immediate neigh-
bour on the opposite side to the A56 is a derelict building
with the inscription 'Hanging Bridge Chambers, 1881' over
what's left of the front door. There was once an actual
hanging bridge over the chasm that became the A56, but it
moved with the times. To cross the road nowadays you have
to pant up and down a lot of barbarous concrete steps,
wondering exactly at what point it was that England's town
planners collectively lost their marbles.

Moving briskly south, I got into what purports to be the
classy end of Manchester's shopping experience, with some
defensive-looking jewellery boutiques (even the optician's, I
noticed, had a full-time security guard in it) and a hopeless
provincial department store. The one in Manchester is
called Kendals. Birmingham has one too, called Rack-
hams. Both really belong to an age long gone, an age in
which middle-class housewives went out shopping, ate cakes
in department store cafés with their friends and complained
about their foundation garments. But this doesn't stop
Bobby Charlton from warning us that 'Some fancy foot-
work is required if you want to avoid temptation!'

It was, on the other hand, both depressing and gratifying
to note the number of Hard Men loitering about in

doorways and at the mouths of alleys. They pointedly wore T-shirts when the weather turned cold and had that blank, innocent look on their faces that only real nutters possess. Many of them had one or other arm in plaster, something which would have been a fashion statement in London, but up here, I think, meant that they'd broken their arms. Too many fights? Or simply desperately clumsy men, coupled with some unusually heavy swing doors? The Hard Men have at least put on some weight in the last hundred years. At the time of the Boer War, two-thirds of Manchester volunteers for the British Army were rejected as being unfit and only a tenth were accepted. During the First World War, the smallest soldiers in the British forces came almost uniformly from Manchester and its satellites: the legacy of the abominable living and working conditions produced by the Industrial Revolution.

The girls, by way of contrast, were tricked out in an agreeable, if rather large-boned style: tight sweaters, big hair, appetising make-up – a style that London women with their in-your-face fashions don't attempt any more. Once they hit middle age, however, the Manchester girls all seem to fall apart. The sweaters, the slap, the bosoms, disappear – and any woman over, say, forty, will almost certainly be completely grey-haired and worn out like an old wallet.

About half-way down, the character of Deansgate starts to change and the shops get scabbier and lower rent and the number of small and not entirely viable companies perched in third-floor offices increases. The buildings also grow more violently and horribly Victorian Mercantile in character and more and more run-down. This process reaches some sort of climax in what used to be the LNER depot (no trains there now, of course), which is itself part of a red-brick five-storey building running for almost a quarter of a mile along Deansgate's eastern side and which is nothing less than an architectural nightmare.

This is partly due to its colour (a drunkenly hectic red);

partly due to the incontinent mess of detailing all over the outside; partly due to its overwhelming, positively American, scale; partly due to the fact that much of the brick and tilework hasn't softened one jot with age so that it still comes at you with full gingery aggressiveness; and partly due to the fact that where it has aged, it hasn't mellowed, it's just fallen to bits. This is one of those Manchester buildings with small bushes growing out of the guttering. Its windows are broken, or blackened with lorry soot. It affords the passer-by odd, depressing glimpses of a life within, most of which, judging by appearances, takes place in pokey offices washed with smudged off-white paint, lit by defective fluorescent lights and concealing some kind of impropriety about the fire regulations. Edward Hopper territory, if you like, but without the colour, sex or genial candour.

But come further with me, down Deansgate. Watch out for Salford, mark you: this lies on the right, separated from Manchester proper by a sluggish black channel called the River Irwell. Salford, I believe, maintains the quaint pretence of being somehow vitally different from Manchester. But at first glance it's hard to see why it should bother. Three observations merely: did you know that the late Jim Morrison has been spotted working in a video shop in Salford? That The Great Morrissey had Salford in mind when he sang 'The rain falls hard on a humdrum town/This town has dragged you down'? That the first thing you see when you cross Albert Bridge over the Irwell is the Salford Social Security Office? Salford in a nutshell.

Then, right at the bottom of Deansgate, something strange happens. What civilisation there is starts fading gradually away, until nothing is left but a wasteland. Manchester just frays at the edges. The only thing left by the time you get to the south-western corner of the city is a very large museum. Following the same logic that put the Cathedral on a promontory moated by sixty-mile-an-hour traffic and condemned Victorian buildings, the Museum of

Science and Industry has been sited in a moonscape of
gravel traps, suspended demolition work, redundant canals
and the occasional hundred-year-old building. I might point
out that the Museum of Science and Industry is imaginative,
absorbing, diverse. It contains the first railway station in
Britain – the one at the end of the Manchester–Liverpool
line which the Duke of Wellington opened in 1830. It has
some excellent sewers. But to get to it is like walking through
the outskirts of Paris after the Prussian bombardment.

Indeed, the long, deserted, punishingly straight Liverpool
Road (home to the museum) led me so far away from the
rest of human life that I thought I might never see my hotel
again. On one side there was an endless, blank red-brick
wall. On the other side, every now and then, there would be
a pub or a newsagent's – low, sad buildings that Dickens
would have recognised – before the rubble and the canal,
way below, would reappear. About half-way along, a brand-
new hotel has been built in the shape of an industrial
warehouse. It was offering concessionary rates, as well it
might.

A solitary figure came towards me. 'Excuse me,' he said in
what I took be a broad Mancunian accent. 'Am I going the
right way for the Town Hall?' He was in fact heading for
Wigan, so I turned him round and he panted off, red-faced
and disorientated, in the direction from which he had just
come.

I'd reached the south-western corner of Manchester and
here at the quiet limit of the world, there was nothing but
was lonely, ugly and abandoned. Somewhere to the east was
the G-Mex centre (once the old Central Station, now an
exhibition centre) standing in its own patch of wasteland.
South of that was the barren hinterland around the Deansgate Station. Over to the north-east was the dirt and decay
of the Oldham Road. To be honest, I too felt lonely, ugly
and abandoned.

I would point out, incidentally, that this experience was

not exclusive to Deansgate, the Cathedral or the Town Hall.
Wherever I went, more or less, in the square mile of central
Manchester, I would find a route equally grim and oppres-
sive. Whether it was up Mosley Street, along Oldham Street
and into Cannon Street; or along the Rochdale Road, down
High Street, through Fountain Street and back to the Town
Hall; or sweating along Portland Street, down Chorlton
Street, along Whitworth Street, up Peter Street and into
Deansgate again, it was all the same. I never knew quite
where I was because the gargantuan buildings blotted out
everything except themselves. The people were sparse and
hunched. The trams hooted mournfully. Manchester was
pervasive.

To make it worse, the sun was shining. Now, Manchester in
the rain is dispiriting. But Manchester in the sun is so
relentless, dusty, hard and treeless (the only green space
in town is the Peace Gardens, which are the same size as the
front page of the *Manchester Evening News*), all it makes you
want to do is stick your head in a glass of lager and leave it
there. So I did that.

I ended up, Bobby Charlton style, somewhere near
Chinatown (what is this Chinatown, anyway? One block
with a Chinese archway and some restaurants does not
amount to a Chinatown. Gerrard Street in London is more
like a Chinatown, but even that's barely a Chinatown),
blundered into a pub and started to swill beer.

That's one thing there's an abundance of in Manchester: places to have a drink. The streets bear testimony to
this in many ways. A barred and silent warehouse will
frequently turn out to have a neon Budweiser sign
glowing in a lower ground window and a bar hidden
down a flight of stone steps. Opportunistic wine bars crop
up in unlikely places, hiding under banks and in upstairs
attics. Outside the window of my hotel room was a
particularly lavishly appointed young persons' bar, filled

with television screens and the sort of seats that are designed to take a good deal of punishment. It was offering 'Naughty Nicker Nite', in which a nicker (or pound sterling) would buy you anything from a Snakebite to a Vimto Special. At around midnight I watched (with a mixture of bewilderment and deep respect) five well-built girls come out of the main doors of the Naughty Nicker Nite Bar in a conga line and proceed to head off down Oldham Street. They were singing, 'We're going to a disco, we're going to a disco, da-da-daah-da, da-da-daah-da.' Big lads, real men with their arms in plaster, jumped to get out of their way.

I was in something more middle-of-the-road. It had crossed my mind to do a Mass Observation job, inspired by that anthropological classic *The Pub And The People*, published in 1942. In this, the Mass Observation team descended on Bolton, ten miles north-east of Manchester, and wrote down how quickly the locals drank their gills (quarter-pints) of beer and (and I'm not making this up) what percentage of them wore flat caps on Saturdays as opposed to Sundays. There is even a table of the number of seats per spittoon in Bolton's pubs, plus snippets of con-versation, such as, 'Theau come wi' no bait, we g'en thee three tins o' bloody maggots, and then theau wants more.' But having just spent a lifetime toiling the streets of the city, I simply couldn't face the urban anthropologist's burden of totting up how many times the regulars farted, or how often they used the words 'elbow grease', or where they stood in relation to the pub's fag machine. So I sat and stared glassily as two Bet Lynch barmaids chafed the regulars and pulled pints ('Yer big dozy pudding. I know what you were up to last night').

In the early evening, the place was occupied mainly by office workers and the odd resting petty criminal. One bunch of weary-looking middle-aged men in grey trousers contained an authentic northern prat: a spindly little geezer

with a moustache who was clearly Manchester United's
Mr Memory Man. It didn't matter whether his colleagues
tried to start more interesting conversations of their own or
just gazed morosely into their beer, he went on talking
United.

'League Champions, right? Sixty-four, sixty-five, right?
Sixty-six, sixty-seven, right? Stunning record. One of *the*
indisputably great footballing performances. But it don't
stop there, does it? European Cup, sixty-eight, are you with
me? And what was sixty-three?'

'Haven't got a clue,' said a balding man in specs.

'FA Cup, right? And who scored in sixty-eight when they
took Benfica to Sketchley's, four-one? And this is Benfica I'm
talking about, European Cup Winners, sixty-one, sixty-two,
right? I'm not talking Accrington Stanley, right?'

'Bin a warm day, today.'

He made *me* feel good, if no one else. I interpreted his gas
as authentic Northern Chippiness. This was something
which had been on my list of things to experience the
moment I'd got on the train to Manchester and found
myself surrounded by a group of five controversially
minded Lancastrian dotards who spent the entire trip
squabbling among themselves. Since the prat was talking
to a passive, if not acquiescent, local audience, I suppose the
chippiness was more latent than expressed. But I lapped it
up all the same. Had I got up and blurted out something
about Tottenham or Arsenal, then I might have got a real
dose of it. But as it was, I was too hot and weary even to tear
open my crisp packet.

'And what was the first League Championship? Pre-First
World War?'

Later on, though, the pub's character changed. The office
workers shrugged their cares back onto their shoulders and
returned to their homes in Altrincham and Cheadle, to get
into pointless fights with their wives and children and to
dream of being rich. By ten o'clock at night, there was a real

this-is-another-country feel to the place. It was about half full and the clientele was mainly composed of awesomely decrepit men and women. Not tramps, exactly, merely people who were short of a good few teeth, had a taste for heavily torn and stained clothing and the kind of hair that looked as if it might have been used for something. In the first half of this century, wrecked old Manchester plebs used to tie rashers of bacon over their chests in the autumn to protect themselves against the winter's smog. These people still appeared to be wearing the bacon. Moreover, a woman in her forties or possibly fifties (or possibly thirties if life had dealt her a really bum hand) was standing in front of a crowd of seated drunks, brandishing a plucked chicken (still with its feet, head, legs and so on) and performing indecent acts upon the corpse. She was getting some big laughs.

'I told 'im to stick 'is 'ead up 'is arse but I didn't think 'e'd fookin' take me literally!' she barked, sticking the bird's head up its back passage. 'Dark up there! Fookin' dark up there!'

'Fookin' dark!' agreed another woman, nursing a mild and bitter.

'I think I'll 'ave a look meself!'

Her audience was in that state of extreme beeriness in which people either cackle uncontrollably and then slump tearfully on top of each other, or start chucking glasses about. She took the chicken's head out of its bum and had a look up there.

'It *is* fookin' dark up there, an' all!'

More gales of scented laughter, then she dropped the chicken and sat down heavily on an ageing greaser who had forearms like Popeye, all covered in tattoos. She got a round of applause. Further down the pub, a short, grey-haired woman was head-butting a fruit machine.

The semi-derelicts then began to move in a vaguely concerted way, a sort of seated swaying motion, as if we were all on a boat in the English Channel. After a while, it dawned on me that I wasn't feeling frightfully bright myself.

I even wondered if some of the younger, less hopeless ones might not decide to tell me to buy everyone else a round. Things had degenerated quite a long way and what at five o'clock had looked like no more than an averagely beaten-up city pub had now taken on an irrational, aggressive character. So I clumsily gathered up my gear and fell out of the front door into the windy Manchester night. The chicken woman started up again and a very large man came out from behind the bar and dragged the grey-haired woman away from the fruit machine. ('You'll fookin' break it, Pauline.')

Now, was this any worse than an average night in New Cross? Of course not. I can remember spending an afternoon in a pub in Brixton – a quiet afternoon, by Brixton standards – where every man Jack was either too pissed to stand up or was just sober enough to stagger across the floor in dance paroxysms brought on by the jukebox which played nothing but Abba at tremendous volume. One customer's speciality was to pull the front of his T-shirt over his face and then launch himself from his tottering barstool with a cry of 'Montego!' before landing flat on his back on the floor. He did this six or seven times in the space of an hour. His drinking companion (well, his closest drinking companion; we were all, necessarily, his drinking companions, one way or another) thought this was so amusing he regularly toppled off *his* barstool with laughter and Montego had to try and help him up again.

Was the woman with the chicken any worse? No. But what was bizarre was the fact that this was happening just round the corner from what must be the least insalubrious part of town: the stretch containing the Town Hall, the Art Gallery, the Portico Library. It was as if one of Peckham's less well-run boozers had been dropped with its full comple-ment of regulars next door to Harrods. I couldn't under-stand what this beery dump was doing in the heart of cultural Manchester. Nor was it the only one. In fact,

almost every boozer I passed was full of shouting drunks and
spilled beer.

Down South there is normally a boundary you have to
cross, a *cordon sanitaire*, between the savage bits and the
tolerable bits and everyone knows where these boundaries
are. Except for foreign tourists, of course, whom I keep
finding trapped in the grimy maw of Hammersmith, asking
pathetically for directions to Kensington Palace. In the
South, almost every town or city has a smart bit where
they keep the restaurants and the prissy shops. There is
invariably a street or two of groomed private houses with
large cars outside. It is the up-market neighbourhood.

Much of Bristol, for instance, is a dreary mess, but you
can't mistake Clifton, where the Chablis set live. And if this
is true for Bristol, it's also true for Plymouth, Brighton,
Gloucester, Reading (provided you include Caversham),
Portsmouth, even Southampton, although I admit that
Southampton's pushing it a bit. There is contrast. There
is smart, there is middling and there is poor. You can draw
them on a map.

But up here, there didn't seem to be any distinction.
Manchester simply hadn't got the same interest in cultivat-
ing a smart part. Instead, it seemed to divide itself along the
lines of: big and still in a state of repair/big and collapsing/
small and rough/just rough. This may, of course, simply be
proof of my new friend A.J.P. Taylor's claim that 'Manchester is the only place in England which escapes our
characteristic vice of snobbery'. In other words, the place
is so uniformly, democratically rough and run-down that it
would be futile even to contemplate a 'smart' part of town.
But I don't think he meant that and I don't believe
Manchester would see it that way, either.

Then again, once I'd got out of the pub, I came across a
party of tourists being haled around the centre of town,
unaccountably late at night. They had foregathered by the
main doors of a high street bank, where their guide was

explaining to them the principles and practicalities of a hole-
in-the-wall cash dispenser. It's not exactly what you'd call
classy.

To get an impression of what a Mancunian finds classy, you
have to leave Manchester altogether. Actually, the smart set
has been emigrating from Manchester – either by choice or
necessity – for years. A guide to Manchester, published in
1839, made the point that 'The increasing business of the
town is rapidly converting all the principal dwelling-houses
. . . into mercantile establishments and is driving most of the
respectable inhabitants into the suburbs.' In 1820, Manchester had 126 warehouses. By 1829, it had over a thousand.
Would you want to live next door to a building the size of the
Royal Festival Hall, covered in encaustic tiles and full of
rats? So the Manchester middle classes left Lancashire
altogether and went to squat on the Cheshire side of the
line in places like Cheadle Hulme, Macclesfield and Wilmslow.

I also had the idea that when bourgeois Mancunians
wanted to relax, they went off to the Derbyshire Peak
District, about twenty miles away. So I actually went there
once with my wife for a nice weekend (in the credulous way
Londoners tend to approach the North when they want to
use it for recreation). But when we got there it was so
breathtakingly dull, I couldn't believe it could have any
currency with today's Mancunians. Buxton was quite nice –
like Bath, but falling apart and not so many cars. And I
enjoyed the spectacle of queues of local Buxtonians forming
by a well-head of some sort where they filled up plastic
containers with the warm, faintly malodorous spring waters
of the region.

We also caught the famous Peak District well-dressing
ceremony, but this, it struck me, was something of a triumph
of skill over content. Well-dressing entails using petals and
leaves to make seven-foot by four-foot pictures of local

churches, religious scenes and pastoral interludes. These are
then placed at the heads of many of the local wells. Very
clever, but are they worth it? Apparently not, judging by the
mutinous faces of the schoolchildren who'd been dragooned
by their teachers and vicars into making the things. 'Is that
near here?' I asked one of them, after examining a repre-
sentation of a church. 'Can't you bloody see?' she said,
pointing at the building directly behind her.

On the other hand, well-dressing is one of the few regional
customs I can claim to have seen with my own eyes, so I do
feel some kind of gratitude towards it. I mean, the very idea
of customs and traditions sounds phoney to Londoners,
given the restless, evanescent nature of the madhouse we
live in. So to find one apparently more-or-less spontaneously
surviving gave me something of a kick: something of the
sensation of tapping the vein of history which imbues
England with its unique sense of self.

In fact, London – according to my handbook *Events In
Britain* – actually tops the charts for extant old customs,
having no fewer than forty-five recorded. I have to say that
I've never come across any of them, but they are listed.
Yorkshire and Lancashire are equal second, both with
eighteen. In particular, Lancashire offers the Easter Sunday
Nutters Dance, at Bacup ('Dressed in black breeches, white
barrel skirts, decorated clogs, with their faces blacked, the
coconut dancers . . . dance through the streets of the town to
the accompaniment of the town band'), and the Cockle and
Mussel Feast at Clitheroe, which 'Occurs before the first
council meeting, where tinned shellfish are served to the
councillors'.

But are these events real? I suspect not, any more than
those in the Yorkshire list. These range from the Goathland
Plough Stots, to Planting the Penny Hedge or Horngarth, to
Burning the Bartle. Implausible enough, you'll agree, but I
must say I wouldn't have minded seeing if the Whitby
Ancient Gooseberry Contest ('Gooseberries of astonishing

size compete in one of the oldest horticultural events of the country') actually took place. And I would have paid money to watch Shrovetide Skipping, at Scarborough: 'Hundreds of people of all ages gather on the Southlands Promenade after midday to skip with huge ropes until nightfall.'

Nevertheless, they were dressing their wells in Derbyshire. They were also selling thousands of dense, flavourless Bakewell tarts, in Bakewell. And our hotel put ruched curtains in the lavatory and served some perfectly nice lamb chops in a jam sauce, just to impress us because we were from the South. It didn't really add up.

Macclesfield, on the other hand, is not too bad a place, although its tone was compromised for me when I discovered that it was the home of a popular entertainer called Mr Methane. Mr Methane is an extremely tall ex-engine driver whose real name is Paul Oldfield. His act, if you couldn't guess, is to fart musically and rhetorically in the manner of the late Joseph Pujol, *Le Pétomane*. His debut was at the Screaming Beavers Club in Macclesfield and he was such a hit that he immediately went out and 'Had a lot of business cards made.' Anyway, despite the fact that Mr Methane is now moving upmarket (farting *The Nutcracker Suite* to student audiences – 'They listen. They will hear the tone changes' – that kind of thing), he made Macclesfield seem a bit too earthy, a bit too raw. So I went to Wilmslow instead.

Now, Wilmslow – too big to be a village, too small to be a town – is a weird settlement, but it does give you an idea of what constitutes class in a Lancastrian sense. This is where the comfortably heeled Mancunian lives when he's not setting up country club leisure facilities in the Algarve or helping to export bathware fittings to Lagos. Wilmslow is also where wealthy Mancunians park their women, children and social dependents to keep them quiet. As a consequence, while the Mancunian men are away doing their business,

Wilmslow during the day is a hybrid of *Hello!* magazine and *The Stepford Wives*.

As I swept commandingly into the centre of town in my rented Ford Fiesta, I was at once carved up by a well-presented woman struggling at the wheel of a sixteen-foot Mercedes. This was followed, shortly after, by a near miss with a pink and white Japanese jeep, driven by a twenty-year-old blonde, clad in no more than a handful of pulse-quickening black garments and wearing an entire drawer of gold jewellery on her fingers. There were throngs of BMWs, Mercs and Jags wherever my eyes nervously swivelled. There was big hair. There were clearly large sums of money behind the place and as a consequence, everything had an awful, unnatural, costly sheen to it.

This even extended to an uncannily well-maintained 1960s branch of Barclays Bank. Barclays do their business in Wilmslow in an interesting experiment in novel concrete forms and whimsical Roland Emett extrusions which anywhere else would have been demolished or turned into a discount jeans outlet, but which in Wilmslow was proudly kempt and flying a flag. If Manchester itself is disintegrating, there are still enough wealthy Mancunians to preserve Wilmslow and its inhabitants in their entirety. In fact, one of the few things a Yorkshireman I met could bring himself to say about the area was, 'Typical Lancashire: three Rollers and mean as shit.' It was surprising to see so much evidence of money. I had taken it to be (almost as an article of faith) a part of the country which was flat broke. To be honest, I felt like a bit of a bum myself.

Having parked my car (there isn't a great deal else to do in Wilmslow except drive your car, park it, then get back in and drive it and park it somewhere very slightly different) I breezed over to a modish wine bar. I fidgeted with the menu and opted for a BLT. 'D'you want chips with it?' asked the comely waitress, giving the lie to the wine bar's evident pretensions as a place where trendsetters foregather over a

self-denying espresso. As well as chips, there were an awful
lot of portable phones being brandished by young men and
women. The young men and women said things into their
phones like, 'Yeah, Dave, it's Pete. Trix says it's okay for
Saturday but she's got to get her car back from the garage,'
or, 'Pete, it's Tessa. I can't make it on Friday but I'll have
the car on Saturday, so tell Mike I'll be there,' or, 'Trix is
coming on Saturday but Mike's car is still over at Tessa's
with Pete's car keys.' It seemed to be one long social whirl,
interspersed with casual work as a wine-bar waitress, a bit of
driving and parking in some surprisingly new BMWs and a
little light shopping in the interim.

Of course, everyone looked fantastic, in that consciously
perfected way that you don't find in London any more. The
men patted their haircuts and kept the dirt off their chino
pants. The women, young and old, wandered around in
layers of make-up, their hair glossed, their figures ideally
curvaceous. The whole town smelt of perfume, deposited by
the women of Wilmslow as they trawled from parked car to
cookshop to hosiery boutique in search of something to buy.
I dug into my BLT and scanned a copy of the *Wilmslow
Express*, while the wine bar's insouciant young chef bellowed
out of the kitchen window, 'I've got this New Zealand girl
staying with me and by Christ, she's the stupidest tart I've
ever come across.'

On page one of the *Wilmslow Express* it said: 'A thirty-
year-old woman was savagely beaten by a group of females
outside the Wilmslow Moathouse at the weekend.'

The nearest London equivalent I could think of was the
area on the city's northernmost edge – Hadley Wood,
Potters Bar, Radlett – where there's a similar air of permed
desperation. Here, too, the money is splurged all over the
place in the form of cars, huge Tudorbethan houses owned
by pornographers and gardens tended by retired burglars.
But even these places are tainted by the presence of the
Great Wen a few miles away. What gloss they have is

inevitably compromised by the presence of the smelly beast down the road. Wilmslow, on the other hand, appeared to be perfectly self-sustaining, perfectly independent of anything, countryside or city. It was just there, preening itself and doing its best to look nice for when the men got back.

Naturally, there is only so much of this kind of thing that one can take in a day. So I polished off my BLT and headed back to town, nearly losing part of the Fiesta on the front wing of a Roller whose driver was so small, I could barely see her head over the edge of the car door. I wondered why it was that a group of women should savagely beat another woman, in Wilmslow of all places. But then, places like Wilmslow are just enigmas, waiting not to be solved.

FOUR

I went back from Wilmslow via Moss Side with my teeth clenched, looking for contrast. Not that long ago, a twenty-one-year-old man was shot dead while riding around Moss Side on his bike. When they came to examine the body, it turned out that he was wearing a bullet-proof vest (the bullet entered his head). This should make a change, I thought. From my southern perspective, I couldn't work out exactly which the most violent, crime-ridden part of the UK was. There seemed to be something of a battle for this reputation between the North East, Greater Manchester, South Yorkshire and south-east London. Certainly, Moss Side seemed to have its publicity worked out, the words 'Moss Side' now acting as a universal shorthand for drug mayhem in much the same way as South Bronx and South Central, Los Angeles do for the wilder parts of the States. As I write, Greater Manchester's ambulancemen and women are deciding whether or not to wear flak-jackets when on duty. It was with a certain amount of perspiration bedewing my upper lip, therefore, that I took a turn off the A5103 into the place where the monsters were.

It turned out to be full of the sort of small, terraced Victorian workers' cottages which in London would have been ripe for colonising by the impoverished middle classes: two-up-two-down places with modest pretensions and a hint of L.S. Lowry about them. The problem was that they were alternately boarded up or burnt out, as if a marauding army had passed through before marching on BBC Manchester. What shops there were were either abandoned and covered in rusting wire mesh, or marginally active and covered in rusting wire mesh. There were a lot of hard-looking youths hanging about, kicking pebbles across the street and scowling at me whenever I caught their eyes. There was also what struck me as an unusual number of burning mattresses on the street corners.

I'd assumed, of course, that Moss Side would turn out to be the name of some gargantuan abortion of a late-1960s council estate. I was anticipating a predictable estate mixture of degrading utilitarian architecture, smashed-up supermarket trolleys and graffiti. But to find that Moss Side is actually the name of a homely plot of urban cottages made it somehow more eerie. It looked fine, it looked almost normal: but it evidently wasn't.

In fact I was starting to feel as conspicuous as an advertising dirigible. I wondered how long it would be before someone noticed the extreme newness of my rented Fiesta and the extreme, twitching whiteness of its driver. When a drugs baron in a black BMW with wide wheels, whiplash aerials and four-inch-diameter exhaust pipes cut me up at a junction, it was all I could do to stop myself from leaping out and shouting, 'Take the car! It's not mine anyway!' My sole aim in life for the twenty-five minutes I spent in Moss Side was to keep moving and not to miss the green traffic lights back onto the A5103. By the end I was practically bent double with nervous flatulence. Did I get out of the car at all? You must be joking.

I did wonder whether there might not be some overlooked possibilities for tourism, though. As I crawled tensely around Moss Side, I was listening (somewhat abstractedly) on the car radio to a local radio station which featured a DJ who sounded like a jovial version of George Harrison. He was running a competition which betrayed a peculiar set of priorities. First prize was a trip on a train (nice northern,

regional touch, well away from the ca[...]
East) down to London, where the wi[...]
the National Gallery followed by afte[...]
believe how staid and parochial this so[...]
Gallery (in London's tawdry, fume-infe[...] 58.
Square) followed by a real London visito[...]
of hot brine plus two leather scones and a [...] cake):
as enticing as a dose of gingivitis.

But think how Manchester could get its own back. First prize on any youth television programme (the sort where celebs and presenters alike give every appearance of being jacked up on coke and barely able to lace their own shoes, let alone talk coherently) could be a trip down Moss Side way. Here the lucky winners could see the gangstas at work, learn something of their fascinating craft, set fire to a small nineteenth-century terraced house and get shot at. Manchester's tourism could do with that kind of bold, self-confident initiative and I for one can vouch for the fact that the menace of Moss Side is nothing if not enlivening.

So what does an economically troubled, beaten-up, chilly, belligerently ugly city stuck in a nondescript part of the country do? It tries to host the Olympics. The very day I got off the train at Piccadilly Station, members of the Olympic Selection Committee were rolling into town to assess Manchester's bid for the Olympics in the year 2000. All round the town centre there were flags, banners, posters, proclaiming, 'British Olympics Bid Manchester 2000'. In fact, some of them were still there when I went back several weeks after the bid had collapsed. They were that serious.

Manchester had first tried to get the 1996 Olympics and failed; after Birmingham, coincidentally, had tried to get the 1992 Olympics and failed. Apparently the Birmingham bid was doomed from the start, being described as 'A lot of Labour councillors and their wives knitting'. Manchester's 1996 failure was subsequently dressed up as a rehearsal for

...ing with various justifications added for the sake ... . The Prime Minister (then Margaret Thatcher) ...n't been behind them, they argued. The chairman of the British Olympic Association hadn't been behind them. There were good reasons why the first bid should be seen as no more than a toning-up exercise. But *this* time, with the 2000 bid, *this* time they were going to be truly professional and awesomely sure of themselves. The ninety members of the International Olympic Committee would have no choice but to hand them the card and tell them to get on with it.

At first, I found the whole notion of Manchester's hosting the Olympic Games unintelligible. Certainly, they have some smart new trams to get you around town. Certainly, they were working on a £9 million, 3,500-seater Olympic velodrome (this is a stadium in which people race bicycles). Best of all, perhaps, they got John Major to commit £75 million of Government money, which, from a Tory administration, is an act which almost defies belief.

But the *place*. After Birmingham, I was almost beside myself with relief. No bright new Hyatt Hotels here. No intimidating sense of civic purpose so far as I could see. Manchester was spot-on, so far as this snotty Londoner was concerned. Manchester raised ugliness to new heights. It was ugly on a heroic scale. And it had a kind of morbidity about it which, dare I say it, Gustave Doré would have enjoyed and which I positively devoured. *This* wasn't going to make me reassess my scheme of things. Manchester was absolutely delivering the goods in its manifestations of northernness. Unlovely, down-at-heel, coarse, charmless, too cold, too dusty, too chippy, it had everything I needed to set my bigotries in marble and parade them around the suburbs of London. I had only to look around to see what an intrinsically sad place it was. Judging from the expressions on the faces of the Olympic Selection Committee as they were shooed into the Town Hall (once the BBC had left), they'd also seen quite enough on their way in from the airport and were making a mental note never to travel further north than Paris in the future.

And this is without even considering the opposition running for the 2000 games against Manchester. Peking, one of the main contenders, is drab and charmless too, but it is a capital city. It was given better odds than Manchester; of course it was. And Sydney, the winner – well, it stood out a mile. Given the choice, would you rather huddle against the cold winds of the Pennines while gazing out over Salford? Or would you prefer to lounge on a beach while fine, strapping wenches and bronzed hunks pour heavily oaked white wines and tear the legs off lobsters for you? Especially if you were one of today's venal, bubbleheaded top athletes? I felt sorry for those poor Mancunian devils who painted their faces in anticipatory triumph and laid in a stock of fireworks to celebrate their victory, only to be reduced to tears when they lost. But even I could have told them Manchester wouldn't win. The only British city even half capable of hosting the Olympics is London. But London can't manage it because London has physically collapsed. How did these people ever allow themselves to believe that the IOC was going to give them the job?

Even as I was wandering around the city, though, contradictory thoughts entered my head. The heroic scale of Manchester's awfulness is not an accident. The city is heroically awful, but it is heroic. Its monumental traders' palazzi and obnoxiously vast hotels (the Midland and the Britannia are almost bracingly hideous) are monuments to a weird but inimitable vision. They're also monuments to human suffering and endeavour.

At the start of the nineteenth century, Manchester was on the way from being a Georgian boom town to an industrial leviathan. It was also becoming a notorious stopping-off point for writers in search of human degradation. Robert

Southey (yes, him) passed through in 1802 and wrote: 'Here in Manchester a great proportion of the poor lodge in cellars damp and dark, where every kind of filth is suffered to accumulate . . . Imagine all this multitude crowded together in narrow streets, the houses all built of brick and blackened with smoke; frequent large buildings among them where you hear from within the everlasting din of machinery . . . Imagine this and you have the materials of a picture of Manchester.'

By 1844, a French commentator called Léon Faucher had arrived. Spoiled for choice when it came to depravity, he made the observation that there were 330 brothels containing 701 prostitutes and that 'The factory girls are strangers to modesty. Their language is gross and often obscene; and when they do not marry early, they form illicit connections which degrade them still more than premature marriage.' There were 920 beer sellers and 624 pubs. He quoted an observer who claimed to have seen, in the space of forty minutes, 112 men and 163 women enter a single tavern. The women, apparently, were even more desperate for booze than the men.

And of course there is Frederick Engels' *The Condition of the Working Class in England*, published in 1845. This is the capstone of Manchester's career as an object of horrified fascination. *Inter alia*, Engels observed 'Everywhere heaps of debris, refuse and offal; standing pools for gutters, and a stench alone which would make it impossible for a human being in any degree civilised to live in such a district.' Worse still was an area known as Little Ireland somewhere to the south-west of the Oxford Road. Hereabouts, 'Behind broken windows mended with oilskin, sprung doors, and rotten door-posts, or in dark wet cellars, in measureless filth and stench, this race really must have reached the lowest stage of humanity.'

With this as a background, it's hardly surprising that Manchester became a home of sedition and radicalism. The city in the nineteenth century was hit by a succession of riots.

The weavers rioted in 1808. There were food riots in 1812, when a mob tried to set the Exchange on fire. 1816 saw more food riots and the beginnings of the Reform movement. The Blanketeers marched in 1817 and in 1819 there was the Peterloo Massacre in which the King's Hussars variously hacked and trampled to death between six and fourteen (depending on whose account you read) Lancashire folk. In 1826 there was yet more rioting and in 1829 Manchester fell into the hands of a mob which looted shops, destroyed the contents of three factories and burnt a fourth to the ground. In 1849, a mob of Irishmen went on the rampage after one of them had gone to pay his tributes to the corpse of his grandson only to discover (upon opening the coffin) that the doctors had cut the grandson's head off to use for medical research, leaving a brick in its place as a makeweight.

And yet, out of all this, came Radicalism, Chartism, Richard Cobden, the Free Trade Hall and the Manchester School of political philosophy. Cobden, in particular, held that international peace could not be bought by force of arms but by commerce and the arts. In this respect alone, he was ahead of his time and may still be ahead of ours. From the swamp, in other words, comes forth the lotus flower of a great political and economic movement, leading ultimately to the somewhat weedier manifestation of the Labour Party.

This was naturally very appealing to my new friend, the late A.J.P. Taylor. As a self-proclaimed dissenter, he viewed Manchester's rebelliousness with suitable generosity. He didn't stop at praising Manchester's radicalism, however. For him, 'Manchester is the last and greatest of the Hanseatic towns – a civilisation created by traders without assistance from monarchs or territorial aristocracy.' He even made the point that 'A society based on money has the great merit of freedom from class.' This got him a rebuke recently from the ex-Manchester *Guardian*, along the lines of, You call the United States class free? But I take him to mean that a society based on money has the great merit of freedom from entrenched, ossified class structures. That you can, if rich enough, buy yourself into the top drawer. As (within limits) in the States. Whether this is a good thing in itself I don't know. But if you absolutely must have a hierarchical society, I would rate the cash system more highly than *Burke's Peerage*. It has a certain appealing transparency about it.

'Manchester,' burbled A.J.P., 'cares no more for the Royal Family and the landed gentry than Venice did for the Pope and the Italian aristocracy.' Look again at the *Guardian*, the only national broadsheet which consistently holds to a radical or semi-radical position. Or at the very least, the only national broadsheet which consistently reviles the Tory party. Consider the Free Trade Hall, a building named after a proposition. Can you imagine that in London? The Welfare State Hall? The Universal Suffrage Theatre (now retitled The Royal Universal Suffrage Theatre)? Look again at those buildings. A hundred and fifty years after they first went up, many of them now untenanted and disintegrating, they look like tombs rather than commercial powerhouses. But as examples of frozen energy (rather than frozen music, thank you) they fill you full of amazement. Some Mancunians must have been giants. What dreams did these people have? And do they still have them?

Pig-ignorant southerners like me generally fail to distinguish between Yorkshire and Lancashire. We can't tell the accents apart, any more than we can tell the Black Country apart from Birmingham. And if in doubt, we tend to lump everything north of Birmingham up to, say, Sunderland, into Yorkshire. Lancashire is the forgotten county. Only the cheese rings a few bells, that and some popular entertainers. And John Lennon singing about ten thousand holes in Blackburn, Lancashire. But once I began to get Manchester under my belt, it dawned on me that this is a place of pronounced, even noble characteristics. Manchester is not an accident. It shares several things in common with other northern cities, but it is consciously stranger and more overpowering than any of them.

Then there are the famous Mancunians and other Lancastrians. Some of these are, of course, better than others. Jimmy Clitheroe I can live without, after years of ruined Sundays spent listening to *The Clitheroe Kid*. Clitheroe was an extremely short Lancashire comedian who settled in Blackpool in a bungalow which he shared with his mother and a tame frog called Freddie. I can draw a veil over Wigan-born George Formby as well. The best thing about George Formby was that the Soviet Union awarded him the Order of Lenin in 1943.

But then what about Gracie Fields (Rochdale) or Al Read (meat maker from Salford and Lancashire 'droll' comedian. 'I come from a long line of sausages' was his joke)? Better still, Robb Wilton, a Merseysider by birth, but subsequently an all-purpose Lancastrian. (Why, incidentally, am I not going to Liverpool? Too big, too mad. The Naples of the North West. I couldn't face it.) When Robb said, 'The day war broke out, the missus turned to me and said, "Well, what are you going to do about it?"' I feel he spoke in some way on behalf of all married men. Ted Ray came from Wigan and was quick, but irritating. And then, of course, there was Eric Morecambe (born John Eric Bartholomew, in Morecambe), who in his day was very fair, although I felt that Morecambe and Wise (Ernie comes from Leeds, significantly) were never quite the same once Sid and Dick had left.

I ended up preferring Les Dawson ('I won't say our council house is a long way from the centre of town, but the rent collector's Norwegian'), who came from Manchester and settled in Lytham St Anne's. And what about Ken Dodd? Indisputably some kind of comic genius, but too Liverpool, not downbeat enough. Forget Tommy Handley

on that basis, too. It's that combination of miserableness and
irritability that Wilton and Dawson had seeping from their
crags which expresses so much for me.

If I'm going to be really expansive, I would even include
Granada TV's *Coronation Street* in the tradition of droll
Lancastrian humour. It comes direct from Manchester
and is an obscurely sophisticated programme, both genteel
('I'll behave with the utmost of decorum') and bathetic
('You've had six months to explain. Ever since we got back
from the Lakes'). At the same time, it's the most regularly
watched television show in the country, with a weekly
audience in the 18 millions. And it's been going since
1960. Now how do you account for that?

Then there are the other Lancastrians, men who aren't or
weren't comics, but who nonetheless display a number of
impressive and interesting quirks. The Great Morrissey
springs to mind (he once, wistfully, needless to say, envi-
saged himself as part of the Great Tradition of Lancashire
entertainers), as does Howard Jacobson. Jacobson now does
a cranky Manchester Jewish intellectual thug act, which is
less funny than his first book (*Coming From Behind*), but
certainly keeps him in the public eye.

L.S. Lowry, by way of contrast, was simply bats. Despite
rising to the position of chief cashier with the Pall Mall
Property Company in Manchester and retiring with a full
pension, he never told anyone in the art world about his
nine-to-five job. This was because he had a horror of being
thought an amateur. He wore filthy, paint-stained clothes in
the street and looked like a secretary bird with a hat on. In
his house in Longdendale, Cheshire, he kept a number of
clocks, all of which told a different time. When asked why, he
answered, 'Because I don't want to know the *real* time.'

And what about Manchester's Chief Constable James
Anderton, the man who, in 1986, made a speech to a police
officers' seminar, in which he launched a moral crusade
against AIDS, explaining this outburst to the world a few

days later by saying that he had been moved by the Spirit of God? Who then said in a radio interview in the following year that he believed that God may have been using him as a prophet? And who subsequently called for the outlawing of homosexuality and the return of flogging? Straight from the pages of Dickens, one would have said.

And then there was Harry Pollitt, one of the last breaths of Manchester Radicalism. Old Harry came from Droylsden, on the eastern edge of the city, and became famous as the chairman of the British Communist Party. He was a political militant of the demagogic variety, a species which no longer exists in this country. In 1925, he was imprisoned for twelve months after an Old Bailey trial for seditious libels and incitement to mutiny. When he came out, he found he'd missed the General Strike. When Britain declared war on Germany in 1939, he rushed out a pamphlet entitled 'How To Win The War'. A couple of days after that, Stalin (who had a thing going with Hitler at the time) purged him from the party. But he came back, celebrated his sixtieth birthday with a party at the Lime Grove Baths, Shepherd's Bush ('Leader yes, but also bone of the bone and flesh of the flesh of the toilers') and died in 1960 with a portrait of Stalin hanging defiantly in his semi.

The point I'm making is that all these people – successes, sometimes global successes, every one of them – are not just northerners, ey-oop, lumpen northerners, no matter how much people like me would like to condemn them to that undifferentiated state. They're not Yorkshiremen, are they? They're not as tediously canny; they're odder.

Some have concluded that the weather and the Pennines are behind it all. Yorkshiremen get the east wind blowing off the North Sea and across the gritty Moors and end up, as a result, like Michael Parkinson. Lancastrians, on the other hand, are fanned by the damp zephyrs of the Atlantic. This gives them a moist, bedewed view of the world which translates into humour, whimsy and song. In Lowry's case it also translates into execrable paintings.

As theories go, this doesn't impress me enormously, any more than the notion of abominable grinding poverty – another Lancashire speciality – being a fruitful ground for artistic talent. In fact, most generalising theories concerning nationalities or regionalities are apt to sound unconvincing. What remains from the epic, tomb-like grandeur of Cotto-nopolis and this curious collection of talented, entertaining people (I excuse Chief Constable Anderton from this en-comium) is the impression (for me, anyway) that there's a kind of forgotten greatness lying around, the relics of a civilisation. Bizarre, this, after all my metropolitan horror at the place. But there it is: a kind of absorbing, heroic doominess.

Anyway, how many great Yorkshire comics can you name? Apart from Sandy Powell?

Is this why they thought they could host the Olympics? Pride and eccentricity? Back in the city, I searched for a curry-house and was rewarded with an evening of what I took at first to be self-important Mancunian chippiness, but which on second thoughts was probably something deeper. There is an Indian restaurant opposite the Town Hall in whose furry darkness I sat, soaking up northern self-promotion. On one side of me was a group of two Mancunians, a Canadian and a Swede – all businessmen of some persuasion.

'You must 'ave 'eard of Mott the 'Oople,' cried one of the Mancunians.

'Nope. Can't say that I have,' said the Canadian.

'Who is Mott the Hoople?' asked the Swede.

'Well what about Bryan Ferry? You must 'ave 'eard of Bryan Ferry?'

'Well, I was always kind of a Bob Dylan man myself,' said the Canadian.

'I can't believe it! First 'e 'asn't 'eard of Mott the 'Oople,

now 'e 'asn't 'eard of Bryan Ferry! Great northern pop
stars!'

On the other side a single Mancunian businessman
grappled with an evil-tempered American. (It was that
kind of curry-house, by the way. The sort where you have
to sit in a lounge area to order your meal, where the decor is
gloomily sumptuous and the waiters produce more and more
variations on the same meal on countless tiny metal trays.
'You've never eaten Indian?' the businessmen would have
said to their foreign counterparts. 'Well, you'll like this
place, then. Got a lot of style.')

'So how's Manchester compare with Birmingham, then,
eh?' yelped the lone Mancunian. 'It's a lot better, isn't it?'

'Gimme that plate,' said the American. 'What did you say
this stuff was called?'

The American, the Canadian and the Swede must have
wondered what the matter was with these people. God
knows what they made of Manchester. Even allowing for
a day spent in the G-Mex centre examining designs for rapid
transit systems of the future, or cooped up in one of
Manchester's great, hideous Victorian *palazzi*, the visiting
foreign businessman will inevitably get a glimpse of the rest
of the city in which he finds himself. And then what will he
make of it? How's he going to know about Robb Wilton?
Even the meanest Iowan dullard could tell at a glance that
Manchester was Cottonopolis in Ruins.

'Gerry and the Pacemakers! Now they were a group!
Remember Gerry and the Pacemakers? Like the Beatles?'

'I remember the Rolling Stones,' ventured the Swede.

'What? You can remember the Rolling Stones, but you've
not 'eard of Gerry and the Pacemakers?'

'Well, I was only fourteen or fifteen at the time,' said the
Canadian.

'Well, so was I,' cried a Mancunian. 'But I can still
remember Gerry and the Pacemakers! Or what about the
Swinging Blue Jeans?'

The American was starting to lose his temper with the food.

'What the hell is on this plate?'

'Er, I think it's spinach.'

'Waiter! Can you take this away?'

'But you've got to admit, haven't you, Manchester's got the business?'

'I liked Birmingham.'

'Yeah, but Manchester's on a different level altogether. Isn't it? I mean, it's on a different plane.'

Meanwhile, across the room: 'The 'Ollies! For crying out loud! Manchester's finest! Everyone's 'eard of the 'Ollies! "He Ain't Heavy, He's My Brother".'

'I was always more of a Joan Baez man, myself.'

They never gave up. The bill came and went and still the Mancunians sweated on, trying to convince their interlocutors that their view of the world was the one that mattered. A Londoner would have been far more complacent: London's a bit grimy, yes of course, fairly heavily polluted, incompetently organised, how right you are, dirty, dark and dangerous in actual fact. But how many symphony orchestras have *you* got?

But these boys were sincere. Manchester really meant something, something barely communicable to an outsider, but vital to them. And what do you know, but several months later, after all the huffing and puffing of the failed Olympic bid, Manchester won itself the British nomination to hold the Commonwealth Games in 2002. Now it's all set to build a spanking new stadium with Government money and establish itself as Sports City of the North. I was wreathed in sneers at the time, but I don't think I am now. In fact, I don't know what to make of Manchester. Of all the places I saw in the North, Manchester is the one I'd be most interested in revisiting. Odd.

On my way back to the hotel, I passed the bank where the late-night tour party had admired the workings of the cashpoint machine. Someone had thrown a portion of mushy peas and chips at it. I would have suspected the ghost of Richard Cobden, assuming that in a rational heaven they actually know how useless today's high street banks are.

FIVE

B y the time I got to Wigan, about twenty miles west of Manchester, I was feeling rather more sophisticated. I was by now elaborating an idea – no, an *ideal* – of northernness. Following my mildly revelatory experiences in Manchester, I decided that northernness had to contain the following things: ugliness; shortage of funds; a complete absence of smartness, or evident class; the odd splash of grandeur; a civic presence and no trees or open spaces. Having got hold of this notion, I wanted to test it and Wigan was the first place I could try it out.

Why Wigan? It could have been Rochdale, Oswaldtwistle, Ramsbottom, Todmorden, Blackburn, anywhere with a resonantly northern handle. But in Wigan's case, I also had a short but specific personal agenda. Forget Orwell's *The Road to Wigan Pier*, I thought, I've read that (or rather, I've read the first, interesting half and skipped the arguments about Socialism).

What *was* on my list was the Wigan Casino, the great soul music dance-hall of the 1970s. I had decided to visit this for reasons of pure musical snobbery. Twenty-odd years ago, it was one of the few places in Britain to spurn the overblown banalities of early-1970s pop music and plough a furrow of defiant musical purism, playing nothing but hard-core American soul and rhythm and blues music. In this proud endeavour it sustained a unique northern working-class dance-hall culture and became a shrine to black dance music.

To be honest, when I was a teenager, I myself was
exclusively interested in the white, overblown banalities of
groups like Yes and Deep Purple. Obscure northern soul
singles and the places that played them could go hang
when I was a volcanically pubertal fifteen. I also wanted
girls to find me intolerably attractive, which perhaps they
would have done had I played them soul classics such as
'Long Gone' by Debbie Fleming or 'R & B Time' by E.
Rodney Jones and not wasted my energies on *Goodbye Cream*
and a pair of Hom underpants. 'Everybody seemed to be
following London,' said a Casino-ite in an interview in *The
Sunday Times*, back in 1976. 'All of them southerners telling
us what to do . . .'

At the time, I didn't care. But now I find that defiance,
that sense of purpose, powerfully attractive; middle-aged
irritability looking for an acceptable outlet, perhaps. I've
also come to my senses and realised, years late, that the only
music that has ever really *moved* is black music, that black
music has been the soundtrack of the twentieth century and
that one must pay homage to it when one can. 'The week's
not the same if I miss Wigan,' a boy called Gary had said.
'It's part of my life. I'm miserable if I miss it.' Nowadays I
can imagine nothing finer than a night of pounding soul
music corybantics, sad old fart that I am. 'We work hard,
bloody hard, and we want to work hard on the dance floor.
The faster the better.' What could be nobler than this
worship at the altar of devil rhythm, I thought?

I went to the Town Hall, first. This was in fact a pointless
exercise as the young man who collared me as I blundered
around the entrance hall had never heard of the Casino.
Oddly enough, I didn't think this sinister at the time.
Instead, he showed me the council chamber (done up for
reasons too deep to fathom in shades of pink and lavender)
and said that they'd 'Moved out of the old Town Hall to get
everything under the same roof'. So there were two Town

Halls? For a town with a population of a quarter of a million?

'Well, the old one's probably going to be bought by the Pentecostals, but you never know.' He looked over the Maison Raymonde colour scheme of the council chamber. 'I think it's nice, this, isn't it? Sort of fresh.'

The present Wigan Town Hall actually dates from 1903, and lives in Library Street. The old Town Hall is about twenty years older and lives a block away in Rodney Street. Both are built in an expressive Lancashire Hideous style, the new Town Hall being just a little heavier on the baroque curlicues (it would go nicely in a Saul Steinberg cartoon). It is also very large, overbearing and made of red, bomb-proof brickwork. In this particular, it is strenuously challenged in the ugliness stakes by the brand-new Wigan Magistrates' Courts, which are also red-brick but combined in a shape of such blank, monstrous brutality, they could easily pass as a toxic chemicals plant. The old Town Hall, by way of contrast, is starting to look a little sad, as is the rest of Wigan.

I was pleased to find, though, that it conformed neatly to my recently acquired preconceptions. There is no greenery, barring a patch of turf called Mesnes Park. But this is not enough to make a serious difference. You couldn't call Wigan verdant, unless you'd just come from the surface of the planet Mercury. Because of its size, it's not difficult to find a viewpoint in the middle of town from which to glimpse the countryside around, but there's no way of combining the two. No one has ever tried to lay out a cathedral close or a garden suburb in Wigan.

Mostly, Wigan is a lot of hilly streets with gales blowing down them and crowds of beaten-up-looking people. There were quite a few surprisingly short women, who looked as if some heavy object had fallen on them a while back. Like Manchester, Wigan also had a prominent bingo and amusements centre, with plush velvet in the windows on which was disposed a generous assortment of gewgaws – cuspidors, presentation tyre jacks, that sort of thing. It also had a businesslike model railway shop in the heart of town. Manchester had one, too. Do all northern towns and cities have a model railway shop in their equivalent of Oxford Street? Was this another item I could add to the check list? Do they betoken some common nostalgia for a time when a place knew what it was there for?

I walked around a bit more, purchasing a can of Sparkling Vimto on the way. Vimto is a quintessentially northern soft drink, made in Manchester, which tastes like seven packets of blackcurrant jelly dissolved in Perrier water. I could feel it liquefying my teeth even as I drank it and began to wonder if perhaps it wasn't also staining my mouth like gentian violet on a dose of impetigo.

After a bit, and burping Vimto under my breath, I reached the local history centre. This pointedly directed me to the signature of one E. Blair in the carefully preserved register of the old Wigan public library, but I was having none of that. I marched up to a pleasant Wigan lady sitting behind a pile of postcards and commemorative Wigan key rings and asked where I could find the Wigan Casino. She looked doubtfully at me, and said, 'Oh, no, the Casino's long gone. It's long gone, isn't it, David?'

A man with a beard and a corduroy jacket sprang from behind a stack of books.

'Oh, yes,' he said. 'They demolished it in . . . when did they demolish it?'

He disappeared. The nice Wigan lady went on, 'No, they demolished it a long time ago, knocked it down and put a horrible little one-storey box in its place.'

'I've found it,' cried the man in the corduroy jacket. He was in a small gallery above my head by this time, clutching a leather-bound cuttings book. 'It was 1980. The licence ran out and they couldn't renew it. Too many young people.'

The nice lady humoured me with a smile.

'It's just past the multi-storey car park. Where it used to be. You can't miss it.'

I thanked her, bought a postcard and went straight to the site of this great institution. There, indeed, was a shit-brown one-storey box (covered with notices announcing that it had been painted with anti-climb paint) standing in its place. It was home, apparently, to a local training initiative. Youth entertainment to youth training: all part of the strange disappearance of fun. I stuck my head round the door, finding a roomful of dazed-looking council apparatchiks. 'Is this where the Wigan Casino used to be?' I asked.

'I don't know.'

'We don't know.'

'You'll have to ask Mr Thorpe. He's out at the moment.'

I smiled winsomely at them and closed the door. As is the way with these things, a bit of space left over from the Casino's demolition had been designated a car park for the apparatchiks' cars. That was it for the Casino: a shit-brown box and a dwarf car park. The North's rebellion, flattened and daubed with anti-climb paint. That also put paid to my reason for being there. A sense of failure started to creep up on me. I stood in the car park and toasted the memory of the Wigan Casino with what remained of my Vimto. This caused me to experience the unusual feeling that my jaw was dissolving.

Having thus disposed of its only authentic landmark, Wigan is now in the position of having to rely on a soft-skinned southerner (in the form of George Orwell) to put it back on the map. It has done this by means of the Wigan Pier experience, 'The Way We Were' (admission £4.10, not including a programme). And that is it, for Wigan. It's thrown its whole identity behind the late George Orwell. The *Wigan Mini Guide* has got the blasted Pier on the cover page. Even as you drive around the town, you keep coming across road signs pointing you towards the world of Wigan

Pier. I'd tried to avoid it, tried to truffle out a little piece of indigenous Wigan history, I'd failed and I freely admit I was depressed. George Orwell, born into a family of middle-class colonial civil servants, educated at Eton and a Londoner by trade, is now designated the official figurehead of Wigan.

In case you'd forgotten the kind of things that Blair/Orwell wrote about in *The Road to Wigan Pier*, let me remind you. There was Mr Brooker, with whom Orwell lodged during his stay in the town: 'At any hour of the day you were liable to meet Mr Brooker on the stairs, carrying a full chamber-pot which he gripped with his thumb well over the rim.' There was the infested offal: 'I heard dreadful stories from the other lodgers about the place where the tripe was kept. Blackbeetles were said to swarm there.' There was the last straw: 'On the day when there was a full chamber-pot under the breakfast table I decided to leave.'

There were the other houses: 'The smell, the dominant and essential thing, is indescribable. But the squalor and confusion! A tub full of filthy water here, a basin full of unwashed crocks there . . . and in the middle always the same dreadful table covered with sticky oilcloth and crowded with cooking pots and irons and half-darned stockings and pieces of stale bread and bits of cheese wrapped round with greasy newspaper!' There was the woman glimpsed from the train: 'She had a round pale face, the usual exhausted face of the slum girl who is twenty-five and looks forty, thanks to miscarriages and drudgery; and it wore, for the second in which I saw it, the most desolate, hopeless expression I have ever seen.' As a local Wigan Trade Unionist recalled: 'You see, when they've left the upper class, they've got to go right down into muck and start muckracking . . . Did he have a taste for that sort of thing?'

I won't go on. George Orwell was a fine writer and probably a great guy, but would you have him as your town's mascot? What's wrong with George Formby? He was

at least born in Wigan. I admit that Formby's stock has
fallen a bit in the last thirty years; in fact, his fan club now
seems to consist entirely of middle-aged men who strum
ukuleles along to George's musical numbers in films like *Let
George Do It* and *Turned Out Nice Again*. Not, perhaps, the sort
of crowd a go-ahead council wants to attract. And I doubt if
anyone under fifty (apart from me) knows who the hell Ted
Ray (the other Wigan comic) was. So no museum of *Ray's A
Laugh*.

The only thing that did cheer me up about Orwell was the
fact that he too had been thwarted in his search for an
authentic piece of Wigan's past, having gone looking for the
actual Wigan Pier – a jetty projecting into the Leeds and
Liverpool Canal. Having failed to find it he lamented: 'Alas!
Wigan Pier had been demolished and even the spot on which
it used to stand is no longer certain.' Apart from that, I
really didn't want to know.

I'd also made a mental note to avoid museums, especially
theme museums. And yet, inevitably, I gave in and went,
like any other visiting schmuck, to *Wigan Pier – Where History
Comes Alive!*. If the Wigan Casino was ever authentic, this is
ersatz. If the Wigan Casino had life, this is moribund. If the
Wigan Casino had movement, this has dummies. The
Wigan Pier living museum promises to take you back over
a hundred years to experience (through exhibits, reconstruc-
tions and *tableaux vivants*) the life of an ordinary Victorian
mining town. It even purports to be on the site of wherever
the real Wigan Pier would have been, had it been anywhere
at all; it is housed in a warehouse which might be brand new,
or relatively old, but rebuilt with the most audacious
insensitivity since Colonel Seiffert got his hands on central
London.

Inside, there are such treats as a scanty mock-up of a
telegraph office (two dummies in waistcoats, keeling over a
telegraphist's desk). A little label nearby, trying to drum up

excitement, reads: 'Wiganers kept in touch with the world through a fast and efficient telegraph network run by the Post Office. The receipt of a telegram was a major event.' There is also a reconstruction of a windowless pub with a couple of stiffs playing dominoes in the pitch dark and another preserved corpse leaning awkwardly against a fake fireplace. All the old material dotted about the rest of the museum (flat-irons, milling equipment, mining kit) looks new or freshly purchased from an antique salon Down South or, at a pinch, in Wilmslow. Only the newer artifacts look genuinely old. '*Aha! Ein Fernsehapparat*,' said a German tourist, eyeing a cabinet of knackered old tellies approvingly.

While I was there, there were also some actors performing dramatic vignettes of northern life. They wore clogs and practised tap-dancing, while going on about the death of the mill supervisor (in a playlet entitled 'Popped Clogs'). After the male lead in 'Popped Clogs' had finished being a mill worker I caught him pulling on a frock-coat and hurrying past The Orwell pub (yes) to evict some tenants in another vibrant *mise en scène*. He shouted, 'Get yerself a proper job,' to a barman loitering in the sunshine.

To give you an idea of the extent of the place's short-comings, I have to say that I was actually mistaken for an exhibit. I was leaning against a railing in one of the dingier parts of the experience, making a note in my notebook, when it happened. Now, I know that I habitually stand with the stiff, lifeless angularity of the average shop-window dummy and I must have been pretty inert with weariness (only the tip of my pen imperceptibly moving). Even so, the only way I could have resembled something from the age of steam railways and typhus was if the rest of the exhibition were to have the same concern for period authenticity as an episode of *The Flintstones*. I was wearing jeans, for God's sake. But after a while I became aware of a small crowd of northern schoolchildren gathered round me. I raised my head and gave them what I imagined to be a benign smile, at which they all jumped back with cries of alarm and shouted out, 'Oh! Mister Statue! You *moved*!' Then they turned and ran from me to find their teacher, crying, 'There's one there that moved! I saw him move!'

I finally fled the Wigan Pier sensation, only to find George's moustachioed face gazing down on me from the outside of The Orwell. I half hoped that this would pick up a more literary theme, offering Winston Smith salads or Boxer Burgers. But inside, it was just another pub with fruit machines and draught lager. That was another notable thing about *Wigan Pier – Where History Comes Alive!*: Orwell himself was absent from the experience. Having used his name and the name of one of his best-known books to get you in, they drop him quicker than a ticking Jiffy Bag. I suppose I'd do the same if Orwell had written about nothing but my chamber-pots, my smell and my crawling tripe. But it does at least point up the ambivalence Wigan must feel about the whole business. God knows what Orwell himself would have made of it. Doesn't Wigan feel traduced in some way? Or having been fucked around by industry and commerce since the turn of the century, is this simply the least bad way to go? On an Old Etonian's grave?

Musing on all this, I gave back my rented car and went to Blackpool for a bit of fun.

SIX

'Room two,' said my landlady in Blackpool, 'used to be a bedroom, but now it's a toilet. And room six is now a bathroom. But you can't change the sequence 'cos you have to change the plan and that costs you money.'

She wasn't actually talking to me. She was talking to a geriatric who, up to that point, had been attempting a forcible entry into my bedroom. The geriatric said, 'I keep forgetting it's up one flight and down the next. I keep forgetting that.'

Even allowing for the fact that bedrooms were now toilets and number six was for bathing not for sleeping in, there was nonetheless a number three (not a number five, the number of her room) plainly affixed to my bedroom door. If the old dear couldn't see that, there was no helping her. But then again, Blackpool is apt to have that effect on anyone, even the youngest and brightest. Blackpool is a town which would drive any sane person mad.

My grip on reality was already slackening on the Sprinter train from Preston into Blackpool. I found myself sitting next to a family of white trash holidaymakers, comprising a half-witted father, a battered and filthy two-year-old and a delinquent mother, who kept up a barrage of abuse at her kid, alternating with fleeting observations on the rest of the world.

'Damon!' she yelled. 'Will you *sit down*. I won't tell you

again, Damon! Leave it out! Drop it, Damon! *Pack it in,
Damon!*'

Damon, who had been biting his father's shoelaces, wiped
his nose on my trousers and wandered off down the Sprinter.
The mother turned to her (understandably) dazed-looking
old man and said, more temperately, 'I've got to see the
childcarewomanonTuesday,Ican'trememberwhattime. . .'
She looked up again. 'Damon! You come right back 'ere – '

The train went over some points. She abruptly forgot
about Damon and looked out of the window.

'Eh, look! Look at that fookin' cow! In that field! I never
seen a cow fookin' run before!' She looked at me. 'Damon!
You're gonna get a right beltin' you are!'

And so on, for the longest half-hour I can remember
spending since the last time Michael Howard gave a radio
interview. I thought, What have I let myself in for? Is it all
going to be like this? Why, indeed, was I here? Manchester
had left me stunned and uneasy. Wigan had just left me
annoyed. What on earth did I hope to get from Blackpool?
Final confirmation that Lancashire as a whole is the kind of
place where you wouldn't want to bury your parents? Too
many expectations boiled around my head. I was morbidly
certain that Blackpool was going to be an unsavoury, blue-
collar experience topped off with lashings of Lancashire
vulgarity. I knew that I couldn't possibly enjoy myself. I
was jaundiced, captious, squint-eyed and my bigotries were
as full of vitality as a young colt. Wasn't I making a mistake
in pitching myself like this into the belly of northern
gratification?

Then the train pulled in, the white trash family got into a
small fist-fight, and I got out and found that, unexpectedly,
the first problem with Blackpool is that it's huge. Everything
is on an immense scale, designed to slake the immense
appetites of those who come here.

The approach from Blackpool North railway station, for

instance, gives you no clue as to what's waiting for you on the front. The back streets of Blackpool are a jigsaw of two-storey terraced houses, most of them B&Bs, alternating with chip shops and newsagents. A block away from the front, the buildings start to bulk into chainstores and banks, with the Winter Gardens and the festooned pile that is the Blackpool Grand Theatre thrown in. Another two or three minutes of that and, finally, you get to the sea, only to find that it goes out a mile and never seems to come in again, leaving behind a permanent and astonishing waste of uninhabited sand. There are three vast piers. Each is big enough to contain the population of a small town and has a train to get vacationing oldsters from one end to the other.

The famous Golden Mile is actually part of a promenade which is seven miles long and provides an unbroken strip of amusement arcades, chip shops, confectionery outlets, souvenir shops and bars. The Blackpool Tower (built in 1894 and 519 feet high) looms gigantically over the throng below and the air is dense with the smell of hot grease and the cries of bingo callers. And this is just what hits you in the first half-hour. I was staggered by the place, by its size, by its relentlessness.

No trouble with finding somewhere to stay, though. Since I was there at the start of the season, the place hadn't yet filled up and I had a wide choice of outlandishly cheap lodgings. Some of them were dosshouses, two or three streets away from the front. These offered worn lino and the smell of very old footwear for only ten quid a night. Others bore all the signs of what pass in England for improvements and amenities. This meant they had the establishment's name done in twirly wrought iron over the front door and had put a plastic Christmas cactus in the window. It also meant that they'd invested in a sign promoting the existence of a television in every room.

Moreover, they all advertised a bar, a pool-hall, a lounge and a dining area. These usually turned out to be all in the

same room – what would formerly have been the sitting
room of an ordinary two-storey terraced house – now filled
with discounted bankruptcy stock clutter and sporting a
formica mini-bar in the corner. I aimed high and stuck out
for a guesthouse on the front, which I duly got for fourteen
quid, B&B. As it turned out, my room was at the back,
overlooking not the sea but a garage and a minute yard
where a Dobermann paced obsessively up and down on the
end of a length of chain. Nevertheless, I felt it was worth that
little extra.

I inspected the visitors' book ('The cook can't cook but at
least she's not as bad as the waitress who's even worse. Room
wasn't worth it. Only joking! First class!' signed 'Sharon',
who under 'Nationality' had written 'Carlisle') and checked
the notice on the front door which read 'We do not take
groups of lads. Thank you.' Then I went back up to my
room where I brewed a cup of coffee on a machine which
was bolted to the wall to discourage theft. Then I went out,
turned right at the nearby Baptist Tabernacle and appre-
hensively took the air.

I made the mistake of thinking I could walk from a club
called 'The World Famous Nellie Deans' (sic) at the northern
extremity of the Mile, down to the Blackpool Pleasure Beach at
the southern end. I made it as far as the Tower, which was no
distance at all. There I was overcome by exhaustion and
fumes. Blackpool is the first place I've been to where the
whole town has halitosis. I don't mean the people, specifically, I mean the environment, the air, the very buildings
themselves. The whole settlement reeks of chip fat, beer and
ice-cream, uniformly and without let-up. I felt as if I were
wading through the contents of somebody's stomach. At the
same time, I was becoming more and more unnerved by the
scale of things. The sheer size of Blackpool seemed to increase
as time went by. The more ground I tried to cover, the more
there seemed to be. There are not just two or three amusement
arcades'n'bingo parlours in Blackpool; there are scores of

amusement arcades'n'bingo parlours, all stretching down the Mile, all plastered with coloured lights, each arcade the size of a supermarket, all pitch black inside to make the fruit machines, shoot-'em-up arcade games and bingo callers show up better, all calling themselves 'leisureplexes'.

You can venture into ten arcades in the space of an hour without even scratching the surface of the problem. For every amusement arcade, there are two or three burger'n'fries outlets. For every two burger'n'fries outlets there is one candy'n'rock stall and one novelties gift shop. For every novelties gift shop there is one pub or club. At either end of the Mile, this unvarying mixture starts to allow in the odd hotel, usually boasting a fantasy-land of tufted wallpaper, melamine and repro brass lamp brackets, and with the word 'famous' indefensibly strewn about its promotional literature. And then the pattern of leisureplexes and junk-food shops reasserts itself, on and on, endlessly towards Lytham St Anne's in one direction and Fleetwood in the other.

What am I saying? Why shouldn't the Queen's Hotel, South Promenade, Blackpool, call itself famous twice ('A Royal invitation from the famous Queen's Hotel,' with four bars, 'Including the famous theatre bar')? Why shouldn't Nellie Deans describe itself as world famous, however novel the idea might seem to the inhabitants of Switzerland or Zambia? Why shouldn't Harry Ramsden's promote 'The world's most famous fish and chips'? Blackpool *is* the most famous seaside resort in England. Perhaps its fame is somehow generic and applicable to everything that lies within the town limits, in the way that just about everything the Apollo 11 astronauts took with them to the surface of the moon is now famous.

Before tourism, Blackpool didn't exist. It was simply a great deal of sand with several miles of flats and rough country stretching away behind it. After a while, some enterprising local had the idea of putting people up to stay and the first holiday makers started arriving in the mid-eighteenth century for primitive swimming and recreation. By the 1820s, there were bathing machines and lodgings and a thousand visitors a year were coming for the 'Fine smooth sand, new modelled by every tide, but always firm, smooth and elastic.'

By the second half of the nineteenth century, the railway had been built and this number had swollen to twenty thousand visitors a day in the height of the season. The turn of the century saw the completion of the third pier, the Tower, the first cinema (the Colosseum) and the arrival of several star turns to entertain the mob. Sousa, Caruso and Houdini all performed there, as did George Formby Senior, father of the holder of the Order of Lenin. Blackpool was at its apogee; it had grown great on the back of Lancashire's sweated prosperity and its industry was pleasure.

Of all Blackpool's performers, the one I like best is the poor old Rector of Stiffkey, the Reverend Davidson, also known as 'the prostitute's padre'. Having been defrocked in the 1930s and grown desperate for publicity, he ended up on the Golden Mile, locked in a barrel. Not content to stop there, he then had himself roasted in a glass oven while a mechanical demon prodded him with a pitchfork. These days, by way of torture, Blackpool contents itself with booking up every comic act that in a Utopian republic would be flung over a cliff. When I was there, the forth-coming attractions were: Jim Davidson, Little and Large, Keith Harris and Orville and Bernard Manning. How much would you pay to see any one of them roasted in a glass oven?

The numbers coming to Blackpool are large, though not actually growing. Since the 1930s, between seven and eight million visitors have been coming to Blackpool every year and nothing now seems likely to raise that total. In between suffering occasional visits from conferencing political parties, Blackpool spends the rest of its time trying to drag the punters back from their cheap fortnights in the Balearics with

ever-larger gimmicks: Harry Ramsden's immense, overweening new fish and chip shop; Tower World; the sprawling
nightmare of the Pleasure Beach; the Sandcastle. More than
ever, this is holiday-making on an industrial scale and, like
any other industry in Britain, it has its work cut out to survive.
Some of the slack, apparently, has been taken up by the DSS,
who have been known to pay for the jobless and homeless to be
put up in the town's boarding houses. I trust this irritates the
Tory party on the odd occasion when it has to hold its annual
conference in Blackpool, but I doubt that it does.

Incidentally, I met a Tory supporter who had been to the
last Blackpool-held conference. It was her first time there.

'My God, what a shit hole,' she confided. 'I mean, do
people really come here for their holidays?'

Like many other Tories, she hung up her fur coat at the
Imperial Hotel. This looks like a prison and is built far
enough north of the Golden Mile not to be discommoded by
the riff-raff and the reek of boiling fat to the south. From
there the Tory lady described a narrow and undeviating
course between the Imperial and the Winter Gardens where
the speeches took place, taking in almost nothing of the rest
of town. But even this was too much for her.

'The shops,' she said. 'And the dirt. I thought Bournemouth was bad, but Bournemouth's a *paradise* in comparison.'

I'd intended not to use the clumsy, pre-war trams that churn
sluggishly up and down the seafront (I think I'd vowed by
then to spend as little money as I could in Blackpool), but
then I collapsed and had to get on one. From my windblown
vantage point on an old grid shaped like a boat on wheels, I
was able to spot variations on the Blackpool theme. Two
Gypsy Petulengros, for instance. One inhabited a modern
brick building on the front. The other was in an onion-
domed kiosk on the North Pier. They both claimed to be the
genuine article and both sported horoscopes for minor

celebrities like Margaret Thatcher and Larry Grayson pinned to the outsides of their consultation rooms. Typically audacious, I thought, to offer two unique and original Gypsy Petulengros and hang the insult to one's intelligence.

Then there were the Unhealthy Chemists. These were something I'd never seen before, North or South: chemist's shops with notices written across them announcing 'Medicines & Off Licence', or 'Kodak Film, Scotch Whisky', or 'Medicines & Cigarettes'. I'd have thought that this would have been against the law, but evidently it isn't. Clearly, when a Blackpool tripper needs to attend to his comforts, he's so brutally urgent about it that the local shopkeepers do their best to deal with all his purchases at once. So he comes in with a racking cough and a hangover, buys his headache pills and morning-after remedies and at the same time stocks up on booze and snout to get him cranked up again once the head's cleared. In Lytham St Anne's, the proprietor of a porn shop actually installed Britain's first twenty-four-hour sex-video porn-in-the-wall vending machine, prompted, I guess, by something of the same spirit: a northerner at leisure simply can't wait.

At the other end of the scale was Roberts's Oyster Bar (established 1876). This is the only building on the front (apart from the Tower) which pre-dates the century. It is also the only building with even a scintilla of good taste about it, although anywhere else (even in Lewisham) it would go unnoticed. Somehow, Roberts's has escaped the march of progress and still sports a cramped, Victorian interior, red vinyl banquettes from the 1950s and a very old proprietor indeed. He was so very old, I wondered if perhaps he was the original Mr Roberts, as he tottered towards me bearing half a dozen large oysters and some slices of bread and butter on a willow-patterned plate. I consumed them with a pot of tea, the proprietor watching me uncertainly as I spilt liquids down my chin. I was the only person in there.

Further down the Mile, I came across Hursty. Hursty is a

computer-generated, wart-infested hobgoblin who sits in a television screen at the foot of Tower World and watches the passers-by on a closed-circuit camera, making extremely audible comments as the mood takes him. You can't speak to him, but he can speak to you. Hursty invites physical violence, but the real Hursty, a man on an hourly rate in a soundproofed cubicle somewhere inside the building, is a long way from the street. So he can afford to make your knuckles whiten.

'Hello Missis,' Hursty calls out, 'you look like a stick of rock. Never mind, sir, they say bald men are sexier.'

I watched in awe as a couple of OAPs ground to a halt in front of the television screen.

'What's the matter with you?' demanded the little arse-hole. 'Somebody steal your candyfloss? If you don't close your mouth, someone'll park their car in it.'

And so on. The OAPs gazed at him, uncertain whether or not to reply, until a muscled yob in a T-shirt swept them carelessly on their way ('Don't go. I love you. You prune'). Hursty goes on all day and most of the night, abusing anyone stupid enough to stop and stare at him. For the terminally vacant, he has a fan club and video tapes are available for you to take home.

At another point, I got off my tram and went into a predictably vast Yates's Wine Lodge. The Yates's Wine Lodge occupies the same part of my consciousness as Vimto: a unique and emphatically northern institution to do with quenching your thirst. What did I find? A single room the size of a bus garage, a bar the length of a football pitch with scores of beer taps projecting from it, and a good deal of easy-to-wash floorboarding, covering an open space about the size of an old-fashioned dance floor. In true Blackpool style, rather than offering the punter scores of different drinks to choose from, the bar offered the same five beers over and over again: monotony on the grand scale. Nevertheless, I had been told that the Yates's in Blackpool

served draught champagne and by Heaven, it did. In this
monumentally tawdry place, somebody still thought it worth
selling champagne on tap.

I swayed up to the bar, my tongue still bleary with oyster
brine, determined to get a glass of pop. Unfortunately,
cowardice took over. The building was filled to the eaves
with powerfully built young men in stonewashed denims and
Millets trainers, squiring tough-looking blonde birds who
clearly put their blusher on with the vigour of someone
rubbing down a horse. The air was in a ferment of hormones
('C'mon Karen, get yer fat arse over 'ere'). I couldn't face
ordering myself a solitary pansy's glass of champagne. So I
cleared my throat, lowered my voice to Paul Robeson pitch
and had a pint of lager, which set my oysters dancing rather
more biliously than I'd expected.

And so I passed the time, feeling strangely and insidiously
defiled. I think the last time I felt so deprived of the common
currency of being was when I was stuck in Morocco on a
particularly evil three-week holiday. Then, I got robbed by
a man called Abdullah over a piece of hashish, my travelling
companion went insane in a hotel in Fez and there was a
toilet on the beach at Casablanca that cannot be described.

I suppose Blackpool wasn't quite as bad as that. But it was
so much more than I had bargained for. What manner of
place was this (I bleated to myself in my B&B room) with its
interminable, stygian amusement arcades; its acres of neon;
its drab, flattened hinterland of two-storey B&Bs stretching
away towards the railway station; its wide, parched, shade-
less strip of pavement overlooking the sands; its smell?

Was I just being middle class about the experience? Was
this not so much a ghastly embodiment of northernness,
rather a ghastly embodiment of blue-collar pleasures?
Wouldn't Southend have been the same?

Well I can tell you that Southend, the South's own
Blackpool, is both the same and radically different. Natu-

rally, it has all the appurtenances of a populist good-time resort: the same hot, black amusement arcades; the same burger'n'chip outlets; the same dodgems; the same reek. It too has plenty of sand and lager and isn't afraid to let its knickers down.

But it also has touches of character (I'm only saying this because it's true; because I've been there) which are a million miles from the presiding genius of Blackpool. South-end has a curved foreshore with a modest headland on it. It has a twee quarter, full of Regency houses with wrought-iron balconettes. There are boats at anchor. Its scale is more manageable than Blackpool, less mind-numbing. And it has, relatively speaking, plenty of vegetation.

In fact, it was the lack of greenery that finally did for me at Blackpool. The only patch of seafront with chlorophyll in it is a ragged-looking crazy golf course at the north end. Everywhere else: stones, bricks, mortar and concrete. Can you imagine how depressing that is in a place which dedicates itself to leisure and recreation? I'm not, I might add, kinky for plants. I like the urban scene. But an urban scene untempered by the odd softening leaf has either got to have the visual exuberance of Venice or be in East Germany. In comparison with Blackpool, Southend is like a Cotswold village. I know that one of my preconditions for urban northernness is an absence of green stuff, but the combination of no leaves and the sheer depravity of Blackpool's appearance is intolerable. I'm sorry, but I'm starting to sound like Clive Bell.

Of course, if you planted trees on the Golden Mile, you wouldn't be able to see the amusement arcades or the illuminations so clearly. What's more, the enjoyment of trees is free. As a rule, everything in Blackpool costs. So no trees and no grass.

Actually, I do the place a disservice. The illuminations are free, they draw between seven and eight million visitors a

year and they cost the local rate payers over £1,600,000.
Curiously enough, this is one area where Blackpool displays
more civic munificence than the Black Country, in that
Walsall, yes, Walsall near Birmingham, has its own illuminations, to which the council contributes next to nothing in
hard cash.

Let me retrace my steps a moment and be frank about
Walsall. For all its comparative respectability, it's not what
you'd call a distinguished town. But this hasn't stopped the
local council from doing its best to turn the place into a
tourist resort. It's got a Museum and Art Gallery. It's got an
Arts and Media Centre. It's got the Jerome K. Jerome
Museum (he was born there in 1859). It's got a leather
museum ('See displays of Walsall-made items past and
present'). And by heaven, it's got the Walsall Illuminations
– and has been having them, intermittently, since 1875, in
the seventy-nine-acre public arboretum in the northern
reaches of the town. Which is a source of very mild irritation
to Blackpool.

And what do these illuminations entail? Basically, they
entail draping miles of electric lights over the larches and
sycamores and rhododendrons which are the arboretum's
normal source of interest. They also entail putting up all
sorts of tableaux and grand effects, such as an illuminated
Chinese junk and a Postman Pat scenario. There are over a
hundred thousand bulbs, thirty-six miles of above-ground
cabling and a budget of well over a quarter of a million
pounds. Small beer, it has to be said, when you put it up
against the Blackpool Illuminations but impressive enough
for a midlands town that no one has ever heard of, and
which people tend to muddle up with Warsaw when you do
mention it to them.

I even met the man responsible for the Walsall Illuminations. He turned out to be a funny little bloke with a good
deal of rather arbitrary facial hair and his trouser turn-ups
caught on the heels of his shoes. He kept lighting small

cheroots and coughing into a mobile phone. He was suitably proud of his work, however.

'They're coming from all over, now. Our first booking this year came from Devon.'

Devon, eh? How'd they get to hear about Walsall, down in Totnes?

'We nobbled a lot of coach-tour operators last year when they had a convention in the ICC in Birmingham and got them to put it on their itineraries. Some of them are even doing a two-illumination weekend with Blackpool.'

Their best year so far netted them over 450,000 visitors, but no one can be sure how much money the event will make, because no one can work out the electricity bill in advance. 'We only know how much it costs to run when the power's switched off on the last night. One year, the Midlands Electricity Board turned the generators off instead of leaving them running all night and all the lights went out in the flats over there.'

Then he started on about laser beams. This got him onto Blackpool which had tried lasers but couldn't think of anything to do with them except shoot them in a straight line ten miles out to sea. So we had a laugh about that. Then he grew more urgent and drew savagely at his cheroot.

'We're looking for somebody, somewhere,' he muttered, 'with the technology for 3-D. We want Virtual Reality. If you can do it without the goggles. That'd really be one in the eye for Blackpool.'

Well, of course, Blackpool doesn't give a damn for Walsall.

'We don't consider there's any competition,' said an illuminations spokesman. 'We're aware of Walsall, but we don't really think of them as rivals.'

How could they? Blackpool's show runs for six miles down the esplanade. It uses seventy-five miles of wiring. It has over five hundred scenic designs and features, with sixty large tableaux. It requires a permanent maintenance team of

forty-five. And it usually persuades the visiting mob to spend
over £125 million while they're up to see the lights. What's
more, the Blackpool Illuminations have attracted a galaxy of
stars to perform the switch-on ceremony over the years:
Wilfred Pickles (1950), Jayne Mansfield (1959), Cliff Mi-
chelmore (1963), Tony Blackburn (1970), Terry Wogan
(1978), Johannes Rau, Minister-President, North Rhine
Westphalia (1984) and Derek Jameson (1991). In Walsall,
by way of contrast, they run a competition in the local
paper, the *Express and Star*, the winner of which gets to switch
on the lights, assisted by the Mayor.

Nevertheless, as the Walsall man is eager to relate, the
Mayor of Blackpool visited the Walsall Illuminations in 1983
and was so unnerved by what he saw that he banned the sale
of ready-made illuminations to Walsall in 1984. This and the
fact that Blackpool, according to at least one newspaper
report, needs to spend an additional £7 million on repairs to
the whole illuminations infrastructure (or else they'll go out)
is meat and drink to Walsall. Is there some message here,
about the virtues of free-standing private enterprise, as
against the featherbedding environment provided by town
councillors? Is it just a simple tale of northern rivalry? Or
does it mean that Blackpool's obsession with immensity is, on
this occasion, actually turning into something of a burden?

Back at my B&B, I stared disconsolately at myself in the
mirror over my washbasin. I had a triangular room which
was taller than it was wide. The Dobermann in the yard
outside had started to whine. I'd used up all the coffee in my
theft-proof coffee machine. I didn't want to play bingo. I
didn't want to work the fruit machines or fetch a cuddly toy
out of a pile of gewgaws with the aid of a small crane. I
didn't want to get emetically drunk. I didn't want to go
sequence dancing in one of the hotels.

I had a look through my copy of an entertainments
freesheet called *What's Going On*. 'The paper's title,' it said

in a footnote on page three, 'is a tribute to Marvin Gaye's deeply inspirational album of the early 1970s.' But *What's Going On* was full of ads for reduced bar prices at The BiZness Pubarama (North Parade, Blackpool) and The Seventh Annual Burma Star Weekend at the Empress Ballroom. There was only one thing I could do. I made my way downstairs, allowing plenty of room for the oldster who'd tried to break into my room ('Are you staying here?' she challenged me. 'I can't get the television to work') and headed for the end of the pier.

Of course, I knew that's what I would do, all along. It's one of the things which make Blackpool mercifully unique among English seaside holiday resorts. By and large, the seaside piers around Britain have been falling into rack and ruin over the last thirty years. Brighton, for instance, has two, but only one which actually works. The other partially collapsed into the sea and its rump now stares dismally back at the promenade while the waves slowly dissolve its supports. Elsewhere, too, the pier is not what it was; at Cromer, in Norfolk, the very existence of an end-of-the-pier show has been so remarkable for so many years that every English broadsheet newspaper runs a profile of the event round about June. But Blackpool has three piers, big, colourful and embarrassing – and it has end-of-the-pier shows with, sometimes, real stars rather than deteriorating ventriloquism acts and desperate light tenors. This was a real chance for me to escape my condition of southernness, to sink into the communal bosom of the North, to experience a kind of social entertainment unchanged in principle for generations.

As it turned out, the choice of shows to go to was narrow. Two of my three options weren't even at the ends of piers, merely borrowing some of their cultural references to make everything seem more holiday-like. There was Mike Donohoe's 'Tributes to the Stars' at the Sandcastle Promenade Show Bar: 'Back to the good old days of fun, laughter and song' it said. Then there was 'See The Stars In The Franklyn James Show: Your host and compare [sic] Kevin Bennett; Making the music Ronnie and Brian' at the World Famous Nellie Deans, North Promenade. And there was the Roy Walker Show – 'Host of television's exciting, high-rating family game show *Catchphrase*' – at the end of the North Pier.

Later on in the season there would be the chance to catch The Billy Pearce Laughter Show ('Plus Mr Music Dick Van Winkle, The Acroloons and The Dave Bintley Orchestra') as well as The Stunning Linda Nolan at Maggie Mays on the Central Pier (with 'Special Guest Star Ian "Sludge" Lees'). But for now my room for manoeuvre was limited. Which was, in its way, handy. I couldn't find the Sandcastle Promenade Show Bar. Franklyn James, judging by his promotional stuff, was not only still doing Norman Wisdom and Bogart impressions, he also had slightly too many testemonials from the likes of Cannon and Ball and Howard Keel stuck outside his nightclub to be plausible. So, accompanied by about three hundred pensioners, sots and low-lifers, I went to see Roy Walker.

The poster outside had done a great job of making this look like a big-time show. A real Blackpool razzoo in fact: big blow-up pictures of the stars, lots of spangle effects round the edges, enormous lettering, plenty of 'As Seen On TV's to guarantee an evening of quality entertainment. At a glance, it looked like a return to the days of the Tiller Girls and Val Parnell, with a line-up as long as your mohaired arm – Variety with a capital V. It looked tremendous. But the poster concealed a shocking reality. In actual fact, there were *three* performers: no chorus line, no orchestra, no troupes of artistes. Just three people left alone on stage for a hundred and twenty minutes, looking into the damp barn which is the North Pier Theatre.

The music was mainly provided by a large and astonishing woman who played two synthesisers with her hands, a pedal bass machine with one foot and a rhythm machine with the other. Talent-spotted by Russ Abbot (whose invisible presence bestows the authority of a Papal blessing on at least half of Blackpool's acts) she was clearly using the summer season to get her name about. She also sang, loudly, whilst conjuring up the sounds of the entire Count Basie Orchestra with her limbs, and belting out Ella Fitzgerald's greatest hits.

Further up the bill was a nice boy who played a violin. His act was a kind of musical kitsch, a Franklin Mint version of what music should be like. To this end, he played a Black-pool-sized medley, chucking in the high-tone ('Air On A G String'), the mawkish ('Ave Maria') and the patriotic ('Dam Busters March'; the chimes of Big Ben). Given that there was only him and the solitary woman buried under her Japanese synthesisers to fill a fairly large stage, he did a fine job of it by moving briskly from side to side, jumping up and down and talking to the audience while he played.

And there was Roy Walker, a genial Irish comic who, assisted by Emile Ford's son (Emile rose to prominence in 1959 with his rendition of 'What Do You Want To Make Those Eyes At Me For?'), had to spend the first half of his act playing *Catchphrase*, the high-rating family game show. I would say he earned his money. Contestants for *Catchphrase* were dragged out of the audience and obliged to watch a large television screen on which punning cartoons appeared. They then had to guess the word or phrase implied by the cartoon – in the doghouse; many hands make light work; tomorrow belongs to me – that kind of thing.

These participants were generally old or half-witted or both, but Roy's patience and enthusiasm barely flagged; although there was a certain tension about his shoulders which suggested that he was mastering strong emotions as he tried to corral the contestants milling about his stage. Prizewinners got some tokens to spend on booze in the pub next door to the theatre and, rather insensitively, I thought, free tickets to see Jim Davidson later in the season. Did Roy really want to offer, as first prize, a ticket to see a more popular comedian? Later on, when the general public had cleared off the stage, he clamped a grin on his face and told a few whiskery jokes, including the one about the kid asking him if he'd got a light, Mac: 'No, but I've got a dark overcoat.'

But was it enough? Was I being hopelessly bourgeois, for instance, to expect a programme? Instead of a glossy magazine-like publication, all I got was a chit of paper with the performers' biographical details crammed on to one side and a contestant's entry form on the other. There was also a voucher for the Jim Davidson Show and free admission to Mick Miller's Comedy Store at the town end of the North Pier. The people sitting near me didn't sound uncontainably keen.

'For Barbara Windsor,' said a woman, 'we were right down the bloody front. Can't get any worse than her, can it?'

Her friend wasn't so interested. 'I've been getting the sweats for three years now,' was all she could say. She held up her arms. 'Look! Red patches!'

A couple of seats back from her was an old bloke in a grey anorak. He was either dying or dead. Next to him a middle-aged woman announced, 'It's this trouble with my stomach. When the stomach goes, it goes right to my ears.'

Outside, the rain had started to pour down on a Swedish camera crew filming scenes of authentic British crumminess. There were wires and lights everywhere, tripping up the punters as they came outside for their interval breathers and seventy-pence tubs of ice-cream. The prizewinning contestants fought their way to the bar and drained off their double whiskies and Babychams furiously. "E were good, but not as good as the telly,' announced one.

Then again, they weren't much of an audience. At the end of the second half, Roy had barely finished his humorous monologue before they were up out of their seats and struggling towards the conveniences after over an hour of straining to keep it in. At which point the lights went down and came up again to reveal Roy, the violinist and the one-woman band, now all dressed in tuxedoes, belting out an unexpected finale to about a hundred and fifty in the stalls while a further hundred and fifty battled their way up the aisles to relief.

'They should have ended it at the interval,' a woman said loudly in my ear. Hardly the capstone of a glittering showbiz career.

Still, I thought, as I trudged back to my B&B in the rain, it could be worse. Halting somewhere along the front I watched a man in a black polo-neck sweater, in his late twenties maybe, standing at one end of the sun-lounge of one of Blackpool's second-division hotels, doing conjuring tricks for a group of about twelve OAPs. His eyes were filled with desperation. Having your big number ruined by a mob stampeding to the toilets would have been no hardship to him. He had that look.

The next day, after one of the hottest full English breakfasts I have ever had – I mean, really scaldingly hot – I grudgingly climbed aboard another tram and churned south along the front to Britain's number one tourist attraction: the Pleasure Beach. This, at least, is how it describes itself, drawing, on average, six and a half million visitors a year. I would have said, if anyone asked me, that Alton Towers, or Madame Tussaud's in London, were the most popular draws in the country. But I think they may be the most popular tourist attractions that you have to pay to get into. The great thing about the Pleasure Beach is that it costs nothing to get in. And it costs nothing to wander around forty-two acres of fairground rides and vomit-inducing white-knuckle experiences.

This is, by the way, what the Pleasure Beach is. It is not a beach (and only tangentially connected with pleasure, some might argue), it is a colossal fairground. Another publicity

factoid: it has more 'big thrill' rides than any other amusement park in the world. It also has, oddly enough, a lot of
very old rides. The Big Dipper was built in 1921 (there's a
little plaque at the entrance to inform you of this, along with
a note to the effect that 'The word Big Dipper was invented
here at Blackpool Pleasure Beach in 1923') while the Grand
National (a Möbius strip roller coaster) was built in 1935.
The Flying Machine claimed, astonishingly, to have been
built in 1904 by the inventor of the Maxim gun.

I can't believe that the mob which gradually descended
on the Pleasure Beach after opening time was wholly
comprised of industrial archaeologists, so I suppose the
antique nature of some of the rides is immaterial to most
people. To be honest, there was hardly a normal person to be
seen there. Almost everyone was grossly fat or appeared to
have been sleeping rough. The staff were kitted out in
battered tracksuits or occasionally thematic costumes such
as Arab *jellabahs* and *tarbouches*.

The point is that you can stroll around for as long as you
like, enjoying the Frank Chacksfield-style music playing on
the PA and allow yourself to be lured into shelling out quite
large sums of money for every ride you take. £1.50 per
person for the Revolution – a sixty-second loop-de-loop – is
no peanuts. Likewise £1.20 for the longer but less aperient
roller coaster. Likewise £20 for a single book of tickets which
allows you one go on only some of the rides and static
amusements . . . this is shrewd marketing: after about ten
minutes of watching other people induce terror, vertigo and
nausea in themselves, it's almost irresistibly tempting to do
the same thing to yourself.

I, of course, resisted, but only because I had vowed to spend
nothing while I was in Blackpool. I contented myself instead
with standing underneath the point at which the Revolution
actually looped the loop, some eight feet above the ground,
before soaring forty feet into the sky. I listened to the PA
playing a Locarno Ballrooms version of 'Mr Tambourine

Man', followed by 'Telstar' with strings – blending in nicely
with the ads for the Pleasure Beach's 'Hot Ice' skating revue,
which claimed to have 1960s favourites the Joe Loss Orchestra and the Rockin' Berries on the bill – and watched the
horror on the punters' faces as they lost their contact lenses,
small change and car keys in the sudden tug of gravity.
Apparently, the trade jargon for puking up as a result of
being subject to violent g-forces while being spun round on
your head is protein spill. I realised after a few minutes of
watching the bulging cheeks and grey complexions of the
riders on the Revolution that perhaps they might spill their
protein over me, so I affected an interest in the Grand
National and moved hurriedly away.

As if this were not enough, the sadists who run the
Pleasure Beach were building something even more awful
and terrifying while I was there. They were working on the
world's largest and fastest roller coaster: 235 feet high at the
top of its arch, capable of generating speeds of 85 mph and g-
forces up to four times the force of gravity. It was going to
cost around £12 million and would plainly dwarf everything
for miles around, including the town of Blackpool and the
Irish Sea. They had already managed to lay the foundations:
great concrete slabs, sitting in pools of rusty water or heaps
of rubble, bolts the size of a man's thigh protruding from the
concrete.

I'll confess that the only thing I was prepared to shell
out for was the Tunnel of Love. I had been told that this
was unusual in that the various *tableaux* inside the tunnel
were depictions of places which the Pleasure Beach's owner
had once visited on some sort of Grand Tour back in the
1950s. A woman of some style and taste, I was told, she'd
got Angkor Wat in there, plus the Great Pyramid of
Cheops, the Hanging Gardens of Babylon and what have
you, all rendered in gay pastels and romantic flesh tones.
In the end, despite walking around for three hours, I
couldn't find the Tunnel of Love, although I did find a

notice which read 'If this loo has a queue, Beaver Creek's toilets are for you.'

I made do, instead, with watching a man whose job it was to squeegee the blue-dyed water out of the rafts which had been through the Log Flume.

Then I realised I couldn't stand it any more and left, precipitately. I had to get out of there.

In fact, I got back to Preston so rapidly I consigned myself to several hours of waiting on a chilly railway platform because I was far too early for my connecting train. But even that was preferable to staying in Blackpool. I positively feasted on my British Rail turkey salad bun, priced no less exorbitantly than whatever the Blackpool equivalent would have been, but tolerable because it had nothing to do with the place.

I had the distinct feeling that I was getting the North all wrong. It couldn't consist entirely of vast, run-down, hideous, working-class towns and cities. It couldn't possibly be this awful. Lancashire had thrown me off-balance, whatever peculiar saving graces there were to the city of Manchester. Was I being too prescriptive about it? Was there some way I could junk my bigotries and see things in a clearer light? Perhaps I should never have visited Blackpool. Why go all that way just to opprobriate a place which provides a great deal of only moderately harmful pleasure to millions? Then again, I don't suppose Blackpool gives a flying fart for my good opinion. Who did I think I was, anyway?

I hung around fretting at Preston Station for a long time, before I realised that I'd been sitting on the wrong platform and had missed my train.

SEVEN

This be the history of Newcastle upon Tyne: Romans, the Venerable Bede, the Vikings, the Normans (and their New Castle), fish, coal, making and repairing the boats of the fishermen, shipbuilding, more coal, regional capital, Richard Grainger clearing away the city centre in the 1830s and rebuilding it in glorious neo-classical style, the Stephensons, Armstrong and his armaments, Jarrow shipbuilding, Jarrow destitution, Jarrow march, *The Likely Lads*, T. Dan Smith and John Poulson, disappearance of coal, Lindisfarne (the group), *Auf Wiedersehen Pet*, disappearance of shipbuilding, Jimmy Nail, the North East: crime capital of the UK, *Viz* magazine. It is a litany which suggests that by rights, Newcastle ought to be well on the way from being the Capital of the North to being a sump of human decay and iniquity. Oddly enough, it isn't.

Newcastle is a strange place. On the one hand, it has an air of real mystique about it – people are more likely to say, 'I've never been there, but I've always wanted to go,' about Newcastle than any other northern city. Admittedly, this doesn't give it quite the same clout as Berlin, San Francisco or Lhasa, other cities which people openly wish they could visit, but it's a lot more than anyone volunteers for Wigan.

On the other hand, some commentators have compared Newcastle with Berlin during the Weimar Republic: doomed, hedonistic, riven with undercurrents of violence and social dissolution. Weimar Newcastle is supposedly the combustible product of several generations of economic neglect combining with the natural Geordie instinct to have a good time. The city is, after all, miles from anywhere, ignored by London politicians, an industrial centre whose industries have fallen apart. But then again, it's never been an industrial city in quite the same way as Leeds or Manchester or Sheffield: it's never been a merciless conurbation in a forest of metal-bashing and milling concerns. Instead, it's had the sea to waft ozone through the streets, the sullen grandeur of the northern Pennines and the Cheviots lurking at its shoulder, and the fairies and pixies of early Christianity, fish and spirituality, just a stone's throw up the river. There is nothing typical about it.

So I checked into my regulation dosser's hotel ('English Tourist Board, 1981', it said promisingly over the front door) and swept into yet another ten-foot-by-three-foot room with cardboard walls, while making conversation with the proprietor: 'You'll find Sunderland's very handy for the train, only twelve kilos away. I mean, kilometres. That's just me trying to be clever.' The front door had a set of Tyrolean cowbells attached to it which went off every time I opened it, causing the owner to spring out from a concealed area behind the formica mini-bar in the front room and shout '*Ooooookayyy?*' at me. It didn't matter whether I was coming or going; I still got the Ooooookayyy? treatment. He also did impersonations of owls. I could tell where he was in the building thanks to the hoots and too-wit-too-whoos that filled the slightly stagnant air.

I threw my bag of socks and pullovers onto the busted concavity of my bed, thrummed the walls of my room, stuck my head out of the window to take a draught of Newcastle's traffic pollution (so much fresher than the fetid odours of the West) and left.

*   *   *

I then went and had the most riotous curry I have ever eaten, in a part of Newcastle called Bigg Market.

The centre of Newcastle is Grey's Monument, 135 feet high with a statue of Earl Grey, who is commemorated here for getting the Great Reform Bill passed in 1832, on the top. The monument is stuck like a large pin in the middle of town, holding everything else down. For a tourist such as myself, it's the central point of the compass: everything radiates from it. You know where you are with Earl Grey. You want the Laing Art Gallery? Follow the Earl's left ear down to New Bridge Street. The Tyne Bridge? Take the Earl's left foot down to Dean Street, under the railway bridge, and it's on your left. Bigg Market? This is an area running at right-angles to Grainger Street, which in turn leads directly from the Earl's right foot.

Bigg, apparently, is an old word meaning barley rather than large, but this element of confusion has not stopped the place from becoming famous for the huge numbers of young men and women who descend on it in the evenings in search of a good time. Indeed, even as I bumbled off to my curry (up two creaking flights of stairs with a security camera waiting dauntingly for me on the landing), there were hosts of sprightly young Geordies starting to patrol the streets.

Most of the action seemed to centre on four or five pubs, all of which played deafening rave music while hanging NO DANCING signs over their entrances. I went into one in order to get a pint of lager under my belt but the music was so colossally loud I couldn't make myself heard and had to come out again. There were plenty of young folk in there, mouthing at each other and not dancing, although they were being vibrated gently across the floor by the beat. I have an idea that the barman who couldn't take my order was wearing a deaf aid. The music rolled around Bigg Market and the neighbouring St Nicholas's Cathedral like thunder. Even the chip shop just off Bigg Market had industrial rave music playing to accompany the chippy while he toiled away at his deep-fat basket and his saveloys.

In the centre of Bigg Market there is a large public lavatory, shaped like a railway engine roundhouse, with a conical frosted glass roof through which a pale green light glows. The roof has not yet been shattered by the noise, but it can't be long before it gives out. The toilet is the cynosure of this particular playground: a convenience where after having your buttocks deafeningly trembled, downing several gallons of lager and hoovering up a bushel of curry to replace lost calories, you can discharge the whole lot at around 1 a.m.

Why always this curry, by the way? Why not something a little more *du pays*? Well, not to mince matters, distinctive and interesting regional English foodstuffs can be counted on the fingers of one hand: Stilton cheese, Wensleydale cheese, Frank Cooper's Oxford Marmalade, Worcestershire Sauce. Anything else is either Scottish – beef, whisky, salmon, kippers, haggis – or, mercifully, nothing to do with England at all. And yet, despite this, there is a proposition which states that England's provinces all boast some kind of special local foodstuff, or way of cooking. I guess this is nothing more than the product of regional vanity and the toils of local tourist boards, but it's hard to escape, all the same.

The North thus comes equipped with a shopping list of fairly off-putting edible things which are supposed to be typical of this half of England: tripe (either honeycomb, for the general consumer, or thick seam, for the devotee), jellied cow's heel, pigs' trotters, black puddings, something called elder (which is apparently minced cow's udder), stotty cake (from the North East), Yorkshire pudding, Bakewell tart, Pontefract cake and forced rhubarb, of which Yorkshire is the English home. When I went north, I was told to look out for rough and ready northern butchers' shops, groaning with tripes and knuckles and green tubular bits.

But I never saw anything like that; in fact, I never saw anything except what I see wherever I go in England, that is, curry-houses, Chinese take-aways, chip shops, McDonalds, Pizza Huts, Happy Eaters, Burger Kings and then, dwindling in significance, Italian spaghetti joints, followed by theme restaurants with names like Harry's or Trader Bob's or The Truck Stop, which serve burgers and salads in mildly pretentious ways and sometimes even on wooden plates, followed by restaurants which take themselves seriously and are evidently struggling to bring the Art of Good Eating to Wigan and Bradford and display two-year-old restaurant reviews hopelessly in their windows, followed, right at the bottom, by a handful of vegetarian eateries peopled by dismal anorexics. Oh, and on offer in one of Leeds' pubs, a laughable touristical confection called a briggshot: 'A pot of ale, a noggin of pottage and a trencher of roast beef', which I avoided like a dose of nits.

Chips and beer and curry: that's the food of the North, along with cakes, cigarettes and sweets. Heart and respiratory illnesses are commoner in the North than they are in the South and it's not difficult to see why. The top four regions for heart disease (courtesy of *Regional Trends*, published by the Central Statistical Office) are all in the North of England, located around the great conurbations; the top four places for respiratory disease are exactly the same. If death rates from lung cancer are rated 100 for London, then the North is rated at 130 for men and 136 for women. For deaths from heart disease: if London is rated at 100, men in the North are rated at 114; women at 112. People in the North smoke more (32 per cent of all men and 33 per cent of all women smoke in the North, the highest figures for England), eat worse and are more prone to the ailments that come from smoking and bad diet. There are, in turn, all sorts of reasons for this general and chronic abuse of the body, but illness and death are the upshot.

So what does your traveller from the South do? Does he go in search of tripe and Pontefract cake, both of which are virtually unobtainable anyway? Does he bloat himself out

like a marine buoyancy aid on chips and beer and Snickers
bars and bring on heart failure? Does he take up smoking
again? Or does he eat reasonably priced and sometimes
delicious Asian cuisine, which is not *especially* bad for him
and which is nowadays no less British than leg of lamb or
Stilton? He eats a curry, of course. Besides which, we owe it
to ourselves to support our Indian, Chinese, Thai and Malay
restaurants; because if we don't, our national diet will
become nothing more than take-away pizzas and completely flavourless slimmers' ready meals.

Once past the curry-house security camera, I found myself
in a long, low saloon with an elasticated floor. I had just
missed the Curry Happy Hour, but a panting waiter found
me a table in the middle of the room. Every time someone
passed, the floorboards bounced like a trampoline, causing
precious drops of lager to gambol over the side of my glass.
I'd never been on such a mobile floor before. I wondered if it
was deliberate or just the freak product of the combined
body weight of that particular night's clientele. After a
while, however, I ceased to care, because I was in the
middle of a party.

On one side of the room was a knot of young families –
mothers, fathers, small children, even a baby in a high chair.
They were laying into their tikkas and biryanis with the
remorseless concentration of people who have been told that
the meal is free if they can finish it in the time it takes to sing
'Greensleeves'. Some of them were drinking champagne (not
quite straight from the bottle, but with an equally businesslike relish, and from old-fashioned flat champagne glasses at
that), others were freely downing beer and sweating copiously with exertion.

Having dispatched the main course, everyone bar the
small children then made liberal use of the restaurant's
brandy and liqueur menu, drinking Tia Marias and Greek
brandy out of half-pint mugs with handles. We were all

crushed together like commuters, the floor twanging uncontrollably beneath our feet, food and drink slopping around, a mood of abandon in the humid air. It was torrid, intimate, faintly bestial and rather fun, but it was as nothing in comparison with the pandemonium on the other side of the room.

Here, two huge trestle tables held two separate parties of office workers, all apparently pissed out of their heads at eight o'clock in the evening and hell-bent on making the rest of their time in Bigg Market go with a bang. There were a lot of young and young-middle-aged men, their hair sticky with sweat, their ties snaking widdershins across their easycare shirts, their faces flushed, their mouths sagging open. (On my way to the curry-house, I'd passed a sandwich board in the street, announcing, 'Suit, shirt & tie, Only £99. Why pay over the odds?' An irresistible offer, judging by the appearance of one or two of my co-diners.) There were also some women, wearing those uneasy, fixed smiles that women understandably put on when surrounded by drunken animals. One of the men shouted, 'It's the chimps' fockin' tea porty.'

'Who sang "Blaydon Races"?' yelled another, with what struck me as engaging local awareness. 'I'm totally serious.'

'Nirvana,' yelled his colleague.

'No, I'm totally fookin' serious.'

'Bring us the kebabs!'

Someone started to sing something that might have been 'Blaydon Races'. I was afraid to ask if that was what it was in case the mob turned on me on account of my Finchley twang and playfully dismembered me.

'I'm fockin' *serious*!'

'I've got me fockin' tikka, so sod off.'

One woman in the mob caught my attention. She came in looking abnormally sober, respectable even. She had the look of the boss's PA about her. She was nicely dressed, nicely made-up, modestly adorned and easy on the eye. She

settled at one end of the trestle table, away from the worst of
the chaos and smiled wanly at the lads in the centre
('Another Foster's, Frank. Make that four'). I felt feebly
sorry for her, and idly began to make mental preparations
for what I might do if things turned nasty and the brutes in
the £99 suit'n'tie combinations fell on her.

I hadn't got very far when my food arrived and I buried
myself (almost up to the armpits) in my own chicken
tandoori masala with all the trimmings and an extra pint
of lager and forgot all about her. Twenty-five minutes later,
I surfaced, wincing with fulfilment, to look around and find
that the correct young woman with the wan smile was now
focusing with extreme difficulty on the world around and,
indeed, right beside her. Frankly, she was pissed. Her make-
up was either smudged or had gone missing. Her hair was
lightly matted. Her hand was wrapped round a half-pint of
white wine and soda water and when one of the lads made a
joke, she had to pause for a second to reassemble the gag in
her own mind, before throwing her head back and barking
demonically with laughter.

She then joined in with 'Doe a deer, a fe–male deer',
which someone on the neighbouring table had begun to sing.
The floorboards twanged, the waiters laboured up and
down between flailing arms, the whites of their eyes showing, their teeth clenched. A photograph of the Rt. Hon. Sir
David Steel (really), shaking hands with the proprietor in
more pacific times, was dislodged from the wall.

It was not even a Friday night. Welcome to the Weimar
Republic of Newcastle!

More or less spherical, I assured and then reassured the
restaurant owner that I had had a wonderful time and an
excellent meal (which I had) before tumbling down the
stairs again, past the security camera, my ears ringing, the
boards above me groaning as the young Geordie office
workers pleasured themselves.

Outside I found myself back in the land of the very loud

pubs, in the middle of a sea of young people, swirling around the point where Bigg Market, Cloth Market, Groat Market and High Bridge all converge. The boys and girls were (sweetly enough) in separate, unisex mobs, the boys wearing low-key vandals' smart-casual chinos and polo shirts, the girls in anything from jeans like sausage skins to leather mini-skirts. Quite a lot of the girls were wearing white stilettos, which, I was later told, are known as follow-me-home-and-fuck-me shoes. More to the point, they were uniformly dead drunk. The boys, on the other hand, were no more than soberly frisky. A couple of strapping fellows in jeans and casual shirts held out their arms to block the progress of a group of four pissed young women. The girls must have been using their drunkenness as a cover, for they managed to duck under and around the lads, leaving them clutching air.

'Is that all I'm gettin'?' cried one of the boys. 'I canna go to the boozer with that – '

'You'll to make do,' shouted a buoyantly leggy blonde. She then stuck her tongue out at him, tripped on the kerbstone and fell backwards into the arms of her friends.

It crossed my mind that all this youthful gaiety might be about to degenerate into violence, but for some reason I didn't actually feel threatened. I don't know whether not getting my head caved in in Bigg Market counts as a warm Geordie welcome; or whether I was just there at the wrong time to get thumped. In London, needless to say, I generally feel massively apprehensive around closing time, except in one or two sequestered parts of the city. And in yet other parts of the city, I feel massively apprehensive in broad daylight at half past ten in the morning. Why I should have felt so relaxed in Newcastle defeats me, especially with its reputation as a great place to get your head filled with a mixture of broken glass and someone else's teeth.

* * *

A few years ago, for instance, Tyneside found itself back on the map after a longish lay-off, when gangs of youths ran riot in North Shields after two joyriding boys died in a police car chase. Shortly after that, police in riot gear had to move into the North Shields Meadow Well estate. Following which, a large number of Newcastle's estates were taken over by joyriding gangs. 'Twoccing' (Taking Without the Owner's Consent) was immediately followed by 'hotting' (driving a stolen hot hatchback rapidly, flamboyantly and life-threateningly around a semi-derelict council estate), which was immediately followed by large numbers of television film crews, getting it all on tape for the evening news. The screens of the nation were filled, night after night, with beaten-up Geordies, muttering imprecations and having difficulty in refraining from busting the television cameras. V-signs flew in all directions. It was a vision of Hell. Perhaps if I'd been in a shedful of savages in North Shields or Byker I might have got my arm broken in three places, but in the heart of the city, I felt obscurely, complacently safe.

Just to prove to myself how incredibly relaxed and earthy I was feeling, I wandered into a pub some way away from the racket of Bigg Market for a last-thing pint and some sort of scuffle. I recount this with shame, but it's true. It's the kind of thing that I could never even begin to conceive of doing in London, or anywhere else. I am, after all, a timorous middle-aged man, but up here – well, I sort of drifted into it.

Unfortunately, everyone else in the pub I found was excessively quiet and well behaved and my vague hopes of a bit of excitement were thwarted. Instead, I nursed my frigid lager at the bar and did my best to metamorphose into a troublemaker: back to the counter, elbows wedged behind me against the woodwork, paunch thrust forward aggressively and a look of sullen, end-of-the-day beeriness playing about my blotched features. I farted a bit and toyed with my beer-mat. I may even have said, 'Howay, man, I'm knackered,' as I banged my empty glass down on the counter and swayed out into the night. Pathetic, I know, but Newcastle is a strange place and I was behaving strangely.

As it turned out, the nearest thing I could find to a riot was a small boy being beaten up by a slightly larger girl at the foot of Grey's Monument shortly before closing time. An alcoholic sat on a wooden bench about six feet away and watched with detached interest.

So I went back to my hotel to find the proprietor waiting for me by the door ('Ooooookayyy?') and doing owl-hoots to impress the other guest. Later that evening, he installed himself, with his wife, in the room next to mine, switched on a wireless (tuned to Radio 2) and spent the rest of the night moving the furniture around.

I spent my whole time in Newcastle in a state of more or less constant mild surprise. It wasn't just the odd evening surrounded by eat-drink-and-be-merry-for-tomorrow-we-lose-our-jobs Geordies that left me disorientated. It was the appearance of the place, too. Newcastle is an astonishingly interesting city to look at. Not all pretty, by any stretch of the imagination – this is late twentieth-century England: how could it be anything other than (to put it charitably) a gallimaufry of styles?

Indeed, just to take a case at random, you'd be hard pressed to find a more vicious piece of urban vandalism than the A167(M). This drives a stinking, deafening, multi-lane, flyover-blown motorway through the heart of Newcastle, neatly amputating the eastern suburbs from the city centre before shooting across the Tyne in the direction of Sunderland and the South. Not only does it cut Newcastle off from its own suburbs (rather nice, substantial ones at that), it also infects the neighbouring streets with its awfulness.

Wander, if you can, down John Dobson Street and Pilgrim Street (just to the east of Earl Grey's left ear) and you find yourself dwarfed by vile 1960s office developments,

which are one part light aggregate concrete mix, two parts
Nicolae Ceau̯escu. At the same time, you have to dodge
walls of kill-the-fuckers traffic bearing down on you from all
directions and hold your breath against the reek of car
exhausts. If you come across Newcastle's Laing Art Gallery
in that corner of town – home to a Gauguin and some
preposterous John Martins – you may also find it contemp-
tuously buried under concrete and rubble, lost in the shadow
of the New Bridge Street roundabout. To be honest, I wasn't
wild about the Laing's collection, but it did have a man at
the postcards counter with a fascinating haircut. He had a
kind of Arthur Scargill pubic frizz, swept forward from the
nape of the neck to meet at the temples in a *victor ludorum*
wreath. For a while I actually thought he was wearing a lace
hairnet and spent several minutes crouched behind a pile of
art books, spying on him.

That aside, the whole squalid development in this part of
the city is quite enough to make you give up and go and get
drunk for the rest of your life – and yet the stoical
pedestrians of Newcastle put up with this stuff, swarming
uncomplainingly around brutal underpasses, picking their
way phlegmatically across miles of senseless and unjustified
walkways, simply clambering over the central reservations
of four-lane motorways. I couldn't believe it at around 5.30
p.m., when the shops and offices began to close and hordes
of white-collar workers started to teem recklessly over the
surface of Newcastle like insects, oblivious to traffic, danger
or toxic poisoning, anything to take the shortest route to
their Metro station or bus stop.

But turn your back on all that and what do you find but
Grey Street: as handsome a thoroughfare as anything in
Bath or Oxford.

Grey Street is almost ravishing, an essay in neo-classicism
which manages to be large and chaste at the same time. It's
executed in beautiful honey-coloured stone (and probably
looks better clean than with a more historically entertaining

rime of soot on it) and sweeps imperiously down toward the river, the Theatre Royal poking out like a discarded wing of Blenheim Palace, unchanged in its general appearance for over a hundred years. It's ironic that John Dobson, who designed Grey Street, should have ended up lending his name to something as hideous as John Dobson Street, but he's lumbered now. The fact is that if you allow yourself to drift roughly south from between Grey's knees (the Earl's head is a replacement, by the way, put there after a thunderstorm knocked the original one off in 1941), down Grey Street or Grainger Street, you can have a great time. The city landscape is a wonderful, inventive mess, full of huge bits of Victorian ironware, plunging perspectives from the heights down to the river, obsessive mercantile stonework.

At random, I observed an inordinate number of musical instrument shops (isn't that heart-warming? The thought of a city which dedicates itself to playing piano accordions and electric fuzz guitars?); a tiny, old-fashioned tobacconist tucked under a gargantuan railway arch; the 'Northern Goldsmiths Company, Ring Shop For The World', with a little marble globe stuck on the outside of their shop to drive the point home; a deserted baroque-style office, former home of the Tyne-Tees Steam Shipping Company with the original painted legend still visible on the outside – 'Regular liner services between Newcastle and London, Antwerp, Dordrecht, Ghent and Northern French Ports'; a stunning decommisioned Post Office, opposite St Nicholas's Cathedral – the grandest Post Office I've ever seen, four storeys tall, with a façade decorated with pilasters, Corinthian capitals and an enormous processional entrance two storeys high; and opposite *that*, a statue of Queen Victoria which portrays Her Imperial Majesty slumped on a kind of Gothic toilet, the whole thing built with the slender, airy grace of Wellington's funeral carriage and shat upon copiously by pigeons for nearly a hundred years.

gives you neckache, because you spend so
ng back and peering up at large objects or
o glimpse things far below. The Tyne Bridge
an afternoon. This is the one that looks like
ross Sydney harbour, a colossal 'D' lying on its
side, d green. It was opened in 1928 and for a while
was the largest single-span bridge in the world. Its scale
beggars belief, even now. I recommend standing at the
bottom of one of its monumental piers and squinting up
at the huge structure hundreds of feet above you to get a real
sense of your own insignificance, mingled throat-catchingly
with admiration for the people who put the thing up.

Having done that, you can then step into a lift. This is an
obscure, lavatorial and claustrophobic device built into the
bridge's foundations and covered at ground level with algae
and piss. It is also the first lift I've been in to bear the notice
IF THE LIFT BREAKS DOWN STAY CALM, which does
nothing at all to reassure the lonely traveller inside, gagging
quietly on the smell and wondering if anyone would ever
discover him if the lift did break down. A long anxious
minute later and you come out on top of the Tyne Bridge, by
a bus stop, the place where you were now distantly below
you, the river sprawling at your feet, seagulls wheeling
through the girders.

This may sound arch, but the place Newcastle most reminded me of was Lisbon. This is another great city by the
sea, similarly composed of all kinds of crazed architectural
forms, likewise lurching from the cramped to the massive,
full of vertiginous leaps and tarmacadamed cliffs. Both are
pretty shabby, too. Both places feel (as indeed they are) cut
off from the general, diminishing march of civilisation. Both
are slightly mad and both like to eat and drink a fair bit.

Newcastle is, of course, colder and wetter than Lisbon and
it doesn't have terrific pre-First World War trams grinding
up and down its streets. Nor does it have smart-arse travel

writers from the colour sections coming up to sing its praises as a forgotten jewel in the crown of any sophisticated traveller's itinerary.

What it does have, unfortunately, are hacks other than myself coming from London to do pieces for the *Guardian* which go on about (and I quote) 'Social damage, the chronically high levels of unemployment, spinning off into poverty, the crime, the alienation . . .' Making it sound less like Lisbon, in other words, and more like Moss Side on Sea.

One reason why I'm so partial to the city is that a friend of mine is loosely a Geordie (half Durham, half Newcastle by upbringing) and his tolerant parents once let me sponge off them years ago, on my way to the Edinburgh Festival. So I associated the place with the holiday mood, right from the word go. I can remember even now being shown round some kind of scuzzy Geordieland working man's club twenty years ago and being told how to ask for 'Newquay Broon' and how to rap out such lines as 'Howay, man, I'm knackered,' and 'Hadaway and puke, man' (whatever that meant) in such a way as to ingratiate myself with the large and threatening north-easterners who found my David Bowie/Anthony Blunt accent and my little wire spectacles highly diverting. I can see it now, Newcastle after dark, in the rain, the desperate, hormone-driven search for sin . . . I might even have gone to Bigg Market, but if there were any girls around at the time, they signally failed to interfere with my pimply young body.

My pal and I also took the bus up to Edinburgh and spent three hours flogging along the A1 being rubbished by a gang of Tyneside yobs in the back seat who had taken a fancy to our travelling companion. He, unfortunately, was obsessed with Anthony Blanche, Evelyn Waugh's charismatic fictional poove from *Brideshead Revisited*. Our travelling companion wasn't just gay, he was an incontrovertibly screaming nance whose idea of fun was to twit the yobs

by calling out, 'I *adore* the *eau-de-nil* of your cardigan', or,
'My, my. Aren't they *frisky*?'

Actually, having said all that, I can't think why I should
be so predisposed towards the place. Perhaps it is instead
because, like everybody else down here, I am a victim of the
North East's PR campaign.

This got started back in the 1960s when Dick Clement and
Ian la Frenais produced *The Likely Lads*. James Bowlam
(Terry), in particular, crystallised an idea of Geordieness in
the minds of millions of southerners to whom the idea of
Newcastle had never previously occurred. It was a deft and
memorable performance, shaded just the right side of
extreme oafishness, and won him thousands of fans. Then,
no less attractively, there was *Whatever Happened To The
Likely Lads?* followed by *Auf Wiedersehen Pet*, with interim
contributions from The Animals, bloody Lindisfarne, Chris
Rea (Tyneside's gravel-voiced human narcotic) and Jimmy
Nail as haunted, would-be heavyweight actor and star of
Spender. Admittedly, Nail went a bit far in his Spender
incarnation, with a look of perpetual ruminative hurt in
his eyes, rotten harmonica playing, frankly risible scripts and
hair like deepfried shag tobacco, but he could still redeem
himself and the rest of Newcastle.

Was there anyone before Clement and la Frenais? At this
point, it all goes blank and the only Tyneside cultural
manifestation I can summon to mind is the woman who
used to croon 'Thou shalt have a fishy on a little dishy whan
the booooat cooms in' on the Uncle Mac radio programme.
And the Venerable Bede, twelve hundred and fifty years
before her.

Sunderland stand-up comic Roy 'Chubby' Brown ('I'm
that fookin' tough I wipe me arse with sandpaper'), on the
other hand, was discovered quite recently by the southern
quality press, but on the strength of his video *Roy Chubby
Brown: The Helmet Rides Again* I think we in the South may
not yet be ready to learn everything he has to teach us. *Viz*

magazine, conversely, has shamelessly colonised huge quantities of southern readers who like to treat farting, crapping,
vomiting, swearing and wanking as acceptable sources of
hilarity. I have to confess that I, too, have bought the odd
Viz – for the cultural critique, you understand (Student
Grant, The Fat Slags, Johnny Fartpants, etc.) – and if a
brilliantly realised, scabrous sociopathy is your idea of a
good time, then *Viz* is the magazine for you. This is also true
if, like almost all British men, you enjoy jokes about soiling
your underwear.

At any rate, these people have successfully laboured to
convince the South that Tyneside and the rest of the North
East is a haven for down-to-earth, sometimes soulful, more-
or-less warm-hearted hooligans with only a mild disposition
towards brutality: acceptable Liverpudlians, if you like.

In fact, Geordieness has gone a long way towards rendering itself the marketable face of the North. Indeed, it's now
evidently superior to imported Yorkshire, with all Yorkshire's attendant bluff, pomposity and meanness. Geordie
voices – where Yorkshire would once have done – now
persuade us to buy camera film or shampoo or sausages.
Geordie voices now denote frankness tempered with warmth
on Radio 4 (Brian Redhead could never make up his mind
whether he was from Manchester, which he wasn't, or
Newcastle, which he was. The Geordie bits kept emerging
in a savoury manner whenever he wanted to sound warm,
concerned, sincere). Geordie local politicians manage to
imply community and common sense in a way that whining
Lancastrians never can. The very word 'Geordie' now elicits
from Tonbridge stockbrokers and bankruptcy lawyers the
response, '*Marvellous* people. Such *resilience*.' Geordies, as
seen from a distance of three hundred miles, are everything
southerners demand from northerners: poor sods with a
derelict economy, glorious countryside, a nice line in self-
deprecating humour and a wonderfully beguiling accent.

* * *

And the city lives up to its own publicity. The day after my
Weimar Republic curry, I tottered into a second-hand bookshop and found a book I'd been looking for for years (Michael
Frayn's *The Tin Men*, if you must know) plus some old *Picture
Post*s. Kismet, I thought. This place is going out of its way to
make me like it. So I went off to the nearest pub to examine my
haul and have an authentic cheese bap (a bap in Newcastle is a
large Northumbrian bun filled with kapok) and found myself
instantly among true layabout Geordies, quaffing their beer
and looking with amusement at their watches.

'I'll never make it now,' said a big fellow in a donkey
jacket, apparently talking about his bus. 'I'll have to catch
the one at four o'clock.'

There was a general shuffling and relaxation around the
table.

'That's the afternoon gone, then. Are you having another
pint?'

The big fellow frowned a bit and stared unconvincingly
out of the window.

'A half.'

'Howay, man! Two pints, for Christ's sake!'

'I'll give the wife a call an' tell her I'll be a bit late. Can
you make that a lager?'

Moreover, the accent, comical and mournful, was firmly
in place, as specified. Newcastle was *Newcassel*; market place
became m*o*rket place; Harvard University would have been
H*o*rvud Yoon*iv*orsity had they got round to the question of
which MBAs were worth the candle, and so forth. Occasionally, and particularly when you've got a group of
middle-aged Sid the Sexists unwinding after a morning's
light graft, Geordie sounds like ordinary English spoken
backwards. Even more occasionally I found myself thinking
that I was among Scandinavians. It's an accent that makes
everything sound interesting, in much the same way that
Fats Waller can make even a piece of old hokum like 'Dinah'
worth listening to.

A veteran of the last war actually insisted to me that when the Eighth Army were campaigning in North Africa, the Geordie regiments weren't required to use the same code words or radio security as other combatants. This was because, since most of what they said was incomprehensible to other English speakers, it was presumed to be completely unintelligible to the Germans.

The obverse of this may also be true, in that Geordies may not be able to understand anyone who doesn't speak Geordie. Having crammed my insides with kapok and cheese and steeped myself in some kind of deceptively feeble-tasting pub-made beer which actually had me singing tunelessly under my breath ten minutes later *and* gave me double vision, I toiled uphill back towards Grey's Monument. There, a group of Dutch tourists had cornered a young man in a collar and tie. He was clutching what looked like a bag of food (which may have been the root of the trouble) and was asking, with rising desperation in his voice, 'Yes, but what exactly is it you *want*?'

The Dutchmen pressed amiably in on him, like fans mobbing a minor television actor.

'We want food,' they said, 'to eat.'

The young man backed against the little globe on the front of the Northern Goldsmiths Company.

'What do you mean?' he shouted.

'Yes!' they said. 'Meat! Food! To eat!'

The young man rolled his eyes and cried, 'Yes! But what do you *mean*?'

A failure to communicate? Is the Geordie demotic a one-way street? Or was it just rank stupidity on his part? Given that he looked like a bank clerk, I would suspect the latter. It is a matter of record, incidentally, that the command in Dutch for the cavalry to mount their horses is *Scromble op dem beesties*. So even if the tourists had spoken in their native tongue, he ought to have made a fist of understanding them.

* * *

On the down side, there was, of course, T. Dan Smith. T. Dan
Smith has been called 'The most eye-catching figure in
municipal government since the days of Chamberlain',
which is admittedly a pretty listless compliment to pay
anyone. He was known to his friends as Mr Newcastle; to
his enemies as the Mouth of the Tyne. At one stage, he even
took to referring to Newcastle as the Brasilia of the North. But
the fact is that T. Dan not only brought a certain revivalist
civic spirit to the North East ('making it fizz', apparently), he
also became one of the few Geordies that southerners have
heard of, when he went down for six years in April 1974 on
charges of corruption. This was despite (or because of) being
Chairman of the North East Planning Council and a member
of the Royal Commission on Local Government.

Working hand-in-glove with the architect John Poulson
and a north-eastern big-time political operator called Alderman Andy Cunningham, he worked up a network of corrupt
business and political relationships in which Poulson would
supply the money and T. Dan would apportion it in the form
of bribes to the appropriate local government functionaries
in order to secure lucrative building contracts for Poulson's
firm. Smith once wrote an interestingly asyntactical memo
to Poulson which read, 'The basis of success in any region,
the North East success has proved to me, is top contact and
someone on the ground to drink pints and make friends with
the rank and file.'

After a while, of course, the drinks started to cost several
thousand pounds a round and a legend was born. It also led
to some of the repellent new road and office schemes which
have so defiled the looks of the city. Smith was released from
jail after serving three years of his sentence and promptly
announced that he was heading a project to stop youngsters
drifting into crime.

The episode as a whole left a certain mark in the mind of
your average southerner, giving the region something of the
smell of Tammany Hall about it. I'm sure that any taint of

corruption was blown away years ago by the crisp North Sea breezes, but history has a way of turning into myth if you're a long way from the source of the story. Londoners look up to the North East, gauge its distance from the rest of the world and assume that if they're not actually greasing each other's palms and bunging slush all over the place, it's only because it's expedient for them not to do so at that particular juncture. A hopeless calumny, a vile misrepresentation, I'm sure: but that's how it can look.

Bearing this in mind, I then had a brainwave as I was walking down John Dobson Street. I spotted the Turkish Baths. These form part of a long, dun-coloured building which looks a bit like Churchill's Admiralty bunker with windows and which principally houses the city swimming pool. It had outside a banner saying, 'Newcastle's Best-Kept Leisure Secret'. Turkish Baths, I thought: this is where the city's big shots are going to be, sitting in the steamroom chewing wet Havanas and talking in a secret language about bungs and slush, or whatever they call graft in Newcastle. This is where I need to go.

To be honest, I like Turkish Baths as well; and I was mildly astonished to find a working public *hammam* in the city. So far as I know, the only public Turkish Baths still going in England are in Harrogate, London (just off Westbourne Grove) and, of course, Newcastle. There are some good baths at the RAC in Pall Mall, but a member has to sign you in which can be a bit tricky to organise. And then your enjoyment is marred by having to sit around in the *tepidarium* listening to jumpy estate agents drivelling on about unshiftable properties in the Regent's Park area. Back in the North East, Lord Armstrong – inventor, industrialist and munitions king – built a private Turkish Bath into his house at Cragside, so maybe Tynesiders are particularly appreciative of a bit of killing heat, given the fact that the place is so cold most of the time.

But a private *hammam* is a luxury I would seriously press on anyone, North or South, for whom a million pounds is not an unimaginable sum. If you've never sweated it out in a steamroom or reduced yourself to a daze in the *laconicum* (the smallest, hottest dry room – usually about the size of a large cupboard, excruciatingly hot and rank with the smell of boiled armpits), followed by a brisk dive into the plunge-pool or a spell under the needle-jet shower, then you are missing a treat. It is an Edwardian pleasure which the modern world cannot compromise. You cannot rush a Turkish Bath.

In fact, one of the best bits of the whole three-hour bath experience is the nap and cup of tea you enjoy afterwards in the lounge area outside the hot rooms. Here you get a little curtained cubicle, a bed and a reading lamp and can sit and drink your tea and read the paper and feel all the knots fall out of your shoulders. And, contrary to popular belief, Turkish Baths are not packed out with emotionally un-stable gays escaping from an Armistead Maupin story. If anything, they tend to attract fat old geezers from the rag trade. That's been my experience, anyway.

So I went in and asked the prices. A sweet blonde girl at the counter leant forward and said, 'I'll let you into a secret.'

She enunciated it with such lilting north-eastern promise, I could hardly bear to discover what the secret was. I wanted to leave it there. It was a beautiful moment. But she went on, 'Last ticket's at seven o'clock. So come at five thirty so's you get the benefit.' Or five *thorty*, as she put it.

Inside the baths at five thirty prompt, I found a group of lads being initiated into the mysteries of the *hammam* by a pal.

'I canna stay in here,' announced one of them. 'Me bollocks is fryin'.'

I left them to it and went off with a towel round my middle in search of cabals of old men talking politics, only to stumble across a couple of sweltering bank employees.

'I believed in Thatcher,' proclaimed a dripping fatty to his mate. 'She was brilliant, she was. Brilliant. She didn't take anything from anyone.'

'Aye,' said his mate.

'But now. It's all gone. They've thrown it all away.'

'Aye. Look at the Soashul Chorter. They've torn it up and the bank can just push us around, now.'

I was a bit surprised at this, given the almost uniformly Labour complexion of north-eastern politics and the fact that the last two decades have seen the economy of the region unravel like an old cardigan. The thought of Thatcher getting any kind of approval up here sounded wrong.

I was also disappointed, because Down South we have no political analysis other than to say that the Tories may have got a few things wrong but at least they're not the Socialists; or to remark, more fatalistically, that the Tories simply beggar belief and why don't we all emigrate? Until recently most of us down here couldn't envisage a world in which the Tories didn't call the shots (although it's remarkable how many otherwise leaden, parochial and unreflecting Conservatives can be seized by the imaginative process when they contemplate the horrors that a Labour Government would inflict on us all). Up on the Tyne, a Labour stronghold, I'd hoped to come across a genuine voice of the people laying into the political system, positing a real alternative, but a fat nude man flannelling on about Thatcher wasn't it.

'Aye. Dave's on twelve and half grand, basic. At his age.'

'That's what I'm saying.'

I trudged across the burning floor of the baths, hitching my towel irritably across my paunch. In the steamroom, I thought I detected a suspicion of Tammany Hall, perhaps the ghost of T. Dan Smith, as an old boy and a young shaver compared notes.

'You know that Broon?' said the old boy.

'Aye.'

'He's a miserable man.'

The old boy slapped his neck with the edge of his towel. The young shaver examined the sole of his foot.

'Aye, he's full of wind and piss, he is.'

'Well, you don't know him.'

'I was a councillor with him. He was terrible then.'

'I'll give him your regards.'

That wasn't really enough, either. So I flat-footed my way to the *laconicum*, emerging after a while as a shrieking raspberry demon and throwing myself under the needle-jet shower. Close to heart failure, I then wove my way out to the comfort of the temperate cubicled area and went in search of a cup of tea. There was a table with the component parts of a cup of tea spread across it – kettle, cups, tea-bags, little plastic buckets of UHT milk with foil lids. You had to put your tea together yourself. Here, another bloke in a towel, looking suspiciously like *Top Gear*'s Jeremy Clarkson, started talking to me. Unlike Jeremy Clarkson, this one wasn't an egomaniacal fart, but he was probably slightly mad. He fiddled with the sugar lumps and spoke as I waited for the water to boil.

'I run me own business,' he began. 'I started it a while ago.'

I thought he was going to try and touch me for a fiver, but he went on, 'I was married with two kids at the time and the Government was paying me £94 a fortnight. Well, it was too much, I couldn't spend it all, so in 1980 I took elocution lessons and became a Con*sor*vative and since then I've never looked back.'

I stirred my tea-bag around and wondered what it was he did, exactly. He was suitably vague about what his business involved, but he did own up to having 'Three properties in the city at one time. But I flogged two of them off and now I'm down to one.'

I drew on my tea and he asked me how I found Newcastle. I burped out something along the lines of how much I liked it and he went on, with relatively congenial provincial chippiness, 'Aye, it's not so bad, is it? We'll send you back with a food parcel to take Down South. Don't tell everyone in London, they'll all be coming up. It's the public transport, you see. You can take the kids on the bus all day for fifteen pence.'

I rolled my eyes appreciatively. Fifteen pence? That's astonishing. Why, in London, you can't even die of pneumonia for fifteen pence, I vouchsafed. He obviously thought to detect a hint of scepticism in my voice and bridled a bit.

'And I'm not saying that just because I'm a Geordie,' he said, wagging his finger. 'I've been all over the world. I've got a Dutch brother-in-law. He lives in Canada, actually. I like Canada. It's a bit like Norway, only half the price.'

He fiddled with his towel and peered at the entrance to the hot rooms.

'I've got three kids, now. Two girls and a boy. The third's the last. Never again. It's awful hard for a man, having kids.'

And he walked back into the heat. I took my tea off to my cubicle, where I read the Newcastle *Evening Chronicle*, giving the Jeremy Clarkson lookalike plenty of time to finish his Turkish bath and leave. When I went back in, he was nowhere to be seen. I wondered if I should have asked him about T. Dan Smith, but my ticket still had an hour or so to run, so I decided to get the benefit instead.

EIGHT

The next day I debated whether or not to go all the way up to Berwick-upon-Tweed just so that I could claim to have travelled to England's northernmost town. But then it occurred to me that I'd already been there a couple of years before and found that it was a place of dyed-in-the-wool weirdness, where every other building was an impossibly large and cruddy junk shop, flogging off the possessions of everyone who'd had the initiative to get out of Berwick-upon-Tweed, either to forge a new life, or in a hearse. I bought some Shellac 78s there, it was that sort of place.

Instead, I went to Jarrow, for no better reason than that my Day Rover go-anywhere travelcard allowed me to. The self-made Jeremy Clarkson impersonator hadn't exaggerated: the public transport in and around Newcastle is astonishingly effective and outstanding value for money. It is, if not exactly a model of how a public transport network should operate, at least about as good as you can do in England.

The Tyne and Wear metro railway goes underground through the city, before emerging north and south and heading overground as far as the airport in one direction, South Shields (where it connects with the splendid Tyne ferry) in another and Whitley Bay in yet another. Bits of it recycle the old branch-line railway network, sometimes, as at Whitley Bay, using the original Victorian railway station. More often the stops are indestructible concrete challenges to the vandal's energies. The trains are modern, comfortable, frequent and swift.

At the same time, the bus services which fuss around the metro's hinterland are plentiful and cheap. Indeed, you can find yourself spoilt for choice when picking the best way to your destination. I stood indecisively for several minutes in North Shields at one point, wondering whether to get back onto the metro to Byker or catch a bus which was hovering invitingly at my shoulder. And having established a kind of rhythm, swinging from metro to bus to ferry to bus to metro, I rather wanted to spend the rest of the day going to places simply because I could. And all for three quid.

The only problem is that it's very hard nowadays to appreciate how good a good public transport network is, even while you're using it. In Heaven (I am convinced of this) there are no private cars. Can you imagine a double-yellow-lined A-road going through the middle of the Celestial City? But our expectations of travel are more and more conditioned by the car. If we go anywhere not on foot, part of us instinctively hunts for the comfy seat adjuster, the heater switch, the radio which schmoozes away in our ears, the glazed solitude of the traffic jam. There is no comparison, on a cold, wet, windy day, between standing at the Jarrow bus station, wondering which particular arsewit has smashed in the glass panes of the bus shelter (allowing the storm to blow savagely upon my unprotected self) and sitting snugly in a rented car with a softening Fruit & Nut in one's hand, no matter how slow, inefficient or environmentally harmful the car might actually be.

There is likewise little to be said for standing at the bus depot outside the Gateshead Metro Shopping Centre waiting for the number 100 bus to take you, however expeditiously, to the centre of Newcastle, while being obliged to watch two lads standing next to you, gobbing unthreateningly but nonetheless wetly and persistently onto the concrete two feet away. Nor is there much to be said for being

hurled around on the top deck of an old RouteMaster by the
potholes which fill England's roads. Or for sitting on the
damp patch left by the previous sodden occupant on a metro
train seat, while trying to wipe the steam of twenty other
breaths off the grimy train windows. And what you do if you
have two bags of shopping, a pushchair and a lava-bowelled
one-year-old with you, defies the imagination.

But a good public transport system is more than just an
item on every liberal's wish-list, it is intellectually beautiful.
Imagine a really effective national railway system, with all
the complexities such a thing entails, the sense of order and
structure it requires. The whole thing is a vast, elaborate
mechanism, obeying a rigorous system of rules in which the
smallest parts are intimately related to the largest. It is
hierarchical, ordered and organic at the same time. This is
one reason why the French, with their belief in large, ideal,
collective solutions to real problems, have put so much
money into their railways. Railways satisfy the French
theoretician as well as the unthinking French commuter.

The English, on the other hand, like roads and cars
because they reflect every Englishman's right to be a
bourgeois anarchist. To put it another way, the English
road system is the opposite of the structured, Platonic world
of public transport. It's more like the microscopic world of
blood flow or parasitic infestations – a messy, striving,
microbial shambles, with millions of tiny individuals forcing
themselves down blocked arteries and passageways in a
fevered rush for survival. Biologically speaking, England
more and more resembles a large organism increasingly
taken over by a mobile parasitic mass (cars), which drives
more and more tunnels and ducts (roads) through its host's
body, until, eventually, the host organism turns up its toes
and dies (today's economy/environment/society).

So. Public transport is an incomparably superior way to
get around and one day, all England will have a system as
good as Newcastle's. Unlikely, of course, as long as we have a

Tory government, since cars are to the Tories what guns are to the Republicans in the United States. This is what I told myself as I shivered on the station platform, feeling chilly, high-minded and envious in the way that only a Londoner who's lived for years with the penny-pinching farrago which masquerades as a public transport policy in the capital can do.

I stopped at Jarrow. Here God turned on His morning shower and I found myself wetly picking my way across patches of waste ground, searching for signs of the Jarrow Marchers. Well, there was a sort of bas-relief on the platform of the metro station and there was a small plaque on the outside of the Town Hall, but other than that, the place gave the impression of having been razed to the ground shortly after the last war and rebuilt with the contents of T. Dan Smith's corporate dustbin.

'The great achievement of Jarrow,' Melvyn Bragg recently wrote in a staggeringly long magazine piece, 'is caring.' The great visible achievement of Jarrow is to be extremely flat and barren and have a desperate new shopping centre where every other unit is boarded up (there was, though, one shop there with the name 'It's Canny Textiles', which seemed to be doing a good trade in off-cuts of net curtain). It's the kind of place where from the moment you arrive, you start thinking about having a shotglass of something alcoholic. I was there shortly after breakfast time and even then I could hardly wait for the pubs to open. Old Melvyn spent much of his time looking for Bede and Socialism, but I think he must have been able to get out of the rain.

In Jarrow, in high summer at nine thirty in the morning, my extremities were turning violet and I was reduced to blowing on my nails like Dick the shepherd. My hunched, miserable posture and the fact that I was wandering around aimlessly on an acre of weed-strewn concrete clearly made me look like one of the locals, because after a while a chap in a blue anorak came hurrying up. I thought perhaps that he might have caught a glimpse of my expensive southern pallor and was going to rob me, but instead he said, 'Excuse me, mate, is this the way to the Job Club?'

It's nice to blend in, sometimes. In all other respects, I felt as if I'd landed on the moon. This was not just because poor old Jarrow is bleak, flat and deserted, but because it seems to bear no relationship to Newcastle, barely six miles away on the metro. In this respect alone, it was entirely unlike the satellite towns of Birmingham and Manchester, which borrow many of the big cities' visual tropes and architectural turns of phrase, replicated on a smaller scale. You can see, for instance, that Wigan and Manchester are of the same stock. Walsall and Birmingham are not entirely dissimilar. But Jarrow doesn't look a bit like Newcastle. Once you leave the city boundary, you leave everything to do with Newcastle. The rest of the habitations strung out alone the Tyne – Gateshead, Byker, Wallsend, Jarrow – are all ineffably small-time, places of their own desperate making.

This tendency continued out to the mouth of the Tyne. I wandered on to South Shields (standing at the metro stop next to an old guy who looked remarkably like Champion Jack Dupree: in fact I was convinced it was him, except for the fact that Champion Jack settled in Halifax, not Northumberland; and he's been dead for several years) and found more of the same.

South Shields, it turns out, is home to the nation's first permanently stationed lifeboat, installed some time at the end of the eighteenth century. It also once had a horse-drawn tram and, judging by pictures taken a hundred years ago, the streets were crowded with people in dark worsted, going soberly about their business. Nowadays, it seems oddly vacant. It has a mildly respectable pedestrianised shopping precinct, a few bits of curlicued civic building dotted around, the metro line crossing the main street at roof-top height and knots of morose-looking blokes standing in the rain, trying to get the most out of their cigarettes.

It felt, as well it might, like a deeply small town stuck like a piece of punctuation at the end of economic life. Somewhere around here, somewhere between Newcastle airport and Sunderland, there is supposed to be large-scale industrial redevelopment going on, bringing new purpose to the fag-smoking men – men who otherwise have no option but to breed out of themselves, over the next couple of generations, the deep-rooted conviction that a man is not entirely a man unless he works for a living.

The Nissan factory at Sunderland has, of course, become the best-known car works in the country, overtaking Leyland's Longbridge and Ford's Dagenham as a kind of industrial epitome for our times (much as Consett steel works did, when it closed back in 1980). But Nissan can only do so much for South Shields. Even as Nissan takes on a few more car-fettlers, the last pit in the region closes down, or the last shipyard completes its last order and you get the feeling that revitalising the region's economy is like pushing a pea uphill with your nose.

The Northern Development Corporation, charged with the thankless task of boosting the place and getting some big money in, talks up all the local companies who make television sets and kids' toys and what have you, but the immediate beneficial effects of Samsung and Fisher-Price on a place like South Shields are hard to spot.

Let's face it, the economy of Newcastle and the North East has always been a bit on the contingent side. It started to take off in the sixteenth century, when north-eastern coal was moved by sea to the great maw of London (from this time onwards, 'Taking coals to Newcastle' becomes a waggish irony), and about three hundred years later the

place had become an industrial and financial centre. It was
never on the scale of Birmingham or Manchester or Leeds,
but was big for the region. Coal was dangerously and
brutally mined. Tyneside shipbuilders built an awful lot
of ships, all with increasing inefficiency.

And then, in this century, the structure came apart: if all
you have are coal and ships and no one wants coal or ships,
what do you do? Now the cranes line the Tyne from
Newcastle to South Shields, doing nothing. When I was
up there, the receivers had just been called in to take over the
running of Tyneside's last major shipyard, Swan Hunter,
who had lost a vital Ministry of Defence order to Vickers at
Barrow-in-Furness. Over seven hundred jobs were axed in
the first three months, leaving an uneasy workforce of
around fifteen hundred men waiting for the few remaining
Government contracts to run their course.

This sense of the daylight slowly departing is even more
marked once you cross the Tyne to North Shields. I stood on
the heaving ferry boat, my collar turned up against the cold
(this was August *and* I was indoors) and watched as nothing
very much came into view. Someone had told me that North
Shields was *the* place to have your car stolen or your head
kicked in (those riots, of course), but having got there, I
couldn't find anyone to do so much as elbow me aside, let
alone steal a car which I didn't have anyway. It seemed a
long way from civilisation. All I could think about was
strong drink.

I found myself at a bus stop, where it occurred to me that I
didn't have to be where I was and that I could, at no further
expense, be somewhere else. I dithered for a couple of icy
minutes and then caught a bus which drove perplexingly
through bland suburbs, collecting housewives in C&A head-
scarves, some accompanied by clean, middle-class children.
The rain dripped in through a hole in the roof ventilator.

After a while, I got off my bus, sprinted through what
was now a downpour and leaped onto a fetid but welcom-

ing metro back to Newcastle. I was relieved to be back in
the big city. It was cold, sad and pre-Christian once you left
its purlieus. The hotel proprietor gave me a special
'Ooooookayyy?' as I crashed through the chimes over the
front door and tripped on his doormat. Make that a double,
I said.

Ah, but the countryside. If Newcastle is turning into pre-
Nazi Berlin, the scenery beyond the city and the outlying
towns has a kind of scrubbed purity which I don't think you
find anywhere else in England.

To a suburban dullard like myself, of course, countryside
tends to look pretty much the same wherever you go. I
realise that the mountains of Wales are somewhat dissimilar
to the gentle clefts of Kent, but then I would interpret that as
being the difference between countryside and city suburb,
since Kent, like large parts of Buckinghamshire, Surrey,
Sussex, Bedfordshire, Hertfordshire and even Oxfordshire, is
really a slightly bucolic extension of London. If, on the other
hand, you compare the countryside of Wales with the
countryside of Scotland (Celtic fringe/twilight/mist and so
on), you can see at once that there's no real distinction. In
fact, you might as well be in Ireland, for that matter, except
that Scotland's nicer than either Wales or Ireland, so you
might as well stay in Scotland.

Congruences crop up elsewhere: Dartmoor looks like
North Yorkshire; Gloucestershire looks like Oxfordshire,
which looks like Derbyshire, which looks like Avon, or
wherever Bath is these days. The Lake District looks like
Wales. Norfolk and Suffolk look like Lincolnshire and
Humberside. It's impossible to tell where you are just by
looking at the scenery.

I quite like countryside, mind you. It's nice to know that
it's there for townies to walk across (although I approve of
the Jeff Goldblum character in *The Big Chill* who observes
that 'The countryside's just a big toilet, isn't it?' as he pisses

furtively over the long grass), but I don't really understand it. I couldn't live there, for instance, and I can't imagine how anyone could. All that silence and isolation. The terrible shops. Having to drive for twenty minutes just to get a newspaper or go to the pub. Awful.

Only towns and cities hold the key to where you stand. And I suppose I should argue the same about Northumbria (the remnants of the ancient Kingdom of Northumbria, now covering an area from Berwick-upon-Tweed to Darlington), except that to me, it does look at least marginally different from, say, Surrey.

This may be because Northumbria and me, we go back a while. When I got off the train at Newcastle's very fine Central Station, I was transported, for about half a second, back to my childhood. As I wandered out under the majestic stone-faced portico at the entrance (its two ornamental cannons pointing sternly but whimsically at the roof), I was reminded how, a quarter of a century earlier, I had walked out under that same portico, clutching a copy of *Spiderman* magazine (or was it *The Fantastic Four*?) and nervously looking forward to our family summer holiday, which this time was to be spent among the fleshpots of Embleton, just a few miles up the coast.

Decades later, the stonework looked a little cleaner and the sun was shining (my first view of Northumbria had been through an aerosol spray of rain) but there was no mistaking those ashlar columns, or the clustered forms of Victorian shops and offices just beyond.

The holiday itself was a bit of a let-down, the way childhood holidays usually were. We were staying in a barbarous little pre-fab cottage with a picture window overlooking a field full of unimpressed cows. A man came round in a van and sold us kapok-filled baps from time to time, which bucked things up, but otherwise it was mainly cold and lacklustre.

I also nearly drowned when the undertow on a particularly vicious gravel beach started to suck me out towards Denmark, obliging my father to wade grimly in after me in a pair of flannel trousers and fish me out ('Why can't you just go for a *swim*?'). And prefiguring my trip on the coach full of Anthony Blanche and the Geordie hoodlums, we took a day trip to Edinburgh. There, things were so bad, I had to eat boiled sprouts for lunch. The following year, it was North Devon as usual for us.

I made it up, though, years later, by traipsing across the Kielder Forest and Hadrian's Wall in a snow-drift and, frankly, freezing my nuts off on the beach at Dunstanborough. I've also inspected at first hand the Norman grandeur of Durham Cathedral and I've seen the memorial to a Roman soldier, killed by a hairy Pict, which stands in Hexham Abbey. This is a curiously touching monument, commissioned and paid for as it was by the soldier's parents, thousands of miles away in the Mediterranean sun, mourning the loss of their boy at the margin of the known world.

Now, Hexham: that's a place with a certain kind of magic about it. And I don't mean the sleazy, commercialised magic-for-morons of Glastonbury or Camden Town. I mean that, for a Londoner, the strange mixture of easterly breezes, immemorial stone, light, cold and general space at Hexham can be weirdly intoxicating. Blanchland, a sort of Gloucestershire Broadway of the North, had something of the same tone when I ate tea there once. There was a lot of stonework and openness and brilliant light. I had the feeling that the map must have been lying to me in some obscure way. It didn't look like anything I could remember seeing in England before.

Apparently, Hexham is where the smart set of Northumbria base themselves. Someone (with, admittedly, extremely distant Northumbrian connections) told me that the toffs of Northumbria are a distinct variety all unto themselves. Unlike other toffs in England, they don't worry about

London or Home Counties practices, because they're just too far away. Instead, they busy themselves with being rigorously and massively exclusive. From their bleak, backward fastness, rather like Scottish lairds and demented Irish peers, they look down on everyone else with magnificent scorn. Thus, the Northumbrian Waugh crowd lives in a world of its own, holding old-fashioned sherry parties and dancing awkwardly in tiled barns, somewhere in the wilderness between Hexham and Alnwick.

Not that it was always perfect up there, even after the memory of the drear family summer holiday had faded. Staying in a hotel just outside Hexham, I was treated to a piece of real north-eastern-style hospitality as I tucked into my Full English Breakfast one snowy morning.

'Haven't you finished yet?' demanded the proprietress.

'No,' I said, in my most commanding Home Counties accent. 'And I'd like some more tea please.'

So she wordlessly took the pot from my table, refilled it, replaced it and, on her way out, opened all the breakfast room windows so that the snow blew over my toast. I don't know what I'd done wrong, other than be a Londoner.

And in Bamburgh, my wife and I had to share our dinner with an egregious local Tory MP, a southerner dumped in a northern seat. The hotelier there wanted us to eat our supper at six o'clock so that he could get us out of the way for the local constituency Tory party bash which was due to take place amid the battered chintz and greasy flock of his lounge/dining room. But we stuck out for an eight o'clock meal. By this time there were scores of plum-faced farmers and solicitors shouldering their way across the floor, demanding freshen-ups for their gin and tonics and something not too strong for the wife.

We were jammed into an inglenook by the unlit fireplace, where we hacked irritably at the chef's special gammon and

pineapple balanced on our knees. This was bad enough, but
the southern Tory MP caught our accents above the noise of
the rabble and immediately pushed his way through the
mob to where we sat. He then started talking to us in that
curiously obtuse, obsessive way that distinguishes MPs when
they're not addressing large numbers of people but think
they're being intimate, instead. He was obviously homesick
for the Smoke, despite spending most of his working week
there. To this end, he ignored his constituents for an hour
while quizzing us on the South Circular, the streets of
Notting Hill, John Lewis's in Oxford Street and other such
matters. The din from the thwarted farmers and lawyers got
louder and louder and more and more menacing, as they
saw their man schmoozing with a couple of whey-faced
southerners, so my wife and I eventually made some sort
of excuse and detached ourselves from the maundering MP
As we left, the crowd fell on him with a noise like waves
breaking on a shingle beach.

Be that as it may, I have clear and stirring memories of great
moorland spaces and stunning sandy beaches stretching out
along a chastening Christian coastline, punctuated by
occasional vast castles. The landscape, moreover, looks
clean enough to eat your lunch off, which is something
neither the West Country nor East Anglia can claim, while
the Home Counties don't even try.

So attached am I to this part of the world that I even once
took the wife and kids off to a cottage just near Craster,
where the kippers come from. To describe the weather while
we were there as cold would be to describe Beria as a bit of a
rogue. It was spring, but the cold never left the house (a
squat, stone thing smelling of damp at the end of a row of
terraces) no matter how many pounds we shoved into the
electricity meter.

Worse than that was the coal fire in the sitting room. It
was one of those insanity-provoking Baxi Burnall arrange-

ments, with a metal case and a mica-glass window to enclose the fire. You have to bank the coal up against the back of the flue in a way that defies sense and which takes at least three days to master. We wandered around our freezing hovel for the first two days, our noses blue and our eyes watering, kidding ourselves that we'd get used to it and that it didn't really matter that Daddy couldn't get the Baxi to do anything more than consume hundredweights of kindling and fire-lighters.

But after forty-eight hours of mortification and self-denial we realised that of course it did matter, enormously, and that we hadn't got used to it nor ever would. With savage irony, however, I got the bastard Baxi to light on the third day and built it up into a blaze which could have smelted tin; only to discover that it made no appreciable difference. If I stood right on top of it, it was searingly hot. If I moved eighteen inches away, it was merely tepid. Three feet away and I couldn't feel a thing. The house stayed like a freezer for the whole week we were there. I know it's a banality to observe how searingly cold the North is, in comparison with the Louisiana-like steaminess of the South, but it's not banal to have to live through it.

By way of compensation, we had arguably the finest coastline in England to disport ourselves on. We also had the not disagreeable sensation of having travelled back in time to the 1950s. Places like Craster, Alnmouth and Sea-houses are like very large time-capsules. They betray little in the way of late-twentieth-century building. They're unnaturally clean and tidy, as if modern packaging and modern litter have yet to be invented. They're also astonishingly light on traffic (although Alnmouth has got its share of yellow lines): and nothing dislocates your sense of time more than a town or village with no cars.

Craster was even more densely trapped in amber than Alnmouth. Craster looks like something from *The French Lieutenant's Woman*, but at the wrong end of the country. It has a tiny shingle harbour with a couple of tattered wooden boats pulled up onto the beach (the last herring catch was in 1976) and some rusting metalwork lying around and about. Small, grey stone houses stand back in an arc and overlook the chilly waters of the North Sea. There is a permanent scent of coal smoke in the air and there is hardly anyone about. The only signs of newness are a telephone box and a municipal car park, tucked into the side of a hill.

When I first saw this place, I danced about, thinking I'd found something unique and fragile, something as rare as the cistern of Cleopatra. On further acquaintance, I realised that, however pretty it was, it was also a small, slightly depressed fishing village with its own midget council estate and a pervasive feeling of nothing whatso-ever to do.

This was hardly surprising, given that the nearest place of any size is Alnwick, seven miles away, and however pretty Alnwick is (which it is) it is fundamentally a hick town. It has a splendid golden-stoned castle and many attractive buildings which now house firms of solicitors and estate agents, but it is still a hick town. In fact, the only thing about Alnwick which habitually raises any interest beyond the level of the parish magazine is the annual Shrove Tuesday football game, played on the North Demesne of Alnwick Castle. One year, apparently, one of the players in this competition pinched the ball and refused to give it back; while in 1994, fourteen players pursued the ball into the river Allen in the middle of a snowstorm. Originally, it seems, they used a Scotsman's head instead of a ball, so the whole thing is pretty debauched by Northumbrian stan-dards.

Back at Craster, I asked if I could buy kippers from the famous kipper smokery by the harbour, L. Robson & Sons. This is where England's most famous kippers come from and

I thought that if I couldn't get warm in my own house, I could at least fill myself with herrings. L. Robson & Sons have apparently been having difficulties with the Ministry of Agriculture, Fisheries and Food, who have insisted that they kipper their fish on stainless, rather than galvanised, steel tenterhooks. There is also some problem about the traditional open fires the curers use. In short, L. Robson & Sons have got things to worry about, but I wasn't to know this when I strode purposefully up their concrete drive and rapped on the door.

When I asked for some delicious fresh kippers, the staff just laughed at me. Some old boy came out of the sheds and told me that the place was shut, probably going to be sold and if I wanted kippers why didn't I try York, which had lots of kippers? I asked if there were ever kippers to be had and the old goat said something about coming back later in the season. I formed the impression that kippers were only available over a three-week period in October. So we went down the road to a place whose name I forget, but which had a ferry terminal, and bought some wet Scottish kippers in a polythene bag.

It was no warmer when I was up there on my own. After Jarrow and the Shieldses, I felt like getting away from it all by going to Whitley Bay, just up the coast from North Shields. I had been reading a profile of a poet called Fred D'Aguiar in my newspaper on the train to Newcastle: picture my surprise when I discovered the same Fred D'Aguiar featured strongly in Newcastle's *The Page*, 'The arts paper for the North'. And why was he in *The Page*? Because D'Aguiar had spent a couple of years living in Whitley Bay, just to the north of Newcastle, on a Northern Literary Arts Fellowship.

Moreover, he had actually written a sonnet sequence about that heady time and the love affair he had had there with an unnamed woman ('I knew between us, me and

Whitley Bay/ We couldn't make you stay'). In this sonnet sequence, he describes Whitley Bay as being, *inter alia*, a place of 'Five minute jams and one of most things', which sounded promising. Slender and only slightly interesting coincidences like these are meat and drink to hacks like myself; and it coupled itself with a vague desire to inspect a place I'd actually heard of (filed under 'Sad Seaside Resorts', along with Herne Bay and Bridlington) and which my Geordie friend had told me was where he used to endure his annual family outings at about the same time that I was enduring mine.

Well, Whitley Bay was even wetter and colder than everywhere else. I couldn't understand it. It was the absolute height of summer. In Athens, people were dying of excessive heat. As I stood on what I imagined was the seafront (a large area of grassland with a closed Big Wheel overlooking an even larger expanse of tormented, icy sea), Fred D'Aguiar's words came back to me, in the way I imagine they must haunt many in that part of the world: 'When sea-lit winds loosen a stinging rain/On Whitley Bay, your tears drown out mine.'

Having stared at the North Sea for about a minute, I couldn't take it any more, so I walked at an angle of forty-five degrees against the tempest to the nearest pub. I heaved open the door, squelched over to the bar, past a semi-conscious pensioner (the only other customer) with a small Guinness in front of her and leaned wetly against the melamine. The landlord was standing looking ruminatively out of the window as he polished a glass, saying, 'There's a couple of taxis out there, crashed in the rain. That'll teach 'em.'

There was in fact a large, messy pile-up at the crossroads outside, with queues of cars going in all directions, but he wasn't bothered. Whitley Bay on a freezing summer's day, with only the sea and the shadow of the Cheviots for company, could turn anyone the same way. He then spent about forty-five minutes building me a simple cheese and tomato bap while I sipped my whisky in microscopic quantities, to make it last. I don't know how Fred D'Aguiar coped, although I imagine his sweater collection must have been pretty extensive at the end of the two years.

This is not to say that Whitley Bay is without charm: on the contrary, I had recently come from Blackpool, so I was in the mood to be seduced by it. Unlike Halitosis City, Whitley Bay's tartiness extends only to a crumbling whitewashed cement edifice called Spanish City and one or two comatose pleasure arcades. It was about right, being much the same size as I imagine Blackpool was shortly before the railway came.

There is no pier, therefore there is no opportunity to see Keith Harris and Orville. There is no branch of Harry Ramsden's universal chip shop and there is no Hursty. Instead, there is a sweet little old railway station and a high street that has been pedestrianised in what struck me as an excessively complicated way. The rest of it – again, in contradistinction to Blackpool – is several streets of tidy suburban villas, acres of rain-refreshed grass, some cowering trees and shrubs and the hectic sea. And that seems to be that.

One of my guide books describes Whitley Bay as Tyneside's most popular seaside resort. Now, I realise that Whitley Bay has a smaller local population to draw on than Blackpool (the city of Newcastle contains maybe half as many people as the city of Manchester, with its half a million), but you wonder in what sense, exactly, *is* it the most popular? Is it the most sentimentally thought-of? Is it the one with the greatest number of family associations? Is it the nearest? Is it the only one with a leisureplex (however truncated) that Geordies can use?

Well, I liked it. But I wouldn't go there again, not unless I were being sponsored by Barbour, the Tyneside firm which makes warm, doughty, impenetrable waterproof jackets and leggings. It is not coincidence that their warmest and most ghastliness-resistant coat is called a Northumbria. Time, I thought, to go South.

NINE

By the time I left Tyneside, I was definitely turning into a professional North fancier, a wiseacre. I'd stopped merely *seeing* things and had started to *look* for things which I thought should be there. I was beginning to approach the North with what I thought of as a specialist's eye. The feeling had first come over me around Wigan, but now it had really taken hold. It wasn't anywhere near dementia, yet; just the kind of serene, slightly deranged conviction that religious enthusiasts and Tory think-tank occupants are full of. In Wigan, I was guessing that the North had to have certain things (ugliness, civic manifestations, the acrid smell of industry in decline, no greenery, temperatures from Baffin Island, etc.); but now I knew. Now I was bursting with *convictions*.

To be frank, I could have listed these same preconditions (with the possible exception of the tree shortage) down in London and saved myself the travelling. The difference now was that I knew these things to be true, having seen them with my own eyes and savoured them with my own nostrils.

I was also just beginning to tip over into a state of traveller's jadedness. I was looking, not for novelty, but for titillation. I was becoming finicky, precious, arrogant. I could see myself discussing aspects of northernness with the same creepy donnishness that wine snobs bring to their hobby: 'Well, yes, I think Heckmondwike's got body, but no character, if you see what I mean. I see it as a kind of poor man's Pontefract, upright but lacking in demotic resonance. Can I offer you a Hebden Bridge, or as the locals call it, an "Ebden Britch?"

So of course, clever me, I went straight off to Grimsby and Scunthorpe. Another mistake.

I don't know why I looked at the map and thought, Scunthorpe and Grimsby, they'll tickle my palate. The names had something to do with it: Grimsby, which sounds like an acronym for something you don't want (like Nimby or Yuppy) or failing that, a conflation of 'grim' and a defunct suffix meaning 'town by the sea'; and Scunthorpe, which to a southerner is just one of those richly comic northern place-names, in the same league as Eccles, Ramsbottom and Oswaldtwistle. It is also the place immortalised in the song 'Who Put The Cunt In Scunthorpe', by Ivor Biggun and the Red-Nosed Burglars.

And they're on a latitude with Oldham and Barnsley, north of Manchester and Sheffield and even getting close to Leeds and Bradford. I suppose I could have stopped at Scarborough or Hull, but I thought, no, these places are already on the map. Scarborough is where Alan Ayckbourn keeps a theatre and where old Yorkshire ladies sit on the front, fanning their knickers with the cool breath of the sea. And Hull has a large roadbridge over the River Humber and is where Philip Larkin conducted a string of clandestine sexual liaisons, wrote poetry ('Rain, wind and fire! The secret, bestial peace!') and ran the university library. Too predictable, I thought. Too self-evident. I can get to the quick of northernness now (I told myself) by intuition. I also thought that I ought to see the coastline of the North of England once more, before I never saw it again. And I felt that having just been to a city like Newcastle, it was time to try somewhere smaller, duller and more pointless.

And, if you can believe this, for a long time I thought both Grimsby and Scunthorpe were in the county of Yorkshire, which is a serious misassumption for a man in his mid-thirties, but nonetheless the case. This gave the journey added value in my eyes until I found out that they were in something called Humberside, a new county created in 1974. This had its administrative headquarters in a minuscule town called Beverley (under normal conditions the name of a girl) and a total, countywide population of 845,000.

The good news, from my point of view, was that Humberside did notionally form part of the new, post-1974 Yorkshire (althought the bits south of the Humber were clearly there under protest), along with other non-metropolitan councils such as Cleveland and North Yorkshire. Up to 1974, Grimsby and Scunthorpe had been in Lincolnshire, which is not a northern county however you hold it up to the light. Humberside was at least better than Lincolnshire, particularly as the bit north of the river Humber was made up of authentic Yorkshire leftovers. But it didn't alter the central dilemma of the trip, which was that Grimsby, Scunthorpe, Cleethorpes and Mablethorpe are no more North than Birmingham. Or to put it another way, they are North, but only to a devious carpetbagging Londoner like me.

I went first to Grimsby, which proclaimed itself 'The Capital Of Food' on the signs at the edge of town, but which turned out to be both the land of traffic jams caused by extensive and unfeasible roadworks and the commonwealth of carpet shops. Entering the town centre at the speed of a glacier gave me plenty of time to admire the bargains on offer and wonder if I wanted Axminster edge off-cuts more than I wanted branded warehouse clearances or whether I just wanted to lie down on the floor of my car and dream of being rich enough to stay for once in a hotel which wasn't the subject of a council investigation. I counted seven large carpeting emporia during my brief stay on the A18 (some of them more than once, thanks to the one-way system and my cack-handedness with the road map) and began to sink into a light depression.

In fact, I can tell you nothing about Grimsby except that it's not especially big, it's fairly ugly, it has some docks where they land fish and that to the north, there's a huge port at Immingham, where they off-load hundreds of BMW motor cars every day. The roads which lead due west from Immingham are thus distinguished by the great number of car transporters, all laden with tasty BMWs, which thunder off to satisfy the needs of lawyers, accountants and business types who survived the recession, somewhere west of the M1. The roads going east towards Immingham are likewise distinguished by numbers of empty car transporters, hurrying back for their next appointment with Germany's export miracle.

A ballad called the *Lay Of Havelock* claims that there actually was a fisherman named Grim who rescued a Danish king's son when the latter was a baby, adrift in a boat. Once the kid had grown up and made his fortune, he rewarded Grim, who founded the town of Grimsby. If this is indeed the case, you wonder exactly what it was Grim had in mind when he decided to settle there. If a Danish princeling offered you a bundle of money, would you spend it on a bleak, almost wholly characterless fishing port near Hull?

Inertia and a failure to deal positively with the one-way system then led me all the way through Grimsby and on, seamlessly to Cleethorpes. Well, I decided, Cleethorpes is as good as Grimsby from the point of northernness and it has much better parking. As an added come-on, it is also described (in *The Companion Guide To The Coast Of North-East England*) as 'A huge great ding-a-ding holiday resort. There are performing dolphins!'

This is not, however, true. If there are any dolphins,

Cleethorpes is not telling you where they're kept; and it is
not a huge great ding-a-ding holiday resort. It is a small,
ineffably sad seaside town where the clock stopped in about
1962. The only visible signs of modernity are in the road
markings and the advertising hoardings. I was standing on
the front, morosely consulting the Cleethorpes mini-guide,
when a woman with bottled ginger hair wandered up to me.

'Are you looking for something to do in Cleethorpes?' she
asked.

'Well, yes, I am,' I replied, waving the mini-guide at her.

'There's nothing much to do. It's very quiet. Well, it's
dead, really. There's nothing here.'

'But . . .'

'You want to go to Grimsby. They've got the Heritage
Centre there. That's very good. You turn left, go past the
roundabout, straight on, on, on, on, straight on, there's
another roundabout, take a left and follow the signs. Why
don't you go to Grimsby?'

'Because . . .'

'Or you could look at the Clearwater project.'

Well, I'd already chanced upon the Clearwater project,
since that was the name given to a lot of roadworks, dotted
about Cleethorpes, where they were plumbing in a new
sewage system. I thought that I'd already seen Clearwater.

'Well, it's Grimsby then, isn't it?'

It did occur to me that I was merely projecting my own
inner disenchantment onto Cleethorpes and that perhaps it
wasn't the relic I at first took it to be. After all, I could have
sauntered off that very evening to catch the Yarborough
Ladies' Choir giving a concert in Grimsby. I could have
taken in the Country & Western night at Darleys, wherever
that was. I could have hung around for several weeks and
witnessed the second or third Cleethorpes Conker Cham-
pionships, depending on which hand-out I believed. Perhaps
Cleethorpes is a place of riotous hedonism which I'd caught

at the wrong moment. Perhaps I was just in a mood.

But before long, the place started to grow on me. If you're feeling pissed off for some not readily definable reason, then a just-out-of-season seaside resort is actually quite a good place to be. And of all the out-of-season resorts one could visit when pissed off, I would recommend Cleethorpes as having just the right mixture of empathetic charm and charmlessness, as Jane Austen would have said. It has a lot of nicely mournful things to appropriate as objective correlatives for your inner gloom.

It has, for example, the most inadequate and least necessary pier I've ever seen, which strides all of twenty feet out into the Humber estuary and then stops dead to make room for a barn-like affair called the Discotek. It's so pitifully short that a tall man could stand in the middle of the pier and still shake hands with a passer-by on the esplanade.

Overlooking the pier is an assortment of restaurants which would have looked a trifle *démodé* twenty years ago: The Monarco (sic) Grill; the Marples High Class Tea Rooms; and a nameless place two doors away from the Monarco, which was never open but which sported dingy melamine tables and Utility chairs, bathed in a stale, yellowy daylight and waiting, from the look of it, for a Pathe newsreel team reporting on mods and rockers: 'The respectable calm of a family seaside town, about to be shattered by today's teen-age rebels.'

There is a gargantuan beach, bigger, possibly, than Blackpool's, along which you find, in short order: (1) dead seagull (1) rotted-out hull of a boat (1) bubbling, reeky marsh (1) discarded tampon applicator. The beach is so vast you could use it for nuclear testing without singeing the eyebrows of any of the Monarco's customers (doubtless ordering themselves a nice London Mixed Grill and a can of Long Life). There is a potty little railway station on the front, with a wrought-iron clock tower and an Art Nouveau café hard by, both dwarfed by a tin-clad amusements complex from the 1970s. There is a road sign directing you towards 'Humberston Fitties'. There is one chip shop for every three head of population.

And there is a desperate mid-1950s novelty and gift shop, a little way into town, selling three-inch-high plastic gorillas, kagouls and boxed toy cars whose packaging has been bleached blue by years of sitting in the watery Cleethorpes sunshine. 'Please walk in,' it announces over one doorway; 'Walk out pleased,' it quips over another.

This shabby gentility is something of a reversion for Cleethorpes which, like most seaside resorts, got into its stride after about 1840 and the arrival of the railway. Skegness and Mablethorpe, further down the coast, were for the indigent folk of Lincolnshire and Nottinghamshire; while Cleethorpes was more for South Yorkshire. As neighbouring Grimsby grew, however, Cleethorpes was seen to be no longer suitable for gentlefolk, with the result that, by 1903, the whole area had become, to quote a contemporary commentary, 'The great summer playground of the working-classes . . . conveyed by the northern railways in express excursion trains, every day through the summer.' This may be where the huge great ding-a-ding holiday resort mendacity comes from: some sort of residue of its Victorian and Edwardian heyday. I'm sure I needn't add that if, like Whitley Bay, you compare it with a real ding-a-ding working person's holiday resort such as Blackpool, it comes absolutely nowhere. You could comfortably fit the whole of Cleethorpes into the Pleasure Beach.

My suspicion is that Skegness is the one making a play for the rough trade in this part of the world. My free copy of *Spotlight On The Stars At Skegness* advertised almost exactly the same performers as had Blackpool earlier in the season. I was pleased to note, however, that Sid Lawrence and his Orchestra were booked to bring a touch of class to the proceedings, as was an Elvis impersonator, a comic who

clearly based his performance around the works of the late
Max Miller, and a desperate-looking vent act with his hand
– apparently – up Jack Jones. There was even Slightly
Naughty Jethro.

I couldn't think for the life of me what I was doing in this
place. I must have been the youngest person there (bar a few
spavined yobs who restlessly quartered the town on stolen
mountain bikes) by about thirty years. The oldsters looked
at me with undisguised suspicion. In desperation, I retreated
to my B&B, to sit it out in my room for a while and gawp at
the television.

Now, in American travel books, the television is an endless
source of interest and consolation. The weary hack settles
down in his motel or his high-rise, and what does he find but
sixty cable channels piped to the end of the bed, offering an
amusingly heterogeneous mess of sports shows, cartoons,
pre-Cambrian reruns, quiz games, barely sane chat shows,
CNN and round-the-clock pornography. This then bulks
out a chapter or two very nicely, as the writer settles down
with his notepad and proceeds to draw all sorts of bright
inferences about the state of American society.

This trick can also be turned in continental Europe and
even the Far East – anywhere, in fact, where they have lots
of television to watch. But in England, it doesn't quite work
like that. On the one hand, it's mildly impressive to note how
even the meanest of B&Bs will nowadays offer a television
facility in their rooms. But on the other, cheap hotel tellies
offer only four channels, of which at least two will be on the
blink.

On this occasion, BBC1 and ITV were freaking out in
shades of grey with intermittent blizzards, while the sound
was like that of a man brushing his teeth with a roll of
coconut matting. Channel Four's horizontal hold was shot,
so I had to try and reassess my progress with *633 Squadron* as
background inspiration. I couldn't concentrate and even-

tually found myself reduced to leafing through the *Grimsby Evening Telegraph* in search of some sort of lift while George Chakiris was being tortured in a baroque Norwegian loo.

The *Telegraph*'s front page headline read, bafflingly, TONIC NEAR THE GIN! It then went on, 'A futuristic new medical surgery complex the size of a mini-hospital is to be built in Cleethorpes at a cost of over £400,000.' This, apparently, was the tonic; while the gin was provided by the soon-to-be adjoining Darleys Hotel. Gin and tonic. Hospitality and revitalisation. I puzzled over this one for a long while, before the penny dropped and I turned in disgust to the inside pages. Here, I found what I now recognise as a clutch of entirely typical local paper stories.

The first one concerned a Local Man in The News. At the top of page three, there was a piece about a Grimsby-born publisher who had been cleared of fraud charges. The fact that this publisher now lived in Guernsey and had his offices in Gloucestershire didn't deter the *Grimsby Evening Telegraph* one jot. The thing was, he'd been *born* in Grimsby. No matter that this was back in the 1920s and that decades had gone by since he left the place. He was still bound to it by some kind of unbreakable link of kinship and a twitch upon the thread was all that was needed to get him back onto the pages of the local paper.

A little further down, there was another quintessential local newspaper device: the national story, given a blatantly local twist. PENSIONERS FUEL VAT DEBATE, it said, which was fair enough, given that the Government was at the time getting a lot of grief for putting VAT on fuel bills. But these were, of course, Grimsby pensioners, chipping in to the nation's discourse in their own unique way: 'There is a feeling this is wrong,' said Mrs Helen Hooton (aged sixty-seven) of Clarke Avenue, Grimsby.

Plunging deeper into the paper (page seven), the process was reversed: regional reportage of national stories, under the heading UK NEWS TONIGHT. Now, this is something that regional papers never seem to get quite right. If people want the national news, they can buy a copy of *The Times*. Or they can watch the news on television. But why on earth would anyone turn to page seven of the *Grimsby Evening Telegraph*? Is the paper run on some sort of analogy with the London *Evening Standard*? The *Standard* is without doubt a local paper, but it too carries national and international stories. The point of the *Standard* is that it has a kind of semi-national prominence because so much of what goes on in London is significant to the rest of the country. Blame it on historical chance, but if you have the Law Courts, Parliament, the Civil Service, the Bank of England, London's glittering West End and the greatest assortment of prostitutes in the country in your reporting purlieu, then the odds of carrying a national story are going to be stacked in your favour.

But what process of selection, somewhere in Grimsby, sees to it that on page seven of the *Evening Telegraph* there is a short piece about Somalia, a long one (with illustration) about dissent in the Tory party, two paragraphs on Benazir Bhutto and three on Rolf Harris (with illustration)? Was it just that they had the pictures? Or is there some arcane connection between Grimsby and Somalia?

If there is, then in normal circumstances it would be meat and drink to the paper's regular roving columnist. This is yet another distinguishing feature of local papers: the speaking-frankly, notepad-about-town, man-of-the-people column, usually going under some sort of ragbag heading like 'As I Find It' or 'Speaking Frankly' or 'Out And About With Winstanley'. In the *Evening Telegraph*'s case, it's called 'Odd Man Out, A Weekly Look At Life with Peter Chapman'.

Peter's roving eye, the week I was in town, took in some aerial photography of Lincolnshire; the 350th anniversary of the Battle of Winceby; a Ten Years Ago salute to Stanley Fowler, who had retired ten years before as head of the Grimsby firm of Fowler and Holden (no account of the firm's activities provided) and a tribute on the death of

Charles Loughlin, yet another son of Grimsby who made his
name miles away from the place. I won't bore you with the
details, except to remark that Charles Loughlin was the son
of a Grimsby fish curer and subsequently became Labour
MP for West Gloucestershire. Chapman writes, 'Parliament
watchers – and even older Grimbarians and members of the
Royal Antediluvian Order of Buffaloes – will remember
Charles Loughlin.' Quite apart from the Royal Antediluvian Order of Buffaloes, what is a Grimbarian? Is it a fancy
name for an inhabitant or scion of Grimsby? In the same
way that the people of Newcastle are sometimes referred to
by raving pedants as Novocastrians? Anyway, that's the
kind of thing Peter Chapman comes out with.

After that, it's downhill all the way, with a million and
one small ads for new and used cars, followed by the £50 and
under bargains ('Five dollies, £3.50 the lot – Tel. Grimsby'),
ending up with the sports news – 'Clee Almost Shock Boston'
– and an advert for a pair of earrings costing £395, which
makes one wonder where the money comes from in Humberside.

And this pattern is reiterated almost endlessly, it seems,
throughout England's northern provincial press. For
instance, Newcastle's *The Journal* ('North-East Newspaper
of the Year') had, as its lead story on the front page, an item
about some poor bastard who'd been beaten up so badly, he
thought it was 1986 and was convinced that Margaret
Thatcher was still the Prime Minister. Into what category
of local newspaper news did this fall? It fell into the category
of Local Man Makes News In Completely Different Part Of
The Country: the hapless amnesiac being a Tynesider who'd
actually moved to Portsmouth seven years earlier.

The Jarrow & Heburn Gazette ('Britain's Oldest Provincial
Evening Newspaper') had an eye-catchingly half-baked
One Person's View page – 'Cookson Country, by Linda
Colling' – with stories about a South Shields woman who
had left for New Zealand twenty years ago and a piece which

began, 'Sitting pretty in Pat Redman's kitchen I was struck by her sheer dedication.' Birmingham's *Evening Mail* ('Voted 1992 Newspaper of the Year') looked highly professional but suffered badly from internal identity problems, lurching wildly (as it did) from Bosnia to the Worcestershire ambulance service, to the Studley Operatic Society, to the Indian Government, to CALL FOR MORE FLOATS TO BOOST CARNIVAL DAY. The *Manchester Evening News* ('Newspaper of the Year') smartly inverted a national story into a provincial one (TORY 'FIDDLE EXPOSED' claimed extremely local Warrington MP Mike Hall), and had a classified ads section that was more appealing and attractive than the main part of the paper.

The Wolverhampton *Chronicle* led with the kind of headline *The Independent* would die for: CONCERN OVER ABATTOIR PLANS. While *The Birmingham Post* ('Speaking Up For The New Midlands') cynically splashed a colour picture of Princess Di on the cover page to lure the punters in, before swamping them with pages and pages of bilge about Birmingham City Council. Blackpool's *Evening Gazette* ('Putting the Fylde First') was the usual mishmash of local, international and nonsensical (COAST EROSION FEAR IS CALMED BY BOFFIN), although there was solid back-up from the regular columnist ('Natural Break, with Ron Freethy') and I enjoyed a news story which began, 'Police have recovered two pairs of jeans stolen from a washing line in Clifford Road, North Shore, during the weekend.'

Last, but in no way least, Newcastle's *Evening Chronicle* actually played a straight bat and turned its back on the rest of the world (as, wisely, did the *Wilmslow Express and Advertiser*), leading with a Gateshead man's pools win, followed by plenty of stuff about car crashes and Newcastle United. Even so, why should Tynesiders have to buy two papers a day – one national, one local – just to keep abreast of things? Down in London, we buy the dailies and if we're really stuck for something to do, or we're the kind of people who write to our local councillors about the state of the pavements (I know I am), we get the weekly local rag, which makes no bones about its parochialism and avoids national news entirely (COUNCIL CAVES IN ON EEL PIE RUBBISH DISPUTE, as my own parish pump said recently). But what unimaginable vanity is it that keeps these northern publications going?

What am I saying? Vanity? People *buy* these things, sometimes supporting more than one publication per city. Is it that vaporous thing, regional identity, that makes them do it? Is it because they know up here that however far away London may be, it's not far enough; and that if they don't carry on trumpeting all the little nullities of local life then the South of England will just eat their regional identity alive?

This is, of course, the thinking behind local television programming and those valueless news shows you get on BBC1 and ITV at around six in the evening. The ITV companies are naturally keen to do as little of this stuff as they can get away with, given that five nights a week of 'Sub-Post Office Threatened With Closure', and 'Local Man Talks Of Ordeal At Dry Cleaners' is marginally less interesting than facing the wall and drooling. And besides, in a more rational world, they could be keeping the advertisers happy with high-ranking game shows hosted by Roy Walker.

Evidently, this is not true for the printed word. Newsprint can handle almost any amount of parochial trivia, because newspapers are as much for comfort as for entertainment. A newspaper is something you carry around with you during the day, dipping into it as the time allows, rolling it up, fondling it, looking in it for your old friends the columnists, gradually dog-earing it, thumbing it importantly and reading it with exaggerated attention in pubs when you want to look as if you mean to be sitting entirely friendless and alone in a crowd of people. And if this is what a national paper can do for you, think how warming and consoling a local paper must be. There it is, reflecting your world back at you, making your boring, parochial interests seems like news. There's your identity as a Tynesider/inhabitant of the Fylde/go-ahead midlander written in black and white, proof that you're who you thought you were and that the rest of the world has left you untampered with for another day. Assuming, of course, that you want to be reminded of your tedious provinciality; which, I suppose, quite a lot of people must.

I went out to have my curry and was finishing off the remains of a chicken biryani in a perfectly decent curry-house, when a short, grey-haired man wearing a Service Warm overcoat bustled in. He sat himself at a table opposite me and barked, 'I'll have my usual: a cup of white coffee and make it quick.'

I paid and left and went back to my broken television. *'Why am I here?'* I shouted at a rapidly disintegrating *Newsnight*.

The problem was, as I said at the start, that it wasn't in the North. No matter how many bits of Yorkshire there are in Humberside, it doesn't feel northern. This is partly because everything south of the Humber is plainly still Lincolnshire: that is, flat, vasty and miserable. This is Tennyson territory, after all: 'Tis the place, and all around it, as of old, the curlews call,/ Dreary gleams about the moorland flying over Locksley Hall' and so on. Nothing joyous about the area between Grantham and Goole, just miles of big skies and mournful plains. You can churn down the A1 for hours before anything starts to change and when it does, it's because you're starting to reach the outer fringes of London. Humberside makes you think of Lincolnshire first, East Anglia second and Hertfordshire last.

And the problem with this is that there aren't any cities. South Humberside is mostly open countryside of the most

open and grimly bucolic kind. If Cleethorpes did anything
for me, it at least confirmed the fact that for an old hand like
myself, northernness is an exclusively urban phenomenon.
Around Grimsby and Cleethorpes, the towns peter out too
quickly, leaving you in the middle of that stuff again, that
countryside stuff you find everywhere. Grimsby is simply not
big or industrial enough to have any impact, to say nothing
of Mablethorpe or Skegness.

Travel a few miles west, however, and once again it
becomes immediately obvious where you are: you're in
Leeds, Doncaster, Sheffield, Bradford, Manchester. You
haven't actually gone north, but you're North with a
vengeance, now. You're part of the historical-cultural
construct that *is* the North: Victorian buildings, urban
grime, factories, mines, big lads who stand in the rain
wearing only a T-shirt, tormented industrial outcrops,
back-to-backs under a steady drizzle. It's threatening,
it's a cityscape drifting into endless haphazard conurbations.

As if to emphasise their lack of real northernness, the
people of Cleethorpes, Grimsby and so on talk in comfortable, washed-out tones, as if they've spent a few years living
Up North and haven't quite got the accent out of their
systems. According to the same stupendously unreliable
guide book which told me about the dolphins of
Cleethorpes, Cleethorpes people are called 'meggies' or
'howletts'. I detect the dead hand of artificially preserved
provincial distinctiveness here. This is one of those insights
which is meant to create a Spirit of Place, but which looks
wildly implausible even to a hack like myself, who has every
interest in overdoing the regional differences of the place he's
mistakenly chosen to visit. I can tell you now that if you went
up to even one of Cleethorpes' numerous old-age pensioners
and called her a meggie or a howlett, she'd give you a kick
up the Harris.

* * *

I didn't give up without a fight, mark you. I did my best to experience everything that Cleethorpes had to offer, minutely comparing it with my preconceptions.

I saw it by night. After about eight o'clock in the evening, a kind of stunned silence fell on the place and the air was filled with mist. It was melancholy beyond words. There was a fragrance of coal smoke in the air, the occasional rattle of a shop or office being closed up late, perhaps a distant fanfare of music from some lonely gramophone, followed by silence and then the long, withdrawing roar of the North Sea. The town's discos glowed pink and mauve in the dark, but made no sound. The sea-front illuminations burned in the mist, as men in short overcoats took their dogs out for a last pee . . .

I saw it by day. I marched up and down the streets of Cleethorpes with my chin at a jaunty angle, looking for excitement. It was dauntingly tranquil first thing in the morning – a time when any other town or city would have been a hotbed of traffic, irritation and bad breath. In the calm, I spotted one or two strange-sounding street names: Cuttleby, Grime Street, Yarra Road and Oole Road. I admired some nice wrought-iron arcading. I followed a deserted miniature railway along the length of its track as it meandered from the Leisure Centre to the Lakeside. Showing an enterprising sense of authenticity, the miniature railway had clearly been reduced, just like the real thing, from a two-track to a single-track service, with a bald patch where the second line had run, a mute reproach to the way of the world. Even more authentically, the trains weren't running.

Increasingly stuck for something to do, I marvelled at one of the worst punning shop-names I'd yet seen: a pet shop called PETS´ EM-PAW-RIUM. It is, of course, a feature of all provincial towns to insist on wearisome puns for shop and restaurant names and in that respect Cleethorpes was no more than typical. Still, it took me aback. As well as the PETS´ EM-PAW-RIUM, I also saw Spaghetti Junction (pasta joint) and Hair Today (hairdressing salon). I once saw a hairdresser's called A Snip Off The Old Block, but that was somewhere else.

Swinging back onto the front, I then bought some postcards, but even these were strangely blank and untenanted. One shows the pier and esplanade on a warm summer's day, with no more than twenty people ambling around in their shirtsleeves. Another depicts the Boating Lake, again in high summer, with a hefty, curly-haired woman sitting in a rowing boat, scowling at the bloke opposite her as he catches a crab in the lake's dreamy waters. A dog has climbed on board and is evidently wondering whether it can get out by leaping the gap between shore and boat.

A third postcard shows the saddest scene of all: a pocket funfair on the beach. Another fine English summer's day, to be sure, but the fairy roundabout in the foreground is immobile, while two small children (sitting on opposite sides of the machine, their backs turned towards each other, as if they're in the middle of a row) stare listlessly into space. Behind them, the Big Wheel (occupancy: four people) stands still. Behind that, the infinite sands of the Humber Estuary stretch to the horizon, where only the passing container ships, laden with BMWs for Immingham Docks, betray a life going on elsewhere.

Now can you imagine Blackpool getting away with that? Would Blackpool ever countenance a postcard or a tourism brochure which wasn't covered in pictures of hysterical vacationers, shining lights, beer bellies and jouncing cleavages, all topped off with the graphic equivalent of involuntary protein spill? For a moment I admired Blackpool its thuggish sense of purpose, its nerve, its emetic brashness. Surely, I thought, pleasant, depressing, time-warped Cleethorpes could have found some way to make itself look like a happening place? Equally surely, I thought, wasn't I just projecting my self-loathing at having gone directly from one moribund seaside resort (Whitley Bay) to another (Cleethorpes), without introducing some kind of mediating experience on the way, onto a perfectly decent, harmless little non-northern town?

But Scunthorpe would be different.

I now consider myself rather an expert on Scunthorpe, having stood in its pedestrianised centre for all of, oh, five or six minutes. Scunthorpe ('The Industrial Garden Town', it says at the city limits) is the sort of place where, if you stand in the centre of the town, you feel as if you're still on the outskirts. It's the sort of place whose middle closely resembles the fringes of somewhere like Gloucester, or north Oxford, lots of little streets with two-storey red-brick terraced houses with twelve-year-old cars parked outside. It's the sort of place that ought to have a struggling, low-division football team and it has. Scunthorpe United's achievement was to become Third Division champions in 1957. Since then, obscurity. Scunthorpe's women tend to be short of a few teeth and the men all look as if they've got criminal convictions.

Big time, in Scunthorpe terms, means the British Steel factory at one end of town and the BOC plant at the other. Actually, I take my hat off to British Steel for building a works that fulfils every suburbanite's ideal of what a really hideous factory should look like. This one is vast, rust-brown, inescapable – despite the planting of a few wind-torn saplings between it and the main road – putrefyingly ugly and possessed of all kinds of sinister-looking pipes, ducts, runnels, silos and cisterns. I suppose it must have been making, well, steel (pre-rusted if the outside was anything to go by) but from the looks of it, it could have been making anything from mustard gas to iron maidens. In a way, of course, I was delighted to see that it was there and still working and bringing employment to the knee-faced men of Scunthorpe. In an even more real way, I was delighted that it was hundreds of miles from where I lived.

I drifted off in search of some light relief. Light relief, on this occasion, meant going in search of the Gallery Erotica, a few miles from town. This was advertised in the *Humber-side Visitors' Guide* as a 'private gallery and garden', with 'safe whittling lessons on request'. I found myself driving through an almost surreally empty landscape of very slightly undulating fields, with the Humber estuary glint-ing in the distance, vying from time to time with the estuary of the river Trent for my attentions. A Constable sky hung over me. I drove past Flixborough, which is unfortunately the only thing to have put Scunthorpe on the map in the last thirty or forty years. This was where a chemical plant, making the ingredients for nylon, exploded in 1974. Twenty-nine people were killed and the blast blew out the windows in the Midland Bank in Scunthorpe's high street, five miles away. Going past it now, there's nothing to see except for a clutch of anonymous factories and new, innocuous-looking chemical plants not making nylon products.

Still, my imagination was in ferment as I made my way to the Gallery Erotica. It sounded more like Hamburg than Scunthorpe. I wondered if I was going to be arrested when I got there.

But the Gallery Erotica turned out to be a small red-brick cottage, largely covered in green mould and with a Reliant Robin parked outside. It was home to a sculptor and artist called Ernie and indeed I could make out through a grimy window a few twelve-inch-high sculptures in wood of nude women doing headstands. There was also a poem, typed on a piece of A4 and laid on the windowsill, which began: 'When in the moonlight my lady finds her horse/A Virago she becomes.' Next to that, a notice read, 'Carvings in wood, sensuously realised'.

A pair of Wellington boots stood, empty, in a covered courtyard, but there was no other sign of life. I went up to the back door and knocked and cleared my throat and peered through the windows into a modest but comfortably furnished private home (where a television was on, showing a member of the Government making a speech), but no one came. I walked around a bit more, went round to the front and quizzed the Gallery Erotica sign (half-hidden by lichen and an overgrown bush) to make sure I was in the right place, went back to the courtyard, found no one and then left. I don't think I even had the energy to feel disappointed. In fact, it fitted the mood perfectly. I stood next to my car (back for this one excursion) and stared into space for a while.

I wish there was more to say about Scunthorpe, but I really don't think there is. I wish I could justify mentioning it in some way, but I can't. Scunthorpe is a town of sixty-something thousand inhabitants, where they make steel and chemicals and, and . . . why should Scunthorpe be intrinsically more interesting than, say, Leatherhead, or Slough, simply because of its latitude? I thought I was being clever, picking on Scunthorpe, Grimsby, Cleethorpes, this little knot of establishments, just because they had funny names. And all I had to show for it was a feeling of being left in a place where everything happened somewhere else.

TEN

So I made my way back inland, towards Doncaster, Pontefract, Sheffield, to the Leeds/Bradford conurbation, to Harrogate and York, to the very heart of northernness.

To be honest, I'd been putting it off – partly because I felt from the outset, irrationally enough, I admit, that Yorkshire was going to be the Grail, the epitome of northernness, from which everything else would be a deviation or a diminution, so I wanted to get the rest under my belt while my critical tastes developed and matured for this treat; and partly because Yorkshire is so big, so important, I couldn't face attempting it until I absolutely had to.

It's huge, Yorkshire, far and away the largest county in England. Not in population terms, maybe – there are probably no more than 200,000 more people in all Yorkshire's regions than there are in all Lancashire's (I include in this both Greater Manchester and Merseyside); but in physical size, it's a killer, covering more than 6,000 square miles. Compare that with Lancashire, at something over 1,800 square miles, and you can see how massively Yorkshire leans against its old western enemy. Norfolk's not small, but even Norfolk is only a third the size of Yorkshire. And as for Surrey – you could fit eight and a half Surreys into Yorkshire. It's like talking about Australia.

* * *

Then there's the mythologising of Yorkshire. This is a process which Yorkshiremen over the years have naturally encouraged, giving the place its familiar, ghastly, robust, larger-than-life aspect. And this too has to be dealt with. Going to Yorkshire entails visiting an idea as much as a place. We *know* Yorkshire, even if we've never been there before. Yorkshire attracts phrases and epithets like film stars attract loonies. 'Yorkshireman' immediately triggers off an avalanche of words, including bluff, no-nonsense, down-to-earth, mean, unpretentious, proud, canny (when it's not being appropriated by the Scots), monosyllabic, stage, boring, careful, violent, cloth-capped, pie-eating and beefy. Roy Hattersley (a Sheffield man) wrote in his book *Goodbye To Yorkshire*, '"Careful" is one of the great Yorkshire euphemisms, a word that conjures up all the mystery of the tea-caddy on the Wakefield mantelpiece and all the magic of the ten-shilling note inside it.' Sounds ghastly, doesn't it? But there it is, acknowledged by one of the county's native sons. (Incidentally, why *Goodbye To Yorkshire*? It sounds so off-hand. It's like writing a book and calling it *So Much For Hereford And Worcester* or *That's Enough Of Hampshire*.)

For Yorkshire itself, the following attributes automatically spring to mind: rugged, windswept, bleak, industrialised, coal-mining, unspoilt, wealthy, dark and satanic (cities), picturesque, brooding, of the Brontës, pompous (cities again), chill, off the beaten track, sheep-infested and Dales. In fact, Yorkshire The Idea is so familiar to us that it's like something out of the Myles na Gopaleen *Catechism of Cliche*:

Q: Of what countenance are the hill farmers of Yorkshire?
A: Dour.
Q: And of what nineteenth-century characteristic is the Leeds Town Hall strongly indicative?
A: Victorian self-confidence.

Q: Without which item of clothing should one not
venture onto the moorland at Ilkey?

A: 'at.

Q: And in the proximity of what desirable commodity is
there an attendant quantity of dirt or putrescence?

A: Brass.

You get the picture. More than any other part of the North,
Yorkshire has colonised the southern mentality, standing in
many ways for the whole of northern England. You want to
speak northern English? Then it's on with the motley and
out with the sub-Yorkshire, ee-bah-gum voice that has City
stockbrokers in the suburbs of London and Guildford reeling
with mirth. You want to sketch in a word-picture of a typical
northerner? He wears a flat cap, keeps a whippet, digs coal,
works in a mill, or makes metal things. Or used to. He is
typically mean with his money and close with his words. He
loathes and mistrusts southerners. He enjoys (if that's not too
strong a word) rugby league in winter and cricket in
summer. He is, in fact, a Yorkshireman. No one else can
entertain all these attributes simultaneously. You want a
selection of reach-me-down northern aphorisms? There's
nowt so queer as folk. Where there's muck, there's brass.
There's trouble at t'mill. You don't get owt for nowt. These
all carry the authentic tang of Yorkshire about them. They
all metonymise the North, because they all sound like
Yorkshire. It's a kind of ghastly branding, in the same
way that Texans used to represent all Americans, in *Punch*
cartoons of the 1950s.

This process was of course given a boost in the 1960s,
when the British film industry suddenly discovered northern
realism and started to make large numbers of dingy black
and white movies north of Elstree. Of these, two of the
better-known ones – *A Taste Of Honey* (1962) and *Saturday
Night And Sunday Morning* (1960) – were set outside York-

shire: *Honey* in Lancashire and *Saturday*, supposedly, in Nottinghamshire.

On the other hand, *Room At The Top* (1959), *This Sporting Life* (1963) and *Billy Liar* (1963) were all Yorkshire-based. Thanks to them, London found itself temporarily on the way out, along with its flaccid costume dramas and studios stuffed with Home Counties accents. Going to see *Room At The Top*, with its torrid sexuality (courtesy of Simone Signoret) and its grizzly Bradfordian masculinity (courtesy of Laurence Harvey) must have been like a refreshing toot of cocaine for the jaded cinema-goers of West One.

The northern craze was still going strong enough in 1967 to allow David Halliwell's play *Little Malcolm And His Struggle Against The Eunuchs* to become a hit of sorts in London. Unless you actually know the play, it's hard to convey quite what a frightful lot of bollocks *Little Malcolm* actually is. Suffice it to say, it contains lines such as, 'They sense the pristine animal in me, hee hee,' and 'Out of this calm will erect the penis of our conspiracy!' It is set in Huddersfield and the theatre critic of the *Sun* (and this really dates it) called it 'Both funny and pathetic, a cry for real leadership and a study of an individual case of a kind of all-too-common madness.'

Yorkshire was that big in the 1960s. Even the Prime Minister (Harold Wilson) came from Yorkshire. D.H. Lawrence might have made Nottinghamshire the flavour of the North for an earlier generation, but once you'd seen *Billy Liar*, or *This Sporting Life*, how could you doubt that the North was really located somewhere in the Leeds/Bradford/Wakefield triangle, peopled with a rare and enticing mixture of petty-bourgeois bigots, crop-headed retards and hard blokes who'd nail you for a tanner?

And the good folk of Yorkshire don't seem to mind. Admittedly, the heyday of Yorkshire drama has gone, leaving us only with ITV's *Emmerdale*, a dim little soap-by-numbers which strikes me as being unduly populated with cockney tossers and which only gets eleven million viewers a show (seven million less than the great *Coronation Street*). It is also obliged from time to time to go to the lengths of staging a catastrophic plane crash in order to boost the figures.

But the Yorkshire stereotypes still live on. In fact, those who make it Down South seem happy to live up to their stereotyping – bluff blokes who can take it and dish it out: Michael Parkinson, Geoff Boycott, Sir Marcus Fox (Chairman of the 1922 Committee), Jimmy Savile, Sir Bernard Ingham, Fred Trueman, Alan Bennett . . . it has to be said that, with the exception of Alan Bennett, not a single one of these could do anything other than make fifteen minutes seem like a fortnight, but that seems to be the role they're content to play. For God's sake, Michael Parkinson takes his Yorkshireness so seriously, he actually moved his heavily pregnant wife across the border from Lancashire to Yorkshire (Parky was working for Granada TV at the time) so that she could have her baby in God's Own County. And why was this so important? So that the wretched child would then be eligible to play for the Yorkshire cricket team.

Alan Bennett, being clever enough not only to write *Forty Years On* and *Talking Heads* but also to live in Camden Town, does his particular Yorkshire act strongly censed with ironical distance. No jaw-setting, no-nonsense pooh-poohing, man-of-the-people bluster for him. Individual words, scrupulously turned and finished, do all the work. He writes thus about his father, a Leeds butcher who 'Was plagued by dogs: "Get out, you nasty lamppost-smelling little article," he shouted once as he raced some unfortunate mongrel from the shop.'

His mother, on the other hand, had it in for Vivien Nicholson, the Yorkshire pools winner: 'Her persistent car crashes and the dramas and notorieties of her personal life were never out of the *Evening Post*. "Well," my mother used to say, as Mrs N wrote off yet another of her cars and her lovers in some frightful motorway pile-up, "she's a common woman." No other explanation was necessary.'

It's not as if Bennett ever formally relinquishes the part, either. He can write about Kafka and George III as much as he likes, but Yorkshire keeps cropping up in daytrips from drab northern towns, post-war pig-farming farragoes, in the voices of Thora Hird and Patricia Routledge. But wait: Hird and Routledge are Lancastrians. So clever is Bennett, he doesn't even insist on Yorkshire actors to interpret his writing, any more than he insists on continuing to live in Leeds. He simply allows Yorkshireness to pervade his work like seasoning. This might look like a rare and unsettling pragmatism from a Yorkshireman, until you consider that most well-known Yorkshiremen have regularly made the kind of compromises that the Yorkshire County Cricket Club would rather die than submit to. Savile, Parky, Ingham – they all buggered off pretty quick (as they would put it) when the call came.

Curiously enough, of all the more famous Yorkshire expats, only Frankie Howerd really made the effort to disguise his roots once he'd left the North. Howerd always gave the impression of coming from Croydon or Pinner, somewhere in the Draylon belt of outer London. I was surprised to find that he was actually born in York – although York does enjoy the distinction of being the only northern city that's pleasant and middle class enough to look as if it really belongs in the South.

Have I ever met Yorkshire people face to face, down here? Have I ever got to know them? Do they ever drop their guard and lapse into non-Yorkshire Englishness? I've known a few and they never, to my knowledge, stop being Yorkshire.

There was a Yorkshire girl I once went out with. I met her at college. She was a fine, well-built thing from Brighouse way and she was also completely daft. For a while, she took to wearing enormously elaborate underwear with no out-

wear in public, which turned a few heads but at the same
time made her look mentally unbalanced. She also nurtured
a fixation on Bryan Ferry (a black mark in any book) and
tried, constantly and urgently, to be cool in the way that
Bryan Ferry was perceived to be cool. Since she was built
along the lines of the Bradford Wool Exchange and had
motor coordination to match, she always came across as
large and apt to spill her booze, rather than nervously
elegant. When she opened her mouth, she had a pronounced Yorkshire twang in her voice and liked to come
out with remarks like, 'Bryan's dead fab, totally grooovy',
spreading her fingers wide, Liza Minelli style, to indicate
that this was her being ironic, whacky, consciously parodis-
tic. Either that, or she'd grab a couple of fistfuls of breasts
and scowl at them bitterly, saying, 'God, I wish I was *thin*.'

She grew her hair long for about a year and had all sorts of
Louis XIV curls put into it; but had to give the style up
when she started to find small items of refuse lost in her
perm. After one party, she was mildly shocked to find that
she'd picked up in her hair three peanuts and a cigarette
butt. I was very fond of her.

Then there's a male friend of mine, of whom I am also very
fond, who comes from Cleckheaton and now lives in Bromley.
His approach is to turn the plain-dealing, call-'em-like-I-see-
'em Yorkshireman's *schtick* into a satire of itself; and very droll
it is too. Like Alan Bennett, he is a clever fellow, and also like
Alan Bennett, he can't stop being Yorkshire, however little
need there is for him to be that way. It is a strong and curious
identification and not one I really understand. It's as if I were
to find myself living in Dewsbury, unable to do anything
other than affect a Belgravia accent, quote *The Spectator* aloud
and reminisce about the District and Circle line on the
London Underground.

With all this churning around in my head, I had to decide
where to go. Fortunately, some places automatically ruled

themselves out from the start. York was one. The problem with York was the problem with my hunger for the True Northern Experience. How can York, with its Georgian houses, its quaint Shambles, its thirteenth-century Minster, its general air of having been appropriated by the National Trust, be a northern city? You can't buy pot-pourri in a real northern city, but you can buy little else in York.

Another thing: I stayed there, years ago, with an ex-girlfriend, in a revolting students' house on the edge of York, and that put me off. It was one of those houses where relations between the inmates had got so bad that everyone's food was marked with violently worded stickers: 'Strictly Paul's Jam'; 'Sarah's Bread – KEEP OFF'; 'This is MY coffee. It is NOT to be drunk by anyone else. DAVE'. I mistakenly used a forbidden tea-bag to make a clammy mug of tea and I was arraigned before the kitchen court and made to go out and buy a fresh packet of tea-bags to atone for it.

It was also the sort of house where one of the guys claimed to be able to cast your I-Ching, so I had to go through that. We sat on his seething rug in a bedroom that smelt of joss-sticks and hiking socks, while I solemnly threw some little silver coins with holes in them on the floor and he solemnly looked up the meanings in his Book of Changes and then we all solemnly argued about what on earth the Book of Changes' wisdom ('A time of balance is a time of with-drawal') could possibly mean to a white middle-class English dog who'd pinched a tea-bag.

I was then taken out onto the North Yorkshire Moors (somewhere near Ampleforth, I think) to visit a mediaeval ruin. It was the usual story of a northern-style bright spring day – in London, an invitation to throw off your blouse and tousle your hair – turning out to be colder than central Moscow. The wind blew through my overcoat and my teeth and tongue fought. I stood there, cowering from the blast, thinking all kinds of bitter and unwholesome thoughts, while the ex-girlfriend closed her eyes and placed her hand on a

still-standing chimney breast in the Old Solarium in order to
sense the vibrations.

'Yes,' she said after five minutes of ludicrous empathising
with the stonework. 'This was a happy place.'

We then drove back to York in a fug of ill-humour which
became so unbearable, I left early. So no York for me.

Later on, I visited Harrogate, but Harrogate wouldn't do.
Same manner of drawbacks as York: spa-town gentility,
well-planned and tended parklands, middle-class, dignified
Victorian buildings. To its credit, though, Harrogate does
have a fine Turkish Bath (1897) and I did nip off there just
to draw a few comparisons with Newcastle's *hammam*.

The most obvious distinction between the two is that
while Newcastle's baths are done up in relatively homely
style – about the sort of level you'd expect in a two-star hotel
in Tunisia – the Harrogate Baths are built in a fairly
delicious Victorian Moorish pastiche, with handsome
glazed tiles mimicking in their clumsy way the artistry of
the Blue Mosque and the great gates of Fez. They are also
full of Yorkshire businessmen sitting around in the nude,
talking their heads off and comparing their dicks. I positively cowered in a corner of the *laconicum* (which wasn't
quite hot enough, quite apart from being no more laconic
than a Methodist hymn meeting) while a knot of tough-
looking chaps pointed at each other's crotches: 'What d'yer
call tha' then? Black pudding?'

'Least it's got a bitter body on't.'

One fellow grabbed his joint and sort of hefted it around.

'I'm up for a bit of action this weekend. Me and the wife.'

Oh, God, I thought: soon it'll be my turn and I'll have to
say something about my genitals. I was looking around
hopelessly for some means of escape so that I wouldn't have
to push past the businessmen (I even toyed momentarily with
the idea of climbing out through a hot air duct), when the
topic of conversation lurched into wristwatches and scuba-

diving. More technical, this time, but still with a strong resonance of size being the key thing. And of course, some of them still had their wristwatches on, so they could perform some on-the-spot boasting. One bloke had a thing on his wrist which was the diameter of a manhole cover and this got everyone's attention very successfully.

'Two hundred metres,' he said, 'with a chronograph function. Got it in Singapore.'

'Were you divin'?'

'Not wet suit. Not in Singapore. It's not Bridlington, is it?'

Well, it all struck me as highly Yorkshire: the boasting; the proprietorial emphasis on size, weight, technical specification; the importance of a bargain well driven (Singapore, you see. Cheap import); and, magically, the return to Yorkshire (Bridlington – technically Humberside, spiritually forever Yorks.), the birthplace of civilisation, the Mesopotamia of the North.

I couldn't face Sheffield, either. I'd been *there* to interview a mountain climber who'd crawled down some enormous mountain somewhere, with his leg broken in several places. Terribly stirring stuff, but it seemed like one of life's crueller jests to make you drag your shattered self down a mountain in South America, only to end up in Sheffield.

I have never seen a place more inhumanly ugly. This is not the demented, russet ugliness of Manchester, or even that of Blackpool (how could it be? No leisureplexes). It's more like the ugliness of an unutterable place called Thamesmead, on the outermost fringe of south-east London, where up-to-the-minute 1970s showpiece social housing has, with the passage of time and the shittiness of human nature, become an unpremeditated piece of visual sadism. I know Sheffield is the Rome of the North on account of being ringed by hills (much as Nottingham and Birmingham both claim to be the Venice of the North on account of their

canals), but the *flats*: Rome has got some pretty dreadful
flats (I stayed in one, once. The lavatory was in the sitting
room) but none of them disposed quite so monstrously across
the horizon – in a ring of rusting prefabrication and stained
architectural cliches – as the ones in Sheffield.

Another of my new friends, Roy Hattersley, sees it slightly
differently, of course. 'There is nothing contrived or consciously decorative about Park Hill or Hyde Park flats,' he
says. 'The style is subsumed in the intention that Sheffield's
new buildings are good places to live and work in. They look
confident that their intention is fulfilled and, therefore, right
for men and women of a confident city.' To give him his due,
he was writing before (a) the Tories had bundled us through
the two worst recessions since the war (b) the buildings had
started to fall apart. But even so, it takes a wilful denial of the
truth, which only a politician can manage with fluency, to
come out with that sort of tosh.

Quite apart from this, Sheffield used to be famous for its
lack of hotels and I really didn't want to find myself padding
around Furnival Street or the Cutlers Hall at closing time,
wondering if I could roll my coat up into a pillow and kip
down in the gutter. So I ducked out of Sheffield.

Then there was the countryside. Now, I don't want to start
belabouring myself all over again about whether or not the
countryside offers a truly meaningful experience. But I did
have a few qualms about not seeing rural Yorkshire. Like
most southerners, I am only too aware of the supposed
glories of Richmond, the grandeur of Castle Howard and
the enchantments of the River Derwent. The very mention
of the Dales fills me with longing, no less than the sound of
the Brontë Country and the Emmerdale Territory. I even
have reason to believe that Catterick Garrison is not as bad
as it's made out to be. For some reason, southerners,
particularly Londoners, feel an obligation to know about
the Yorkshire landscape in a way they don't feel a need to

know about the landscape of Northumberland, County Durham, Lancashire, Derbyshire or Staffordshire. Stupid Londoners also feel they need to know something about the Lake District, although anyone who actually goes there ends up regarding the Lake District as a bit of a joke, filled as it is with serious men in kagouls and implacable, four-feet-tall grandmas taking their terriers for a stroll up the near-vertical sides of fells.

But there's a burden of expectation about the Yorkshire scene. Perhaps because W.H. Auden had a bit of a thing about limestone, perhaps because of *Emmerdale* (nothing to do with the French colloquial verb *emmerder*, by the way, which means to piss someone off), perhaps because after years of bigoted Yorkshiremen telling us one way or another what a great place it is, we know no other way of thinking about it.

But I had already been there and I had seen the rolling hillsides and the ferny Dales of Yorkshire, so the argument, for me, did not arise as to whether or not to make a special trip.

The first time I really got my teeth into Yorkshire pastoral was when I found myself renting a pre-war Morris in Hebden Bridge. Don't ask me why. The gimmick was that for £150 you could hire a 1930s car (in my case, a Morris 8 in black and royal blue) complete with a picnic in a wicker hamper and a wind-up gramophone with a selection of 78s, and take an entrancing trip back in time. Very big with geriatric golden anniversary celebrants, apparently.

So I collected the car at Hebden, loaded my musical picnic onto the back seat, got into the thing and drove off in the vague direction of Haworth. Why is it, incidentally, that so many Yorkshire towns and villages begin with a letter which most Yorkshiremen are congenitally unable to pronounce: 'Ebden Bridge, 'Aworth, 'Alifax, 'Eckmondwicke, 'Arrogate, 'Ull, 'Uddersfield, 'Olmfirth? Was Ilkley once

Hilkley, until they gave up the unequal fight with aspirates?

Anyway, I had this horrible old car which could manage about twenty-five miles an hour on modern A-roads, with half a mile of fulminating traffic behind it. The gearbox didn't have any synchromesh so it kept barking and grinding every time I tried to change gear. And the seating position (whether this was true to 1930s form, or merely that the old banger had collapsed internally) was so low-set, I was practically kneeling on the floor while I drove. I flogged it all the way to somewhere called Percival Hall, where I stopped by the deeply photogenic river Wharfe – you see? All the most associative Yorkshire names – and made myself eat my picnic.

I might point out that the rain at this point was coming down like Hollywood rain, dense to the point of solidity and absolutely consistent with it, so I didn't feel much like spreading out the travel rug, cranking up the portable player and slipping on my courtesy copy of 'Let's Get Together' by the Big Ben Banjo Band. I just sat at the wheel, listlessly eating my sandwiches and toying with a glass of alcohol-free sparkling wine (a drink with all the taste of sodium bicarbonate, but none of the pleasure) while a Dutch tourist in a Ford Escort drove up, stopped, got out and took a picture of me eating. He obviously thought I was a typical English mental defective, very much the kind of person the Dutch, by and large decent people, would have found professional help for.

Nothing daunted, I churned through Haworth, but the Brontë Parsonage was closed. The Brontë Hair Salon was open, but I didn't get to see where Branwell formed his early drinking habits, or Emily penned the immortal drivel that was to become *Wuthering Heights*.

What can I say? If you like bleak, unaccommodating scenery, then the Haworth region is for you. As Brontë's temporary narrator Lockwood observes, 'This is certainly a beautiful country! In all England, I do not believe that I could have fixed on a situation so completely removed from the stir of society. A perfect misanthropist's Heaven.' Or, as Hattersley puts it, when describing his own trip to Haworth, the rain 'Did not simply come down. It blew from across the moors, horizontal and hostile, challenging the anoraks and pakamacs head on. It bent round the corners of the Victorian houses and spread across the black cobblestones of Main Street, making them shine like the toe-cap of a guardsman's boot.'

Then again, if you like the Yorkshire Moors, you'll like Dartmoor or Bodmin Moor just as much, although I don't especially recommend Jamaica Inn for your lunchtime stopover if you have an aversion to coach parties, family pets or men who wear nylon next to the skin. I suppose the principal difference, so far as moor-fanciers are concerned, between the West Country's open spaces and those of Yorkshire is that Dartmoor, Bodmin Moor and Exmoor have been left more or less to themselves – formal waste-lands, if you like – while the moors of Yorkshire are farmed, one way or another, and are scattered with villages and hamlets all the way up to the borders with Cumbria and County Durham.

This was actually of some use to me as I drove painfully back towards Hebden Bridge in my Morris 8. I don't know whether cars sixty years ago simply didn't go up hills, or whether this particular example was just a nail, but there are a lot of hills around Hebden Bridge and the old heap simply couldn't take the strain. I was crossing a mountain between Keighley and Hebden, when the scenery slowed to walking pace. There was a powerful smell of burning. Steam burst from under the bonnet and was dragged away by the wind. A certain amount of oil fell out. Then the machine went *bang* and stopped.

So I climbed out, smelling strongly of Rexene (the leather-ette of the 1930s) and fear, and stared uselessly for about five minutes at the smoking engine, the way one does in these situations. Then I realised that there was a tiny crofter's cottage by the roadside and I thought that if water was what the engine needed, I could beg for some from the crofter.

I walked up a stony path to the front door, knocked, and an old boy in overalls opened up. I came on at him like a mildly psychotic Leslie Philips.

'Hel-*lllo*,' I said, rolling my eyeballs. 'I *saaay*, you don't happen to have any *water*, do you?'

The old boy was just starting to nod his head and form some words of acquiescence, when a dog the size of a small horse came rushing out from behind him and went for me with foaming jaws.

'*Let him touch you*,' yelled the owner. '*It's the ones that won't let him touch them that get into trouble.*'

I stood there like a statue while the brute covered me with spittle and sniffed my crotch and its owner went off to get a plastic jerry-can of water. Too numb to speak, I filled up the awful car and crawled back to Hebden.

That night I ate *cordon bleu* Wiener schnitzel in the warehouse-sized restaurant owned by the bloke who hired out my Morris. It was just me, him and his wife.

'We're the first serious schnitzel restaurant in Hebden Bridge,' he confided. 'I got these wine holders in Vienna. They're the only ones in the country.'

He pointed out – on each table – an elaborate wrought-iron bracket with vine leaf decorations, in which sat an inverted bottle with a tap on the end. Ours had some kind of Riesling in it.

'Of course,' he went on, changing tack, 'William Morris was probably the most intriguing man the car industry ever produced. But' – here he pulled out a particularly resistant piece of veal from between his teeth – 'you've got to be partially masochistic to go out in an old car.'

He took a slug of Riesling.

'What do you think, then? Think there's room for a

Wiener schnitzel restaurant in this part of the world? Bet
you haven't got a Wiener schnitzel restaurant in your part of
London.'

The thing is, the countryside of Yorkshire is very nice in its
way, but it's not accommodating. Candidly speaking, the
river Wharfe near Percival Hall is a fine, broad, placid,
darkling sort of topographical feature, full of bends and
lumps of picturesque rock. It invites you to stand up to your
waist in the middle, fishing for whatever fisherman catch in
the Wharfe. Either that, or perch Ruskin-style on some
boulder and limn its grandeur and its sublimity on an A3
pad. But at the same time, it's nigglingly hostile. It's just a
bit too cold, a bit too bleak to be loveable.

And I suppose this is the point. Proud, doughty Yorkshire makes a thing of being handsome without actually
being likeable. Haworth's the same. It's not as if you'd
ever say to yourself, this is the spot for me. I'm selling up
the family home in Barnes and hauling the wife and kids
off to this Shangri-la. Not, of course, unless you were like
the Lockwood character from *Wuthering Heights*, and he, I
recall, was not entirely on the level. And when I breezed
into a pub somewhere to the west of Halifax for a
lunchtime pint and half a pound of indigestible bar
food, I won't say that the conversation halted and every
pair of eyes turned on me in hostile appraisal while
someone nipped round the back for a bucket of tar and
some chicken feathers, but I did feel distinctly as if I
wasn't meant to be there.

And again, there was the Wiener schnitzel/vintage car
hire man: you couldn't exactly call him dour, but for
someone in the leisure and entertainments business, he
was hardly the soul of gaiety. It was quite clear that he
thought me both simple-minded and effete when I stumbled
in on him at the end of my day's touring, twittering and
gibbering about the car bursting and a huge dog which

nearly ate me and having to drink alcohol-free sparkling
wine in the rain and being photographed by Dutchmen.

'It 'appens,' was all he said, giving me a sideways look.

I don't know what sort of temperament you'd have to
have, to want to live in rural Yorkshire for any length of
time. On the one hand, the local tourist organisations make
a big thing out of naming bits of the county after well-known
cultural manifestations in order to make it all that bit more
accessible to delinquent southerners: Brontë Country, Emmerdale Farm Country, Herriot Country, Last of the
Summer Wine Country (around Holmfirth). But on the
other hand, they don't try very hard to fleece you when
you're up there in the way that they do in the friendly,
exploitative West Country or Lake District. They're not big
on pieces of local stone carved into memorable shapes or
packets of biscuits with a picture of an abbey on the front,
which cost the same as a half-bottle of wine. Having got you,
they then seem to disdain you.

Then again, there is a real element of ostentation up there.
The next time I found myself in Yorkshire, cars were once
more involved; only everything was being done on a lavish,
not to say preposterous scale. It was the launch of a new Alfa
Romeo – rather a nice set of wheels – and I was one of the
scores of slavering hacks who'd been invited up to give the
thing a run-around. The hills around Ripon, we were told,
were absolutely the place to put the car through its paces,
test the roadholding, examine the operation of the glove
compartment and so on. So we were flown up from London
to the Leeds and Bradford airport (a real 1950s job) and
bused off to an exorbitant country house hotel in the middle
of nowhere. Even the cheesy London journos couldn't quite
believe the opulence that met their gaze.

'Where does the money come from?' we all asked.

'There's a lot round here,' confided a senior hotel functionary. 'A lot of wealth.'

But it was all fields, mud, drystone walls, sheep, barren expanses. Not a trace of currency to be seen.

'All I can say,' said the functionary, 'is that the local ladies' lecture society uses this hotel. You what I mean? Every week, they get someone in to give them a talk about something, novels or paintings or horse racing or whatever. And they all turn up, big hair, loads of jewellery and that car park'– he gestured dramatically towards some enormous swagged windows, beyond which a gravel car park the size of Rutland lay in the afternoon sun – 'is *completely full* of Mercs, Rollers, BMWs. You name it.'

We all stared out of the window at the huge car park and tried to imagine the ladies with big hair and the cars and the wealth, whistling softly under our breath. A flunky brought round some canapés and some drinks and we stood in awkward clumps, staring alternately at the Chinese rug on the floor and the Grinling Gibbons imitations stuck to the ceiling. It felt more like somewhere in one of the flash bits of Kensington, designed to lure Arabs and Americans into a better, more costly life.

From there, we were taken to yet another fabulous country house hotel. This was much like the first, only, if anything, even grander. It used to be someone's eighteenth-century seat, freshly done up in ruched chintzes and warm apricots. It was also one of those places which doesn't have a reception, but instead, a small, friendly repro King Louis table parked in the corner of a daunting, stone-flagged entrance, with a person behind it who gets up and smiles and says, 'Welcome to Overwhelming Towers, my name's Denise. Is there any way I can do anything at all for you?' By then, of course, it was dark, which made the whole experience even more disorientating.

None of the hacks could work out where all the money came from to fund not one, but two overblown hotels in the space of a few miles. And who knows how many more there might not have been, stretching away into the darkness?

Evidently, wool used to bring in a certain amount of cash to pay for these things – as it did spectacularly in East Anglia, once. But wool *per se*, and the processing of wool, is not enough to flood the countryside with hotels and rich women with big hair. EU subsidies doubtless help, as does the relative wealth and proximity of service industry centres like Leeds and York. And the sheer number of Yorkshire building societies is testimony to the thrift and acumen of Yorkshire businessmen: the Bradford & Bingley, the Leeds, the Halifax, the National & Provincial, the Skipton, the Yorkshire. How many nationally represented building societies can you think of which have a Lancashire or Tyneside provenance? Yorkshire, on the other hand, is home to the country's biggest building society, the Halifax. It's as if they conjure the stuff out of the rock.

Confused and already somewhat light-headed, the hacks (myself included) then drank massively of the free wine provided by Alfa's PR company until we could no longer remember our own names nor see our shoes. Then we tried to find our way along Overwhelming Towers' endless corridors to our palatial bedrooms. The next morning, we had to get up at sparrowfart to drive the cars all over North Yorkshire. The fittest made a thing of ostentatiously eating huge fried breakfasts, while the rest of us panicked crapulously at more than a glass of fruit juice.

We then had to drive, two to a car. I found myself sitting next to the late Maxwell Boyd (subsequently late, you understand, not as the result of the PR's booze) and we still couldn't work out (hungover or otherwise) where the money came from. We drove sweatily around a prepared course, which offered nothing but hills and clefts, as advertised in every Yorkshire prospectus, criss-crossed with drystone walls and tiny lanes. There were sheep, definitely, and crofters' cottages and small, dirty settlements and cold stone farmhouses. There was also what struck me as an undue amount of ordure on the road, causing our powerful Alfa

Romeo certain problems in the tractive department whenever we put our foot down.

But we drove and drove, stopping, unbelievably, at *another* country house hotel for mid-morning refreshments, then at a four-star restaurant for a stomach-bursting lunch. Two of our number had problems keeping up with the schedule, as, owing to their boozing the night before, they kept having to stop their car in order to get out and be sick. Then we were bused back to Leeds and Bradford airport and tipped into a British Midlands jet where we were fed complimentary drinks and a full cream tea in the thirty minutes it took to fly back to London.

'What was all *that* about?' gasped a hack from *Trucks and Truck Fanciers* who'd managed to wangle himself onto the trip. 'I thought they were poor.'

So Yorkshire lay at my feet: vast, secret, unknowable. I couldn't think where to go. I felt I'd done the countryside, so that ruled that out. I'd also shelved York, Harrogate, Ripon, Halifax, Hebden Bridge and Sheffield. Following the problem of Scunthorpe, I knew better than to aim for Heckmondwike, Cleckheaton, Pontefract, Tadcaster, Brighouse, Pudsey, Holmfirth, Adwick le Street, Grimethorpe, Ilkley, Otley, Guiseley or Kettlesing Bottom, or indeed anywhere with an amusing or typically regional name.

I seriously toyed with Batley, however, on much the same basis that I had involved myself with Wigan and its Casino: Batley being the home, once, of the world-famous Batley Variety Club (as well as the centre for the UK's shoddy production; shoddy being a material made by recycling old woollen refuse).

Hard to believe, but back in the early 1970s, all the big cabaret acts – Tom Jones, Eartha Kitt, Englebert Humperdinck, Shirley Bassey and, I think, Frank Sinatra himself – played Batley's Variety Club, lured there by God knows what promises of wealth and prestige. Eartha Kitt even

talked of buying a house in Batley so as to be near the
place. But I knew, as I hadn't with Wigan's Casino, that
the glory days had fizzled out, that the Variety Club had
closed and that it was at one stage apparently of some
interest to a Moslem educational foundation, which
wanted to turn it into a school. So I thought better of
Batley, even denying myself the treat of going to find out
where the Variety Club used to stand and toasting its relics
with Babycham.

For some reason, though, I felt increasingly drawn to
Bradford. In fact, I started to fantasise about the place.
There was something in the name, something resonant
about it, which made me feel that of all the cities of the
North, Bradford would offer the purest, most vital experience. I could see it in my mind's eye: black, run-down,
teeming, coarse, post-industrial, mean, tough, clinging
grimly to a slowly ebbing municipal pride. I saw the streets
crowded with brightly dressed Asian women, haggling over
spices. I saw blackened mill chimneys rising monumentally
into a dim sky. I saw rough-hewn men and women standing
sullenly in doorways. I saw the red-light district, the Town
Hall, the raucous market place, the birthplace of the Labour
Party, the broken alleyways, the rain, the soot, the despair. I
don't know why, but it took shape in my head as an
epiphany, waiting to happen; a northern junkie's final fix.

Most eerie of all, I started to spot similarities between
myself and Jess Oakroyd, a character out of J.B. Priestley's
The Good Companions. Priestley (Bradford's most famous scion)
starts his novel in the fictional town of Bruddersford (a cheeky
Bradford–Huddersfield amalgam), where Oakroyd muses in
a language of eye-watering Yorkshire homeliness about a
land of new experiences: 'When he [Oakroyd] said "Down
South", he seemed to conjure up a vast journey towards the
tropics and at the end of it a life entirely alien, fantastic.

'"Ay, it's different there, Sam," said Mr Oakroyd, puzzling his brains to discover some proof of this difference. "It's altogether different there, it is.'"

Could have been me, speaking about the North, I thought, with a shudder of recognition.

'I'd like to see summat fresh,' says Oakroyd. 'I'd like to have a look at – oh, I don't know – Bristol.'

And this is despite the admonitions of his friend, Mr Oglethorpe: "'I've nivver been farther ner Wetherby, to t'races there. Nay, I'm lying; I have. I once went for a day to Southport to see t'sea, but I nivver saw it, not a drop. It were a take-in, that.'"

I'm not making this ghastly dialogue up, by the way. This is Priestley's own rendering of the demotic, for which I cannot be held responsible. Anyway, just like me, Oakroyd gets a bee in his bonnet and continues, 'It's summat I'd like to see. I'd like to go and have a look so I'd know if there was owt there or not.' And so he does, and meets Miss Trant and Inigo Jollifant and they all become Good Companions, but I'd better stop there.

Obviously, my Bradford dream didn't extend that far, but the place had me in its thrall. My Yorkshire friend from Bromley also inflamed my passions by describing Bradford as the gastronomic centre of England, with a rich and various food market, not to mention an oyster shop and the whole of the Asian quarter, with its mountainous and thrilling curries. Of course, coming, as he does, from Cleckheaton, Bradford was the Big City of his childhood, a place of glamour and excitement. And what looks big time when you're six doesn't always survive that thirty-year trawl into maturity; but he still seemed to rate the place.

In fact, the more I thought about it, the more strongly I convinced myself that Bradford was not just the epicentre of Yorkshire, but the jewel in the crown. It was going to be the embodiment of northernness, a summation of everything I wanted the North to be.

ELEVEN

The strange thing was how unreal it all was when I got there. They've been getting all in a tangle for the last year or so about electrifying the rail connections into Bradford. This is in order to make the service clean, speedy and efficient, in keeping with the New Bradford which the Old Bradford is so keen to promote. When I arrived at Leeds City Station, looking for my Bradford connection, however (hardly any direct services from London, old boy), instead of a smart new electric commuter special, all I found was a scurvy old two-carriage diesel, shuddering and reeking on some faraway platform, surrounded by litter. And it was late.

I got a distinct feeling of shrinkage, as I climbed aboard: from the scale and relative sophistication of the no-expense-spared InterCity service direct to Leeds (with mobile buffet service and virtually functional toilets) to this dreary, freezing old bus. It was an announcement that I was taking a step down in the great scheme of things and that however much expectation I might have invested in Bradford, the rest of the world didn't share my hopes.

And so the diesel shuddered and smoked west out of Leeds, through Pudsey and into what calls itself the Bradford Interchange about eight miles away. This is the bastard son of the Birmingham Bull Ring, a 1970s nightmare which cunningly intermingles the needs of the bus-going public with those of the train-going public in one vast, single building of unparalleled plainness. The trains come into what looks like a large Hornby O-O station at the top, disgorge their passengers, who then tumble downstairs to a basement whose floor is covered in pocked rubber dotted with chewing-gum and splashes of vomit. This in turn leads to a filthy metal and wireglass shed where buses in various states of disrepair wait to carry you off to Wibsey, Odsal, Eccleshill and Laisterdyke.

It's another example of that absurd sense of design which takes its cue from the *Thunderbirds* and *Stingray* television series and which argues that the best way to solve a problem of people, space and logistics is to piggy-back everything on top of everything else and make the finished product look as much like an airport terminal building as possible. The same disease, differently manifested, also used to afflict music centres and radio alarm clocks. These things are distinguished by a kind of rationale which is at the same time highly visible and fundamentally insulting.

The result is that the Bradford Interchange is about the worst possible introduction one could have to a place. I know that this is increasingly true of all railway stations, but Bradford ought to get some sort of prize. And having endured the rubber, the filthy wireglass and the derelict modernism of the Interchange, you then walk out, not into a city, but into an empty space which was clearly once occupied by something, but which is now just flat, sloping and featureless. And then you turn a corner and find you're actually in Bradford. And of course, that doesn't look like anything, either.

I'll tell you why it doesn't look like anything: because Bradford (twinned, incomprehensibly enough, with Mönchen-Gladbach and Skopje) has discovered tourism. Of course. Tourism. Hard to believe that two generations ago, Bradford was the world's central market for wool and wool products; that Bradford was to wool what Manchester was to King Cotton, a place which traded with every country under the sun and where 80 per cent of England's business in wool was carried out. Why Bradford in the first place? Because it's surrounded by sheep, on the moors. Because it sits in a vale engirdled by fresh, lime-free Pennine streams (very good for washing your raw wool). And because there is, or was, plenty of coal to power the machinery brought in by the Industrial Revolution. All these things helped to lure England's wool production away from splendid Norwich, north to Bradford, a place in which no one had previously shown much interest.

This was also the place which drew hundreds of bright entrepreneurial German Jews in the second half of the nineteenth century, escaping from oppression in the Fatherland and bringing a new zest to the region's economy. This was the place where, in the 1950s, thousands of Pathans, Bengalis and Mirpuris (these last escaping from the Mirpur Valley, which had been flooded to create the Mangla Dam) arrived to find a boom town, offering work in the mills and on the buses. Two generations ago, this was a hell of a place.

And then, throughout the 1970s and early 1980s, Bradford's traditional sources of income – textiles and engineering (as in Manchester, the two went together) – disappeared down the drain, shedding more than sixty thousand workers and bringing the unemployment level up to 16 per cent. The Wool Exchange became a museum and the city became a kind of dismal national joke. At around the same time, the Yorkshire Ripper was busily carving up young women, not very far away. What attention the region gained in the press and on television was largely unwelcome. The whole Bradford area seemed to be gradually divorcing itself from the mainstream of human decencies and aspirations.

So, with what must have seemed at the time like breathtaking presumption, Bradford launched itself as a new kind of tourist resort. The newly formed Economic Development Unit (EDU) started to flog package holidays with names like In The Footsteps Of The Brontës and Industrial Heritage and, to everyone's amazement, sold two thousand of the things in their first year. In 1982, Bradford won an award for tourism and in 1983 picked up the English Tourist Board's prize for being England's fastest-growing tourist destination.

In 1983, it also became home to the National Museum of Photography, Film and Television ('Does more business than the Science Museum in London,' I was told) and by the turn of the decade was attracting (if you can believe this) six million visitors a year, who spent over £50 million while they were up there. I even found a free guide, produced by the Bradford Tourist Information Service, breezily entitled 'Mondays In And Around Bradford'. Now that really is taking an idea to its logical extreme.

So I doff my hat to the EDU and the genius which has turned Bradford from the quintessence of morose dereliction to England's fastest-growing tourist resort. And once it's pointed out to you, it's not impossible to see how the idea might actually work.

There is a lot of blasted Brontë country not far away; there is the Keighley and Worth Valley steam-railway; there is Ilkley, famed gateway to the moors; there are also some nice old mill buildings, a sparkling Asian community, the river Aire and what have you. With sudden, vertiginous hindsight, the hidden logic of Bradford's new direction comes out at you like the clapper falling out of one of the bells of York Minster.

The thing is, once Bradford started to think of itself as a place which outsiders might want to visit, it began to clean itself up. It became houseproud in a horrible, middle-class way. I was readying myself to take a great lungful of airborne muck, once I'd finally worked out where I was and where the centre of town was in relation to the Bradford Interchange, only to realise that the muck wasn't there. To put it another way, I was facing a relatively modest city-centre six-lane motorway (called, apparently, Hall Ings), certainly no worse than most

trunk roads and rather better than Newcastle's A6127(M) or
the A3036 at Vauxhall, in London.

On the far side stood the City Hall (1873), the single
building after the Wool Exchange with which Bradford is
most readily associated. And it was – I don't know – it was
cleanish. It was fairly kempt and clad in a rather nice honeyish
stone which, as I looked around, seemed to be all over
Bradford. It was in moderately good order, in the way that
suburban family homes are usually in moderately good order,
nothing zealous, nothing too sedulously clean about it: just,
okay. And the air was only moderately heavily polluted. The
Wool Exchange, too, was smart enough, bar some moss
gathering on the slates. The headquarters of the National
& Provincial Building Society shone dully. The streets were
unexceptionally, vaguely tidy. And there was nothing that
met my gaze to suggest that Bradford was in any way the
crucible of filthy northernness I'd kidded myself into thinking
that it might be. The tourist board had been round with the
hoover and the bottle of Jeyes Fluid just in time for the arrival
of their guests and it rather took the wind out of my sails.

It *is* northern, of course, profoundly so. At a glance, you
have the City Hall, rich in Venetian Gothic and offering a
very fair challenge to the Town Hall in Manchester. You
have the Wool Exchange, with its triangular ground plan,
built on a kind of sloping promontory, so that the pub
underneath it has a normal street-level entrance on one side,
but a flight of dingy stone steps down into the earth on the
other. You have what is known as Little Germany, a quarter
on the east side of town built almost in its entirety between
1854 and 1874 by the industrious German Jewish wool
merchants who settled there: warehouses, offices, cobbled
alleys, all fanning out from the summit of a hill and
cascading down towards the Leeds Road.

You have, as promised, your mills, quite a lot of them,
especially visible from the Undercliffe Cemetery which
overlooks the town. Some of these are still working, still

turning out cardigans and scarves and so forth, but nothing like the days when a man wasn't a man unless he wore worsted. Of all these mills, alive and dead, Manningham Mills is the most impressive, being enormously large and possessed of a suitably huge chimney (250 feet high), around whose summit a coach and horses were once driven. Driving around unsuitable constructions is clearly something of a Bradford speciality: when the sewage system was opened in 1924, four carloads of aldermen (they were in Jowetts, by the way, a local product) were driven three miles underground, along the new sewer, from Bradford to the Esholt treatment works. Mrs Jowett, wife of the car manufacturer, was heard to say as the aldermen finally emerged into daylight at the Esholt end, 'The first load of shit has arrived.'

Then there is the Bradford Alhambra, one of those theatres whose name is tinged with legend, like the Empire, Leicester Square, the Apollo Theatre, Glasgow and the Cambridge Corn Exchange. Not that the Alhambra looks anything like the kind of place where Jewell and Warris, or Nervo and Knox would have performed. I mean, the name Bradford Alhambra conjures up images of a lost world, of variety theatre at its worst and most desperate: the sort of place which successful comics recall having played at the outset of their careers, before vowing never to visit again. And which twilight entertainers suffering from alimony problems, drink and a lousy act are reduced to, shortly before suffering a heart attack in their digs back in Salford.

It's a surprise, indeed, to find the Alhambra even standing, with its Corinthian columns and its idiotic bra-cup dome shining in the afternoon sunshine. In fact, there was a move to knock the building down a decade or so ago. But public sentiment stopped the developers moving in, while at the same time, the notion of Bradford the tourist honeypot was gaining ground. So the city elders decided not only to keep the Alhambra, but to refurbish it as a living testimonial

to Bradford's age-old commitment to culture and all that's
best in live entertainment. A double bonus, in fact, as they'd
already completed a revolting television-shaped concrete
box a few yards away to house the new Bradford Theatre.
Finding themselves with not one but two theatres, they then
had the brainwave of bidding for the Museum of Photography, Film etc., which they got and promptly installed in
what was to have been Bradford's Alhambra For The
Twenty-First Century. (Ironically fitting, that; to put the
television museum in a museum coincidentally shaped like a
television. Modernism has its uses.)

Having had £8,250,000 spent on it (and I am not making
that figure up), the Alhambra is now airconditioned,
palatial, a sea of glass and tasteful bronzed fittings. Most
of the internal walls have been thrown away to make space
for some of the most sumptuous bars I have ever seen in a
public theatre, while whatever held up the outside has been
replaced by curtains of smoked plate glass. Through this,
you can comfortably watch over the police station and the
poor people of Bradford flogging cheap toys outside the
Odeon Cinema, your Campari in hand.

The auditorium is one of those clever refashionings of an
original theatre interior, keeping the gilt and rococo trimmings, but now underpinned with a decent ventilation
system and all the latest in lighting and sound. There are
lots of Muses and Graces and full-breasted caryatids around
and about, framed in blue skies and ormolu. It's all very
agreeable, although sitting inside the Alhambra for more
than an hour can feel like being stuck in a box of *Mozart-
kugeln* and left to die.

In fact, the Bradford Alhambra started to epitomise the
problem I was having with the city – the problem of
bourgeois Bradford. So bothered was I by the Alhambra
that I went and took in a performance there, just to see how
bourgeois Braford could really be.

* * *

And what was on? The Bradford Catholic Players ('An Outstanding Amateur Theatre Company') presenting *Kismet*. The Bradford Catholic Players have been going since 1927, moving from a fairly heavy reliance on Gilbert and Sullivan to stuff like *Desert Song*, *Calamity Jane*, *No No Nanette* and *Showboat*, with occasional excursions into Art, in the form of a *Rock Nativity* and *Waltzes From Vienna*. In other words, a heavyweight troupe. *Kismet* is also the musical in which the songs 'Stranger In Paradise' and 'Baubles, Bangles And Beads' appear and I felt I owed it to my general education to hear them in their proper context, never having done so before.

I spent £4.50 on a ticket and went back to my hotel to freshen up and comb my hair. Even the hotel wasn't the usual sticky-carpeted hovel I'd been frequenting up to that point. It was, instead, a large, pretentious box filled with sad businessmen's double beds, en-suite bathrooms and ducted heating. It was also running a special offer and rather than fight it out with a Bradford street map and use up a great deal of shoe leather just to put up in yet another bedroom the size and shape of Fatty Arbuckle's coffin, I sagged inwardly and put up at the big box. Once installed, I hung up my coat, neatly put away my pullovers, socks and spare shirts, laid out my shaving kit and toothbrush in the hygienic bathroom, adjusted the central heating . . . This was not how I'd prefigured the experience: dull order and the prospect of an amateur performance of *Kismet*.

Oddly enough, I got lost trying to get from my hotel to the theatre. Indefensible, this, since they are barely three hundred yards apart, in exactly the same part of town. I was, however, in good company. As I wandered moronically up Thornton Road, wondering where the hell the Alhambra had gone, a beat-up Ford Fiesta skidded to a halt at the kerbside and a little man with a beard, a black tie and a trumpet case jumped out and darted into the side entrance of a snooker club. About thirty seconds later, he sprang out of the snooker club and leaped back into his car, pulling a wide-eyed U-turn and heading back into town. At this point I decided that I, too, was in the wrong place and started to trudge back towards the City Hall. A bit of ducking and weaving and I made it to the Alhambra – at the same time as the beat-up Ford Fiesta skidded again to a halt, this time at the Alhambra's stage door. The little bloke with the beard and the trumpet ran in and didn't re-emerge. I thought: strange, fleeting kinship of two strangers in a northern town; and, if this is any guide to the level of competence we can expect this evening, *Kismet* is going to be a shambles.

It was, I might point out, the opening night and the place was packed. It was full of friends and relations, large numbers of middle-aged women in floral print dresses, carefully patting their hair into place as they peered into the mirror at the back of the bar. There were a lot of adolescent children, too, all suspiciously rinsed and combed. If it hadn't been Bradford, with everybody sporting cardigans and warm coats, you could have thought yourself for one drowning, saccharine moment, in a Norman Rockwell painting.

'Is he going to wear his russet sash?' one woman (looking like a freshly cleaned chintz-covered armchair) asked her friend.

'It all depends on the stitching,' she said.

Let me say right now, it could have been a lot worse. To quote the Bradford *Telegraph and Argus*, 'From start to finish, the vibrant and colourful show exuded confidence, enthusiasm, maturity and professionalism from all involved.' Moreover, 'The many scene and costume changes were carried out deftly and smoothly to create an aura of colour and effective scenery throughout, and the choreography was faultless.' I can add little to that, other than that Lalume was wearing a very fetching pair of leopardskin cocktail tights and that the lead part of Hajj, the Public Poet, was consummately played by a man called Barry, who wore a beard and clearly knew how to stand on a stage without looking as if his hands were on loan from a not especially close friend.

Only one or two elements caused any real unease. I found the cast's Bradford accents just a trifle uncompromising for Old Baghdad: 'What good will your wealth be when that *chookle becooms* a roar?' demanded Hajj at one point. Then the stagehands brought on a throne in the middle of a scene, which certainly woke up the sleepier members of the audience. And I did wonder once or twice whether the music was about to lapse into serialism. The string section in particular seemed to have fallen under the influence of Schönberg, rather than Wright and Forrest, the original *Kismet* composers. I wondered if my friend the disorientated trumpeter might not take a little stroll down the lane of atonality, but in the end, he plugged away quite consistently.

These quibbles aside, what really distinguishes amateur theatre from the professional sort (and what really gets under your skin when you're watching it), is the footwear. It wasn't the sets ('A Baghdad Street'; 'The Caliph's Diwan'; 'Bazaar of Caravans'), which were just competent enough to pass muster; nor, conversely, the follow-spot operators, who were either new to their equipment or had been experimenting with prescription tranquillisers, judging by the way they dreamily illuminated empty portions of the stage, the curtain and the front row of the stalls; it was the shoes. When Jawan, the Master Brigand, came on, immaculate in lamé bloomers, a frilly shirt and an embroidered waistcoat studded with sequins – and was still wearing Dolcis slip-ons on his feet – you knew you were watching amateur theatre.

Naturally, this tended to affect the smaller parts rather than the leads. The leads quite often warranted a raid on the costume box even to the extent of getting a pair of black suede calf-length boots or some curly *babouches*. But the bit-players were rife with court shoes, brogues, last summer's espadrilles, even gym shoes among the slave girls and princesses. Apparently the Duke of Wellington was obsessed with the footwear of his soldiers. I think this is something that amateur theatrical companies would do well to emulate.

There is one other niggling giveaway to am-dram, even if the shoes don't tell the story. That is, the advertisements in the programme. *Kismet* was blessed with a deeply satisfying programme, forty-one pages long, printed on high-gloss paper, full of pictures and useful information. But it also had (1) advert for Bradford's leading skip hire company, (1) advert for a complete compressed air service (branches in Leeds, Huddersfield, Doncaster) and at least (1) advert for a private nursing home in Carbottom Road. I had plenty of time to read these, marvelling at the dissonance between style and content, as the first-night audience fizzed and chattered and the follow-spot operators woozily flicked their lights on and off at various bits of the auditorium.

And so it went on. The cast churned through 'Baubles, Bangles And Beads', 'Stranger In Paradise', 'Was I Wazir?', 'Baubles, Bangles And Beads' (reprise), 'And This Is My Beloved' and many, many, many more. The orchestra fumbled its way around the score and the crowd scenes threatened constantly to degenerate into free-for-alls encompassing the entire stage; although given that there were nearly seventy players in the production, I suppose the odd moment of anarchy was acceptable. There were moments when my heart leaped fitfully into my mouth (someone's solo was about to go wildly off-key; a delay of more than two seconds had opened up between lines of dialogue) but because this was one of Bradford's top troupes, it never quite collapsed. This, presumably, is the difference between good and bad amateur theatre: bad amateur theatre really does fall apart in the middle of a scene.

Naturally, the punters loved it. One amateur audience is worth seven professional ones.

'I kept having to remind myself that it was Michael,'

announced a chintz lady excitedly to her friend at the interval. 'He just doesn't look the same with that hat on.'

'I don't know how they remember their lines,' said her friend.

'Well, he's been practising,' said the chintz lady. 'Been driving Pat crazy.'

With *critique* on that level, I thought, the Bradford Catholic Players could hardly fail. Indeed, the bars of the Alhambra were glowing, genial, full of easily won delight.

'I think it could hardly have been better,' said a woman in a navy-blue coat.

'As good as professional,' chipped in a moustachioed geezer, whom I took to be her husband.

Then it was back into the theatre for more shoes and bum notes, by the end of which the Bradford Catholic Players were greeted with cheers and bouquets. The Alhambra was suffused with warmth, perspiration and the smell of ladylike cosmetic preparations cooking gently beneath rayon.

And here's something: J.B. Priestley (whose statue stands beefily opposite the Museum of Photography, Film etc., and only a hundred yards or so from the entrance to the Alhambra) actually observes in his *English Journey* that Bradford 'Is theatrically-minded to a most fantastic and droll degree . . . Every second typist is an ingénue lead somewhere, every other cashier a heavy father or comedian.' Now, I only found this out after I'd left Bradford and got hold of a copy of the Priestley book. But it did strike me as mildly odd that Bradford's pastimes and preoccupations should have survived sixty years of tumult and change so transparently. And that I should instinctively have made my way to the beating heart of Bradford's cultural self.

It was also mildly odd to find Priestley describing Bradford as 'A city entirely without charm', and later on referring to the 'Barbaric gloom and boredom' of a Sunday in the city. I mean, apart from Delius (born in Bradford in 1863) and David Hockney, Priestley is Bradford's best-known citizen.

And here he is, stigmatising the place in fine style, as it might be like a very southerner. *The Good Companions* notwithstanding, I found myself rather warming to him; more so because he had the sense to get out of the place as speedily as possible and spend the rest of his life in London.

I left to look for a curry.

After all that genteel gratification, I was ready for something stronger, wilder, something ethnically diverse. I had my copy of *Bradford's Flavours Of Asia* tucked in my pocket and it was a matter of record that the *Daily Telegraph* had recently described Bradford as 'Unquestionably the curry-house capital of the North, if not the United Kingdom. Nowhere in this country is there a greater density of variety of Asian restaurants to be found.'

What's more, I'd got the idea in my head that the whole of Bradford was something of a gourmet's paradise. My Yorkshire friend from Bromley had goaded my imagination to a fever pitch by claiming that, from the point of view of food, Bradford was the one place in England which most closely resembled France. He even told me to cut along to the Rawson Market, where I would glimpse riches beyond words in the form of fresh fruit, shining fish, tender meat and entertaining vegetables. Being completely credulous, I did that and found a large, rambling covered market in which there were, to be sure, some very fresh-looking foodstuffs on display, but all of them of the most mundane and quotidian variety. I think smoked haddock was about as exotic as it got. Nevertheless, when you get an idea into your head, it's hard to shift and despite the absence of *charcuteries*, *patisseries* and *boulangeries*, I clung to the notion that Bradford was all about eating. And there was still *Flavours Of Asia*.

All I can say is that I stumbled out of the Alhambra and went and ate one of the worst curries of my life. I shan't say where, I shan't even anagrammatise the letters of its name, I shall only say that I was the only person in there (hardly surprisingly), that the waiter sat and stared at me for ten full minutes before abruptly starting to his feet in horror and crying out, 'Oh! Do you want to *eat*?' and that my Chicken Bhuna tasted of minced packaging. There are some seventy thousand Asians living in Bradford. Bradford has its own curry college in the middle of town, where would-be curry-house restaurateurs can learn how to do it right. Don't ask me how I ignored the scores of alternative, more delicious curry-houses in town, I just drew an excessively short straw.

Wandering sadly away from my Chicken Bhuna experience, it started to occur to me that I was in danger of turning into Billy Liar. I don't mean that, like the eponymous hero of the Keith Waterhouse novel, I was becoming a cheat, a pathological liar, a cack-handed womaniser, a gutless fantasist or an undertaker's assistant (although most of these options have been available at one time or another), but that I was beginning to feel myself imprisoned by a world of terminal, northern stuffiness. It was fairly late at night, I was in the centre of Bradford, it was cold and as far as I could see, there was no one there but me. It could not have been more unlike my earlier dreams and fantasies if it had tried.

In Newcastle, at around the same time, the streets would have been thronged with drunk teenagers, Dutchmen, minor-league alcoholics and even ordinary people making their way from one place to another. In Manchester, there would be noisy pubs and groups of tourists having cash-points explained to them. But here, in Bradford, it was *silent*.

Worse still, by standing in the street called Cheapside, on the eastern edge of the city centre, I could see clear across town, to the National Museum of Photography, Film and Television. I cannot tell you how desolating it is to a Londoner to be able to encompass the heart of a city in one glance. It weighed on me. There was no violence, no colour, no Hard Man urban dynamism; only the glare of the street lights and a few late buses rumbling away in the direction of Wakefield and Leeds.

Amazingly, nothing much seems to have changed in the thirty-five years since *Billy Liar* first appeared, although the economy of the West Riding has evidently hit hard times unimaginable in the days of Macmillan. As Keith Waterhouse/Billy Fisher/Billy Liar puts it: 'Our main street, Moorgate, was – despite the lying reminiscences of old men like Councillor Duxbury who remembered sheep-troughs where the X-L Disc Bar now stands – exactly like any other High Street in Great Britain. Woolworth's looked like Woolworth's, the Odeon looked like the Odeon, and the *Stradhoughton Echo*'s own office, which Man o' the Dales must have seen, looked like a public lavatory in honest native white tile. I had a fairly passionate set-piece all worked out on the subject of rugged Yorkshire towns, with their rugged neon signs and their rugged plate-glass and plastic shop-fronts, but so far nobody had given me the opportunity to start up on the theme.'

Waterhouse is actually a native of Hunslet, Leeds, but there's the strong suspicion that his fictional northern amalgam, Stradhoughton, leans more on Bradford for its colouring than anywhere else. Moreover, they made the film of *Billy Liar* in Bradford, a fact which the tourist board is only slightly keen to tell the rest of the world. And if you've read the book and seen the film, Bradford and *Liar* fuse together with a slow, tedious inevitability. Waterhouse, of course, like any shrewd Yorkshireman, pissed off to London as soon as he could (aged twenty-two) and has never looked back since.

Billy Liar is a wonderful book, horribly honest and see-thing with frustrations, evasions, hatreds. The film version isn't bad, either. The action takes place in a latter-day North, not the homely, working-class North of Honest Jack Priestley, but a compromised, denatured, suburbanised North of the post-war years. Everything about it screams

petty, boring, provincial: 'I reached Hillcrest at about half
past two to find lunch over and my mother in the kitchen,
making notes for a scene about my not being home for meals.
It was bacon and egg again, the traditional Saturday feast;
the eggshells were in the sink-tidy and there was an air of
replete doom about the house . . .'

My God, I thought as *Liar* started to churn around my
head, I've just *got* to get out of here, which was about as
fatuous a thing as it was possible to think, given the time and
effort I'd expended getting there in the first place.

So the next day, I got up early and went up a long, steep hill
to the Undercliffe Cemetery, which made me feel even more
like Billy Liar, this time as portrayed by Tom Courtenay,
who's from Hull, as it happens, although his ironic demea-
nour and general air of having been slapped across the face
with a fish fillet are more Lancastrian than Yorkshire to my
eyes.

Incidentally, how would you feel, exactly, about a city
which tells you repeatedly to go and visit its main cemetery?
Bradford's Undercliffe is mentioned in all the tourist bro-
chures. Highgate Cemetery, in north London, obviously has
something in common with the Bradford manifestation, but
the kind of people who visit Highgate Cemetery tend to be
young men engaged in writing brilliant first novels, batty old
local historians and freelance ghouls. Is this really the sort of
crowd Bradford's tourist board is aiming for?

Still, I went (file me under freelance ghoul, I would
guess), and as I stepped through the Undercliffe's entrance
gates, the picture changed from a bright, full-colour morning, to the black, grey and white of the 1963 *Billy Liar* film.
After all, these are the natural colours of the Undercliffe
Cemetery in any condition: twenty-six acres of graves,
containing over 120,000 corpses, hundreds of wonderful
pieces of Victorian commemorative masonry (the cemetery
opened in 1854) and a great deal of soot still clinging to the

stonework, because, thank God, the Bradford tourist board hasn't got round to cleaning up any of the tombstones.

I shuffled down broad, death-lined avenues, my eyes filled with the image of Tom Courtenay in a poorly fitting Burton's suit (with the HP clearly still hanging over it) pestering the mildly obese, snaggle-toothed Helen Fraser (who played his fiancée Barbara/aka The Witch) for pre-marital sex. I sat down, like Courteny/Liar, on a chill stone seat, with sooty vaults and monuments rising over my shoulders. The whole of Bradford lay drably before me, thin pencils of smoke drifting up from the few factories that were still active, the chimney of Manningham Mills pointing into the empyrean, the Dales, the bloody Dales, looming behind that and rolling away into the haze.

An old boy, looking unnervingly like Councillor Dux-bury, came past, walking his dog.

'Beautiful morning, in't it?' he called out.

I bit back the temptation to answer, 'Ay, 'appen,' and instead grunted as genially as I could at him, throwing in a friendly leer for good measure.

'Nippy, though, eh?' he went on. 'Bin a frost last night. Best get on.'

He left me feeling 'That he had said something sage and shrewd' (thought Jennings/Liar/Courtenay) 'although I was unable to fathom quite what he was getting at. He was stuffing his handkerchief into his overcoat pocket, preparing to go. I did not feel afraid. I felt a kind of tentative serenity and I wanted him to go on with his old man's advice . . .'

For fuck's sake, I thought, I'm going potty. I half expected to turn and find Helen Fraser's homely mug gazing into mine, a segment of orange poised to enter her lips, a look of bovine enquiry flitting about her eyes. It was quite clear that I was going to have to get out of Bradford a bit more and escape its baleful, petit-bourgeois embrace, if I wasn't going to end up ruling imaginary

countries in my head and stuffing illicit calendars up my
pullover, Liar-style.

Don't get me wrong about the Undercliffe Cemetery, by the
way. It's definitely worth a visit. The views are terrific, some
of the monuments are big enough to double as small chapels,
the details (angels, Gothic encrustations, draped urns,
obelisks) are ever-changing and inventive, the names
(Illingworth, Jowett, Duckworth, Aykroyd) are evocative
and the grime is first-rate. In fact, it points up neatly what's
wrong with born-again Bradford. The city below is simply
not black enough. Victorian masonry – particularly in the
North – almost always looks better with a good covering of
funereal filth on it. It transforms the mundane into something dark and exciting. And if Bradford is serious about
flogging itself to the Americans and Japanese as a living
museum (viz: the 'Bradford Industrial Heritage Travel
News Supplement', several pages devoted to hawking a
suspiciously reconditioned nineteenth-century past) then
grime is an essential.

Grime, and the kind of shopping facilities that used to
provide a backdrop to films and photographs from the first
half of this century: strange little outlets with over-busy
windows and a welter of signs and notices dotted about. A
place like Bradford should be pitch black and choked with
small establishments purveying Damaroids Rejuvenators,
Smokers' Requisites and small, complicated items of haber-
dashery.

Of all Bradford's present shops, the only one which had
the kind of flavour I was looking for was an especially seedy
medical store I found round the back of the Alhambra,
crammed with trusses and cornplasters, no fewer than six
signs advertising Durex and packets of a product called
Neurelax: The Herbal Tonic For Frayed Nerves. That's the
kind of thing that gives a place atmosphere. I stood outside,
peering at it for many minutes, even to the extent of

attracting curious glances from passers-by. After a while, I found myself walking briskly away from the medical store as if I had better things to do with my time, before rounding a corner, waiting a minute for the street to clear of inquisitive pedestrians, and finally returning to the shopfront and peering in again.

Without grime and a mildly deviant medical store, a town like Bradford looks more ordinary than it should. This, after all, is the birthplace of the Labour Party. The site of the first formal meeting of the Independent Labour Party, on 13 January 1893, still exists. It is, in fact, now Guiseppe's Back Yard Restaurant, but it's *there*. This is where one of the great steps forward in the emancipation of the working man and his liberation from a life of killing drudgery was taken: but does it look the part? Does modern Bradford look like a cauldron of industrial brutality? No, it looks like the sort of place where the Liberal Democrats might congregate to fret over the vexed issue of budgets for local council newsletters.

You can see how misguided this industrial heritage strategy is, if you go to one of Bradford's major tourist draws, Saltaire. Now, Saltaire is virtually inescapable. Even more inescapable than the Undercliffe Cemetery. People who've been there tell you to go there. The Bradford tourist office tells you to go there. Hotel receptions the length and breadth of the West Riding are crammed with posters and pamphlets extolling Saltaire. The metro train service stops at the Saltaire station. It's free. So I went there.

I turned my back reluctantly on the Undercliffe Cemetery, but at the same time with a sense of relief, knowing that once I did so, I could forge a new life somewhere else, possibly with the young Julie Christie.

I shambled down the hill back into town, along the Otley Road, passing a 1960s block of roughcast council flats called, poignantly, Scargill House. A middle-aged woman was leaning out of a window on the fifth floor, calling across

the (really quite wide) Otley Road to a young woman on the
fifth floor of an identical block opposite.

'Sandra,' she shouted, 'yer late. Get a *moove* on – '

'All *raight*,' Sandra shouted back. 'I've not 'ad breakfast.'

Further down the hill, there was a row of old-fashioned
back-to-backs called Heap Lane. It felt good to be on the
move again.

I worked my way round to what's left of the Forster
Square Station. This used to be large, important and full of
trains, whose passengers would alight from their carriages
and go straight to the Midland Hotel next door for a
reviving hock and seltzer and a hot lobster. A few years
ago, the demolition men called and now Forster Square is
mostly a huge, flat, weed-filled wasteland with cars parked
on it and one or two massive Gothic arches let into the
hillside with more cars parked underneath: the remains of an
ancient civilisation. And it has a newish Hornby O-O
railway station, like the one at Bradford Interchange, only
even feebler, to serve those of us who want to get to Skipton,
Keighley, Saltaire and Ilkley in not too much of a hurry.

It is also hard against a piquant little 1960s *Stingray*
development, incorporating a disused, flyblown Cinecenta
cinema (the like of which I hadn't set eyes upon for over two
decades) and some really stupidly ugly glass and steel office
buildings. These are indeed so awful that I hope they have a
preservation order put on them, like the Bull Ring's Rotunda, so that they may symbolise old hopes to new
generations and teach us a lesson at the same time about
how, exactly, not to improve the urban landscape.

Unlike Saltaire. As a concept, Saltaire is impeccable – an
entire Dales village, purpose-built in the 1850s, on the edge
of the Pennines and right by the Leeds and Liverpool canal,
around what was then Britain's largest and most modern
cloth mill. Saltaire, the model village, provided clean,
affordable accommodation for over four thousand people

(three thousand of whom actually worked in the mill), as well as a school, a church, a bath house and no pub: the benevolent capitalist ideal, as seen in Port Sunlight and Bourneville. Why was it named Saltaire? Because the benevolent capitalist in question was Bradfordian entrepreneur and philanthropist Sir Titus Salt: a man who was so afraid of public speaking that in the two years he was an MP, he never once addressed the House of Commons.

Of course, it sounds fascinating and, in a very qualified way, it is. You arrive at the same station that Salt's customers would have used, passing the monumental rear of the factory, before alighting from your reeky old diesel train, climbing through cobbled streets, past some charming poor person's cottages and modest shops, all dressed up in a delightful vernacular simplification of the Italianate style. It must have been heaven in 1865 and, apart from the absence of any pubs, it still is, somewhat. The old mill is now being slowly transformed into offices, a café and retail outlets, as well as providing a home to some small, clean, inoffensive firms making specialised electronic equipment. It is the 1990s dream made flesh (apart from the pub): efficient, attractive, conserving the best of the past and combining it with the needs of today.

But to spend half a day there (as I did) is like spending half a day reading the National Trust Gift Catalogue – excruciatingly agreeable, taking you into new realms of benign dullness. It is dull in the way the Peak District and the Cotswolds are dull: acres and acres of cute stone cottages, dear little shops selling honey, a diminutive stone roadbridge . . . and as its capstone, the David Hockney Gallery.

This really lends distinction to Saltaire, the fact that it's home to a gallery dedicated to the prints, paintings and photographs of Bradford's most famous son (after Delius and J.B. Priestley, of course). But what's the problem with Hockney's pictures? They're pleasant but dull, that's the problem. Pinks, yellows, blues, blue guitars, swimming pools, California, nude men, sunshine, strong, primary colours interspersed with occasional, fleeting descents into mild weirdness (*The Rake's Progress* stage designs; the old *We Two Boys Together Clinging* from his art-school days), pictures of Hockney himself, standing on dappled verandas or leaning against white walls, absently fingering his sky-blue T-shirt, smiling that Buddha-like smile of inner contentment and real wealth: it all drifts past the retina, undemandingly, tastefully, affably, unsatisfactorily. Standing in a whole room full of them – a large portion of Salt's mill, in fact – is like being in a room full of well-made puddings. They look nice, they're quite tasty, but you couldn't possibly live on them.

And yet I have the feeling that this is precisely what Bradford would be if it could. Bradford's even trying to re-invent itself (at the same time as it becomes every thinking person's first choice for a northern holiday break) as the easy-on-the-eye Silicon Valley of the North, or Silicon Dale, ha ha, as they refer to it at the Economic Development Unit. Electronics: it's clean, it's modern, it's an economic growth area; it's not worsted cloth. Forget Worstedopolis (as Bradford was once known)! Come, make your business at home in an artfully refurbished Victorian warehouse/mill building/poor house/lavatory, where the handsome stone dressing conceals a multitude of environmentally friendly up-to-the-minute phone lines and airconditioning ducts! Put your clients/family/illicit lovers up in one of Bradford's sumptuous in-town hotels and shrug off the cares of specia-list electronics with a night at the Alhambra, followed by an unforgettable curry! And at the weekends, savour the quality of life unique to this part of the world (and which got us nominated sixth least unpleasant British city to live in, in a recent survey) with a walk across the bloody moors/a trip on the Keighley and Worth Valley Railway/a mooch around the Hockney Gallery, home to some of David Hockney's most unintimidating pictures!

It's all such a betrayal. We've already got the Cotswolds
and the Thames Valley and hi-tech Cambridgeshire, why
try to transmute the awful North into a frigid version of the
same thing? I suppose Bradford would simply mark me
down as a typically perverse southern ponce, too bigoted
and too concerned with keeping the good stuff to himself to
allow the North to forge a new destiny. Why should
Bradford relapse into dirt and decline, just to satisfy the
morbid fixations of a Londoner with a grudge?

Fair enough. But then again, why was Bradford District
home to the Sooty Museum?

Let me tell you a secret: the thing that really tipped the
balance for me, so far as Bradford was concerned, was the
Sooty Museum. Quite apart from all my dreams of Yorkshire
dirt and good eating, I felt I had to visit a place which gave
Sooty, the well-known stage and television glove puppet from
the 1950s and 1960s, not just prominence, but something
amounting to star billing. Not only did Sooty get a plug in the
official Bradford mini-guide, he also merited a full colour
picture (along with Sweep and Soo) in the glossy hand-out
known as 'The Bradford Collection'; and, as I said before, he
was, unbelievably, in charge of the Great British Cities
Celebrity Walk around Bradford.

For a glove puppet with no independent form of locomo-
tion, Sooty described an amazingly complicated itinerary,
far more complex than that of Queen Victoria around
Aberdeen, or Robin Hood around Nottingham. Robin
Hood, to be frank, was something of a slouch, bothering
himself with no more than a couple of streets leading to the
ABC Cinema via a pub called The Trip to Jerusalem. Sooty,
on the other hand, goads the visitor to Bradford all the way
from the Bradford and Ilkley Community College, on the
west side of town, to Treadwell's Art Mill, on the eastern-
most tip of Little Germany.

On the way, he introduced us to the National Museum of

Photography, Film and Television, the Flavours of Asia, the Bradford Ice Rink, the Alhambra, the Colour Museum – virtually everything there is to see in Bradford, in fact, with the possible exception of the Bradford Interchange bus depot. Stranger yet, not only does Sooty have no legs: he doesn't even come from Bradford. He comes from Guiseley, a middling settlement to the north of the city. Or rather, his creator, Harry Corbett, came from Guiseley. I had to find out if this whole Sooty hype wasn't some sort of elaborate northern joke.

Now, no one over thirty will fail to remember the Sooty and Sweep shows of their childhood. The fundamental premise of every show was the same: Harry Corbett, who looked like a balding, low-grade civil servant from the Ministry of Works (and who would doubtless have been an active Mason in his spare time) put his hand up Sooty; Sooty would then, with the help of Sweep (a mentally defective dog) tip crap all over Harry's head. That was it. The simple, imbecilic pleasure of each show lay in watching the build-up to Harry Corbett getting crap tipped on his head.

What, I used to ask my five-year-old self as the television warmed up, will they get up to this week? Will Sooty try and bake a cake, using a badly designed food mixer, real eggs, milk and flour? Will it be time to paint Sweep's bedroom, using real paint? Will it be the day for rock-blasting for Bauxite reserves, using real gelignite? It was a surprisingly successful formula, in those simpler, less existentially doubt-filled days, and Sooty was something of a national figure. Every child under ten knew the tune which accompanied the words, 'Sooty, ever so naughty Sooty', much as they knew the catchphrase, 'Izzy wizzy, let's get busy' and Harry Corbett's invariable pay-off, his face covered with shaving-foam and flour: 'Bye-bye, everybody. Bye-bye.'

Harry, sadly, is no longer with us, but some years ago, a woman called Pat Redmonds decided to take the puppets,

props and dioramas from the shows and house them in a
museum (a decommissioned church school, as it turned out)
in Shipley. Not Guiseley, not Bradford proper, but Shipley,
because that's where the puppets were made. So I went
there.

Inside, in a sequence of rooms smelling strongly of footwear and mould, the museum traced Sooty's life and times –
from the first days when Harry bought a glove puppet in
Blackpool in 1948; to winning a BBC television talent
contest, four years later; to making the glove puppet more
visually distinctive by putting soot on its ears – the whole
saga was there, in the form of tableaux and dioramas in glass
cases, framed snaps of Sooty and the gang, newspaper
cuttings and videos of his shows running in the basement
cafeteria.

It was, frankly, a bit odd. The first tableau you came
across was of a one-fifth-scale domestic interior, circa 1959,
in which Sooty was practising his conjuring tricks at a table,
Soo was reading the paper and Sweep lay apparently dead
at the piano, his face pressed against the keys. Nearby was
another glass case filled with memorabilia – photos of Harry
mugging for the BBC cameras; Sooty going for a ride in a
midget pedal car; old Sooty annuals; and another incarnation of Soo. I stared blankly at this hotchpotch for a while,
only to be frightened out of my wits when Soo started talking
loudly at me in a Home Counties accent. 'Jesus!' I cried,
leaping backwards and catching my leg on the edge of a
chair.

Luckily, I was the only person in the place (I was there for
an hour and no one else came in; which tells you something
about the Sooty Museum and more, perhaps, about what a
sad middle-aged man I must be) so no one heard me. At the
same time, it did nothing to relieve me of the feeling that I'd
blundered into the Museum At The End Of The World, the
last collection of significant objects that anyone could
possibly have thought worth making. It reminded me of

the old Museum of Curiosities in Arundel (pickled snakes in jars; *tableaux vivants* using stuffed dormice; the world's smallest cricket ball, that kind of thing) – a museum which you couldn't in all honesty recommend to anyone; but which you knew would appeal quite strongly to a certain class of wandering deviant. Me, in other words.

I collared the sheep-like woman at the ticket desk and asked her what sort of person, exactly, would think it worth establishing such a place.

'Well,' she said, peering at me, 'it's a lady from around here. She put up the money, you see.'

And?

'All the models on display were made for Harry Corbett. By a man called Bill,' she went on.

Oh?

'Yes. We've been going for nearly seven years.'

That seemed to be it, so far as she was concerned. She went back to counting old ticket stubs. I turned away. On the wall opposite the ticket desk was a notice written in biro, which read, 'The Fan Club is no longer operating. Please do not send money to the address in Bournemouth as advertised.' Clearly, Sooty was having trouble cutting it. Indeed, the air or morbidity about the place was so powerful and pervasive that I suppose I wasn't even surprised when I read in the papers, weeks later, that the Sooty Museum was about to close. Sooty, Soo and Sweep were going into storage, and Ms Redmonds was planning to install a troupe of mechanical cats talking in broad Yorkshire accents. Saddening, though: a last vestige of my doubt-free childhood, swirling down the drain of history. And what (I wondered with a pang of anxiety) will it mean for the Bradford publicity machine? What about Celebrity Walks? Who will show us round Bradford now? Frederick Delius?

I left and went to the pub across the road. This was almost as deserted as the Sooty Museum and refused to sell me a sandwich. Then I drifted lugubriously back to Bradford via the Shipley Conservative Association, which, I was interested to see, had a large sign affixed to it, saying: 'Marcus Fox MP. Enquiry Centre'. I did wonder whether to go in and ask the Chairman of the 1922 Committee quite what he thought Bradford was up to, making Sooty, Hockney and curry their official mascots, but I realised in time that Sir Marcus would probably be in London, trying to prevent what was left of the Tory party from hurling itself once and for all over a cliff.

Back on the platform of the Hornby O-O station at Forster Square, I was feeling a bit desperate. Not another cock-up, I thought. Is this really all that Yorkshire amounts to? Bourgeois gentility, defunct glove-puppet museums, small-time railway halts? I made a decision. I decided to quit Bradford and try Leeds. Leeds would have what I wanted. It was big. It was important. It couldn't possibly be boring.

I trudged back to my lonely businessman's hotel, my heart full of mixed emotions.

TWELVE

My mistake was to ask the barman in this pub in Leeds. I was standing there, watching him pull me a pint of Tetleys ('Leeds, The Home Of Tetleys', as it tells you, unavoidably, on a hoarding by the railway line into Leeds City Station), and thought, I'll ask him what's so special about Yorkshire.

Fatuous idea, I know. If you go up to someone and ask them straight out, what's so great about Manchester, or why's Newcastle so special, or what's the big deal with Scunthorpe, or any similarly witless enquiry, you either get no answer worth recording; or you get an earful of non-sense, intended to impress upon the (clearly) sceptical, pallid southerner what a splendid place he's standing in. It's a futile activity, but I felt an overwhelming urge to do it.

After all, I'd been around, I'd seen a fair bit of the county, I'd spent a small lifetime in Bradford, and it didn't strike me as *that* impressive. There was no clear reason why Yorkshire-men should be so full of themselves and the region they come from. Well, maybe they're not, I thought. Perhaps it's only the professional Yorkshiremen who come south who are so fixated on the place. Maybe the rest of them take a resigned, cynical approach to the whole issue of Yorkshireness: Yes, it's frightfully overdone, gives us a terrible reputation as pointy-headed bigots, the place is no better in the overall scheme of things than Wiltshire or Dyfed, really . . .

So I asked the barman and he repeated my question back
to me.

'What makes Yorkshire so special?' He gazed into the
foaming head of my pint. 'Pride. That's what makes it
special.'

I felt a subsidiary question bubbling up in my throat. I
couldn't stop myself. Pride in what? I asked.

'Pride in being Yorkshire,' he said, placing the pint on the
counter. 'Pound fifty, please.'

And that was that. Thanks very much, I said, both
ironically and without inflection.

The fact is, however, that Leeds may well be the perfect
northern place. I was dispirited after Bradford, scolding
myself for being too prescriptive, for taking a typically
perverse, southern, dilettantish approach to the whole
Bradford question, like a kind of North-obsessed Huys-
mans, hanging around decommissioned wool factories in
search of kinky uplift. It was the problem I'd had from the
very start: the search for what I more or less arbitrarily
thought should be there, coming up against the reality of
whatever was there.

But the longer I hung around Leeds, the more it dawned
on me that perhaps here was the happy combination of
qualities for which I had been searching so long – for which I
had been searching since Birmingham, indeed: the great
false start.

I checked in at yet another desperate hotel, where the
proprietress couldn't stop herself from squinting suspiciously at me (alerted by my untrustworthy London accent) until she finally asked, 'You're not int'theatre are you?
Only we get a lot of 'em 'ere.'

No, not at all, ha ha, I squeaked as she shooed me up
several narrow, winding, odorous staircases to an available
room. The walls of this private midden turned out to be so

thin that, much later that day, I could hear the man snoring in the room next to mine. But I was used to that; in fact, I almost welcomed it. Frankly, I don't know what to do with myself in smart hotel rooms. On the rare occasions when I put up in somewhere with stars next to the name, I waste hours simply scampering from luxury to luxury, gobbling the free chocolates, pressing my slacks in the Corby trouser press, fiddling with the buttons on the television, jotting down redundant *pensées* on the hotel writing paper with the promotional biro, showering unnecessarily (whilst wearing the complimentary plastic shower cap) and gazing hungrily at the contents of the mini-bar, while being too mean to consume any of them. The day goes to pot and at the end of it, I feel enervated and dissatisfied. None of which happens in the cardboard-wall, leaky-washbasin, U-shaped-bed, minimal-comforts establishments I normally frequent. In other words, my Leeds flophouse was most satisfactory.

As was the rest of the city. Indeed, it had everything that I wanted from a northern town, absolutely everything.

Leeds came to life, just like everywhere else in the North (apart from York, Buxton and Ripon) at the time of the Industrial Revolution (did you know, Leeds was the site of the world's first commercial railway? This was the Middleton Colliery Railway, which was laid down in 1758, several years before the Stockton–Darlington line) with a mishmash of textile empires, engineering concerns and related financial institutions. Since the place was surrounded by cheap coal, industries grew up which were large coal consumers: chemical works, glassworks, potteries, brickworks, iron foundries. Lives there a train buff who remains unmoved by the name Hunslet, the Leeds suburb where generations of damn big steam locomotives were riveted and bolted together? By the mid-nineteenth century, Leeds had already made a name for itself as one of the most heavily polluted cities in the country: a testimonial to its industrial success.

At the same time, it was covering itself both ways, by maintaining a strong presence in the cloth and clothing business. Bradford had wool, but Leeds had wool, flax and ready-made clothing, so that when the flax market (as in linen) collapsed at the end of the nineteenth century, there was enough expertise in wholesale clothing to take up the slack. By 1890, some five million garments were coming out of Leeds' factories (heavily staffed by women) and by 1921, Montague Burton's Hudson Road Mills were the world's largest single clothing plant. Think of that, next time you're in Burton's, searching in vain for a pair of trousers that *aren't* made out of no-style crease-resistant polyester/cotton weave.

As a consequence, Leeds has scale – a population in the metropolitan district of a little less than half a million people, spread across a conurbation larger in area than those of Sheffield, York, Hull or Bradford – and it has big buildings. Nothing quite as monstrous as those of Manchester, but quite large enough to be daunting; and, unlike Manchester's *palazzi*, pressed more closely together to create a greater illusion of substance, as well as being in a better state of repair.

Admittedly, things can get a bit ragged around the edge of town, and the painfully long and weary *schlep* I made down Wellington Street towards the inner ringroad interchange and motorway fuck-up revealed an outbreak of gloomy barrenness that Manchester would have been proud of. But this is Yorkshire. This is where tykes toil away at whatever they toil away at, being close, prudent and hard-headed. So it never gets quite as desolate as Lancashire.

Nor is it quite as painfully ugly. Clever Leeds, in fact, managing, as it does, to avoid the dullness of Bradford with its agreeable stonework, without going all the way and turning into a red-brick nightmare. What do you get from Leeds? You get a bit of stonework, you get plenty of senseless 1960s and 1970s abortions around and about – note well, the

City Square with its equestrian statue of the Black Prince and some nude Victorian women, now completely over-shadowed by an outbreak of dim-witted concrete office blocks – you get a good smattering of ugly brick things, some cobblestones and dead alleyways and plenty of fly-blown squalor near the railway station. All this competes with some really rather nice buildings, such as the Time Ball Building (a gleeful 1865 clockmaker's establishment with Old Father Time perched on the outside in wrought iron), the Corn Exchange and a load of terrifically elaborate nineteenth-century shops up and down Briggate. Taken as a whole, Leeds is an eyesore, but an eyesore that seems to be at ease with itself. A William Bendix or Boris Karloff sort of place: ugly without being morbidly introspective about it.

In fact, students of architecture who don't object to a complete absence of anything refined or elegant can amuse themselves for days in Leeds. I found some really entertain-ing ugliness in the north-western corner of the city centre, around the Leeds University campus. If you're ever tempted to take a look around there, I recommend a stunning nineteenth-century mock-Tudor castle (now an Adult Edu-cation Centre) in Springfield Mount, with, just round the corner, a ruined maternity hospital with a foundation stone laid in 1928 by HRH Princess Mary, the Viscountess Lascelles.

For contrast, why not drop in at the nearby abandoned garage, where a pre-war notice still announces A.N. HOL-LAND LTD. LICENSED PETROLEUM SPIRIT STORE, before you drift down the hill into – well, I'm not entirely sure what it is, but I think it's the campus of the old Leeds Polytechnic (now the Leeds Metropolitan University).

Whatever the institution is, its physical form is that of a merciless 1960s concrete shambles, devoid of grass, flowers or living things, with an eye-watering wind howling through its walkways and round its bleak corners. It's a place where *Alphaville* meets the Pennines and quite how any under-

graduate manages to last three years there beats me. This
may be why there are no signs telling you exactly what it is
or where you are: simple shame. There are colour-coded
maps at various entrance points, telling you in an awkwardly conceptual fashion how to get to the Geology
Department or the Centre for Jazz-Fusion Studies; but
not a single announcement of what exactly this huge
cement agglomeration of culture and science is.

Gaiety seekers, on the other hand, should look in at the
Leeds General Infirmary, a little piece of St Pancras Station
in the north, displaying an amusing reversal of the architect's intentions (common to this part of the world) in which
the decorative light-coloured stonework around the doors
and windows and corners has absorbed the soot of decades
and turned black; while the deep red brickwork has
shrugged off the same black muck and is now a lighter
colour than the stonework. The building has, in fact, turned
into a dingy negative of itself, which I see as a charming and
very northern thing for it to do.

The litany goes on: the 1862 Corn Exchange (with its odd
little black-painted desks bearing names such as Kenneth
Wilson Grain and Allinsons), the County Arcade (1900), a
Moorish cloth factory (1878) in Park Square, a breathtakingly gloomy Victorian pub round the back of the Town
Hall, the Tudor Fish Bar just off Briggate, some small red-
brick terraced things around Greek and Bedford Streets – a
cornucopia of tastes and styles, for those of us who get a kick
out of anything awkward and lacking in good taste.

And all, of course, devoid of *smartness*. In Leeds' case, all the
smart bits of town are in other towns altogether – places like
York, Harrogate and Richmond – leaving the hard-wear-
ing, thuggishly unpretentious stuff for the big city. The
Kirkgate covered market, for instance, is a real gem, a
big, smelly, rambling affair, selling great amounts of carpet
remnants and boasting what passes for culinary adventur-

ousness in Leeds: a Continental Delicatessen which stocks almost nothing but Carlsberg Special Brew and huge piles of Scottish Cheddar.

As I blundered gratefully around the Kirkgate market, I pushed some hot chips into my face, feeling pretty much integrated with the social flow as I walked around with fatty fingers and bits of chip adhering to my chin, savouring the crude vitality of it all. A couple of memorably scabby drunks were stuck in the entrance to the Gents' toilet immediately outside the market. One was trying to get up the steps to the street, the other was trying to go down.

'You dick'ead!' shouted one to the other.

'*You* dick'ead! Hee hee!' the other shouted back.

They swayed on the greasy tiles for a bit, laughing and shouting 'You dick'ead!' at each other, before one of them lost his footing and stumbled down into the reeky interior. Cheers, mate, I thought, vaguely saluting him with a chip.

Rounding the corner from the market, I was passed by a policeman and a policewoman, hurrying to arrest a couple of juvenile tykes. By the time I got to where the tykes had been run to earth, there were four coppers, a patrol car, a knot of moderately interested passers-by standing eight feet from the action and two ten-year-old (at a guess) boys standing with their feet in a heap of litter, looking at the coppers with mild, surly defiance. I'd obviously reached them at a point of stasis, with no one saying anything to anyone else and only the garbage coming out of the coppers' radios to break the silence. I don't know what the tykes had done (nicked something from the market? Impersonated a VAT inspector?) but whatever it was, it was clearly deemed more serious than pissing in an extremely public place, which I witnessed not long after, in Merrion Street.

In this instance, the pisser was a very large, blond heavy-metal fan, taking a copious leak over a plate-glass shop window which had a pyramid of electrical goods on display on the other side. His friends, also Def Leppard enthusiasts

from the look of them, cackled with delight as he announced
to passing pedestrians, 'Shoodoop, you. I'll piss 'ere an' like
it.'

Middle-aged ladies with shopping bags looked doubtfully
ahead of them and quickened their pace, while the rest of us
pretended not to be bothered by the spectacle. Nobody came
to arrest him and, with a grunt, he did up his flies and
wandered off with the other headbangers in the direction of
Harrogate. I thought of Manchester and the dossers' pub in
the respectable part of town and drew my own comparisons
between that and the heavy-metal fan urinating over an up-
market electrical-goods store in a refurbished and smartened
part of Leeds.

There's just no barrier of propriety once you get to these
big northern cities: as evinced by another bloke I saw – a
prosperous-looking business type – standing on the concourse of Leeds City Station, bellowing quite unselfconsciously into his mobile phone, 'What do you mean *he's
not there*? Well, get 'is bloody assistant. *Jesus!*'

He was deafeningly loud (even for someone trying to
make himself heard above a main-line railway station)
and completely without embarrassment. Nothing prissy
and middle class about the way he attended to his needs.
You want to shout your head off in a public place? Be my
guest. You want to empty your bladder in full view of the
good people of Leeds? This is Liberty Hall.

What was the non-fiction Book of the Month in one of
Leeds' larger bookshops while I was there? Something about
Italian cookery? A mincing travel book, illustrated with
lavish colour prints of the Serengeti? No. It was *The Effective
Way to Stop Drinking*. If that's not the most shameless title
since *A History of Orgies*, I'd like to know what is.

Ah, but the pride of a place like Leeds: the pride manifested
in the Leeds Town Hall. Now, this is something I don't quite
understand, given the prominence Leeds Town Hall as-

sumes in books about Leeds (a surprising dearth of these, you may be interested to know), and the city's tourist blurb. The way it's usually described, the Town Hall comes across as the spiritual and physical point of convergence of all Leeds folk: the building where the business of the Corporation is transacted and the rates are haggled over by councillors and weaselly apparatchiks, and which directs the lives of thousands.

But it isn't. Apparently, the Leeds Town Hall is not the town hall in the way that the Manchester Town Hall is the town hall of Manchester. The work of local governance goes on in the relatively vast 1933 Civic Hall, a block away to the north (that's the manner of city you're dealing with when you tangle with Leeds, by the way: not one, but two town halls), while the Town Hall is used for recitals or concerts or whatever. In fact, it's like the Birmingham Town Hall; which isn't Birmingham's town hall, either. That, you will remember, is called the Council House. Still, more than any real town hall, Leeds Town Hall is a manifestation of civic pride on a monstrous scale. It was built in the 1850s by Yorkshireman Cuthbert Broderick (who also designed the Corn Exchange) and was opened by the Queen in 1858. And as English town halls go, it is awesome.

It perches on a street called The Headrow, a contour line on the hill which rises up from the river Aire and keeps on rising in a northerly direction to the General Infirmary and the University. Thus the Town Hall is in a good position to gaze down on the centre of Leeds like an indescribably fat alderman in a gargantuan fawn-coloured suit (if you include the dome, the building is almost as tall – 225 feet – as it is wide – 250 feet).

And what a building it is! I stood on the stone-flagged terrace in front of it and had difficulty restraining myself from actually bowing. I mean, Manchester's Town Hall is big and Bradford's is full of a sense of its own importance, but Leeds Town Hall is simply immense. For heaven's sake, the Civic Hall is enormous too, but it doesn't bear down on you in the way that the Town Hall does, with its endless classical piers and architraves and above all, its ridiculous dome (containing a four-ton bell) lofted into the sky by a mob of Corinthian columns like Queen Victoria being given a ride on the shoulders of a rugby team. The effect is, admittedly, slightly diminished by the black netting that's been thrown over the building to stop pigeons crapping on it, with the result that the Town Hall looks as if it's wearing a fishnet bodystocking. But in every other way, its size and its position say, more indisputably than any other town hall I've seen, Do Not Trifle With This City.

As is so often the way, the Town Hall raises civic pride to new heights, while the City Museum lets it down. Once more, I broke my pledge never to go into a museum again, when it came on to rain and I got bored with sheltering in one of the Town Hall's overweening doorways. So I went into the City Museum and discovered precisely the usual municipal city museum dross. Frankly, I don't know why these places bother, except to maintain the pretence that they, like the city museums of every other regional centre of any importance, also have a treasure-store of beauty and culture from which the locals may draw deep draughts of solace.

In Leeds' case, it should be enough to note that the City Museum contains a stuffed guinea-fowl, a Chinese type-writer, a collection of Bulgarian currency and a section entitled 'The Progress Of Angling In Leeds'. This was only exceeded in narrowness of purpose by the monthly display put on by members of the Leeds Philatelic Society. When I was there, its theme was Recorded Deliveries in the UK, 1965–1975, a tale not without its moments of interest, but equally, not the kind of thing to stop strangers in the street and tell them about.

*   *   *

On the other hand, Leeds does make a big noise about its greenery, which struck me as odd, given the fact that there is only one green space in town and that's a ragged salient in front of the Civic Hall. On the postcards, this same patch is covered in grass and brightly flowering bedding plants; but all I could see when I was there were a couple of plantains and some shreds of lawn. Which is how of course it should be, in my ideal northern city. Trees kept to the minimum, no parks, no open spaces. And Leeds is almost completely free of green living things, until, that is, you get right out of town to places like Roundhay Park and Temple Newsam, which, being in the countryside, can afford to show a leaf or two.

And yet, Leeds promotes itself as the greenest city in England, sustaining this claim on the basis of a technical interpretation of 'city' (and 'green' for that matter). The dodge is that Roundhay Park (a large park with lakes), Temple Newsam (a Tudor-Jacobean mansion with a large park) and something called Tropical World (a tropical paradise just off the A58) are all owned by the city and are tended by it on an annual budget of £7 million. So they're Leeds' bits of greenery and indeed, they comprise the largest acreage of parkland forest and wilderness owned by an English city; but they're nowhere near the Town Hall, the Corn Exchange, the headquarters of the *Yorkshire Post*, the Civic Hall – anything, in fact, to do with Leeds.

This doesn't stop the bloke in charge of Leeds' parkland from mouthing off in interviews that 'Harrogate's got bugger all compared with us, unless you particularly want fairy lights in trees.' Harrogate is *littered* with greenstuff, including two hundred acres of grassiness called the Stray, right in the middle of town. Walsall's got more greenery than Leeds. Then again, Leeds council actually persuaded Harry Ramsden's universal fish and chip emporium to fork out £50,000 in sponsorship money for the Leeds Harry Ramsden Heather Garden, so perhaps there's more to this than meets the eye. Waddington's, the Leeds company which makes the

Monopoly game, was also involved in negotiations to
sponsor a Monopoly garden, although nothing seems to
have come of that, yet. I have to say that as a manifestation
of civic sensibility, pitching yourself as the greenest city in
England takes quite a lot of beating, especially if nearly all
your greenery is at least five miles from the city centre. But
then town halls and ludicrous claims are the stuff of civic self-
regard.

Oh, and the local paper. Now, this did surprise me – did you
know that the *Yorkshire Post* ('The Country's Biggest-Selling
Regional Morning Newspaper'), printed in Wellington
Road, Leeds, is actually not at all bad? It gave me quite
a turn to find myself reading a provincial newspaper
unselfconsciously and with genuine interest, but somehow,
the *Post* manages to juggle the national, regional and
international components of the day's news in a surprisingly
confident and grown-up way. It even boasts Austin Mitchell
as a correspondent, instead of the usual blight of correspon-
dents such as Norman Kelthorpe or Jean Clueless.

  The *Evening Post* plays it a little more downmarket,
drifting dangerously on the tide towards the rocks of
provincial rubbish from time to time (SPEAR DANCE WEL-
COME FOR LEEDS LAWYER; 'I'M NO MONSTER' – AXED
CABBIE), but usually stays just the right side of asininity.
And the newsstand headlines around Leeds are amazingly
resonant for such a matter-of-fact part of the world. RE-
VENGE OF TOP LEEDS POLICEMAN'S WIFE was one, getting
in just about everything you could want from a domestic
story that didn't involve politics; while LEEDS BINMEN
SABOTAGE CLAIM was just bizarre.

I ended up in a pub. Being a northern pub rather than a
London pub, its Victorian trappings were probably genuinely old, rather than fresh from the offices of a Covent Garden
design consultancy. The seats were scuffed and faded, the

brass was worn smooth on the counter, the wallpaper was filthy, the appurtenances of modern life (some whiskery loudspeakers for the piped music; a weary-looking cigarette machine) looked tacked-on. The customers, furthermore, were obviously a bit touch-and-go about such things as shaving regularly and buttoning their flies.

It was my last night in the North. I thought, why go on? Why flog myself on to another northern experience, when this one has everything I've ever wanted from the North? At least, if not everything, then as much as I ever felt like having.

I was still a bit doubtful about Yorkshiremen, mark you, about the closed-off quality they seemed to display – a reluctance to give much away, which left me feeling that I was peering in at them from the outside. I suppose the fact was that they were real Yorkshire people in their natural habitat, not showing off for the cameras Down South. They were quieter, off-duty (as it might be), and not much inclined to lay on the Yorkshire cod ('Tha's nivver took owt wi'owt tha teks summat, as we say in Tadhuddersley') to each other. In fact, the best Yorkshire cod I could find was some geezer shouting 'You're right stupid, you are' into a dotard's ear outside the Town Hall, because he had parked a car over the open-air chessboard. And if, on the one hand, this made them seem more like real people, on the other, it made them seem very slightly boring. I would guess, for instance, that the likelihood of finding a witty Yorkshireman is about the same as that of finding a funny Scotsman. This, of course, is considerably greater than the likelihood of finding a musical joke of any nationality that actually makes you laugh, but it's still small.

In fact, I think I found Leeds itself slightly boring. Perhaps it was the spirit of the place: Priestley (not the best person to cite in the circumstances, perhaps) compared Bradford and Leeds and dismissed Leeds in a line as 'More dismal and less interesting.' Even Beresford and Jones' hardback nail-biter *Leeds And Its Region* is overwhelmed from time to time by Leeds' apparent lack of zest: 'The early attainment of pre-eminence by Leeds,' quip Beresford and Jones, 'still requires adequate explanation.'

Was it boring because it didn't seem to have enough immigrants? Like Manchester and Bradford, textiles and clothing drew large numbers of Jewish immigrants to Leeds in the nineteenth century; although by the 1930s, Priestley noted that 'This Jewish element seemed to be far more in evidence before the war than it is now.' And after the Second World War, there doesn't seem to have been quite the same Asian influx as in Bradford. One misses that vague sense of drama. Are they just boring people in Leeds? Leeds has two historically important eccentrics, neither of whom would have caused so much as an eyebrow to be raised in Lancashire: T.S. Kennedy, who was a Victorian traveller and lived in a house designed by Pugin; and Robert Arthington, a millionaire who lived like a hermit in one room of his mansion in Headingley. They're so down to earth in the West Riding.

Or was it the banality of perfection – think of Grace Kelly, Mozart, Henry James, all of them flawless in their way and all in my opinion as dull as ditchwater – which took the edge off things? Was it that sense of let-down you feel in the face of the unimprovable which made my eyelids droop? Was mad Manchester really the Grail and I'd missed it? Or Blackpool? Or Tyneside? Was Leeds just too neat?

I sat there with my pint of mild and bitter, feeling that the time had come to jack it in. At the table next to me, a large man in black was shouting his head off to a couple of female friends. Their conversation overwhelmed me. It seemed to swirl around some central theme, smoggily, without ever quite getting to a point that I could make sense of.

'That's the trooble with the police,' said the large man in black. 'I'd a told 'im to fook off.'

One of his women friends replied, 'I thought 'e were drunk. There's no tellin' what 'e'll do if 'e's effin' drunk.'

'I'd a told 'im to fook off.'

Was there a drunk policeman? How do you tell a drunk policeman to fuck off, exactly?

'Well, it's no use when 'e's in that mood,' said the woman, folding her arms.

This, for no reason that I could fathom, enraged the large man in black. He banged his glass down and started gesticulating with the flat of his hand.

'Fookin' 'ell!' he said. 'I've fookin' 'ad it up to fookin' 'ere! Fookin' John said 'e was fookin' mad!'

So the other woman companion took a thoughtful sip of her small Guinness and said, 'He's got this aversion to bald men.'

This seemed to pacify the large, gesticulating man in black. He subsided and muttered a bit into his pint.

On the other side of this little mob, there was a senile old girl, straight out of Alan Bennett central casting, short of both teeth and brain cells. She was levered into her seat by a middle-aged woman who said, 'You sit 'ere, Mammy,' before the middle-aged woman went off to the bar to get something short and warming. Mammy sat and stared ahead of her, talking quietly to herself, until a look of horrified disgust gradually settled on her features, as she tuned effortfully in to the conversation happening beside her. Every time the big fellow in black came out with a 'fook', she winced a little and said something under her breath; and every time he banged his glass down on the table to emphasise a point, she lifted an inch or so into the air. Eventually, her daughter came back with the small glass of something.

'Take me away from here,' hissed Mammy. 'Put me in another chair. Not here.'

The whiskery loudspeakers started to play the Inkspots, of all people. I drifted into a beery reverie.

* * *

At least, I told myself, I now knew *something* about the North.
I knew about railway stations and hotels and city centres
and pubs. I had seen some interesting sights – none of them
in any of the municipal art galleries or museums, but then
that in itself was worth remarking on. I felt I had a handle on
the place, something I never had before.

The danger was that I had turned into a North connoisseur – or rather, a North connoisseur whose connoisseurship
was founded on fleetingly formed prejudices and basic pig-
ignorance. Whenever a northern voice now crops up on the
radio or television, for example, I twiddle my thumbs and
purse my lips and deliberate and pronounce on its place of
origin, usually completely inaccurately. 'Ah yes,' I say, as a
weatherman gives me the lowdown on my tightening
isobars, 'Lancashire. West Lancashire. Or possibly Derbyshire. Nottingham, maybe. Certainly not Yorkshire, that's
for sure. Certainly not North Yorkshire. Definitely not the
North East, I'd stake my life on it,' and so on, until my wife,
driven to distraction by these ramblings, hits me.

The same thing happens when I learn of someone's place
of birth. 'Aha, a Lancastrian,' I begin. 'Strange, tortured
people, full of a curious intermingling of greatness and
abominable decline, a rawness, an uncouthness about
them, tempered with a subversive and genuinely original
sense of humour,' and on and on I go. In a horribly real way,
all I've done is subdivide my original big prejudice (the
North is strange and ghastly) into many smaller, but equally
untenable, prejudices concerning regional variations within
the North. Then again, this is in many ways what passes for
knowledge nowadays, so perhaps I should just make the
most of it. It has brought me a small amount of kudos round
the meal table, but not quite enough to put me in the
category of Britain's Ten Most Invitable Men To Dinner.

Equally, I still can't answer any of the big questions people
like to throw at me when the subject of the North comes up

(or when I laboriously jemmy it into the conversation). Is there really a North–South divide? they ask, and I immediately answer that of course there is. The simplest way to find out if you're in the North or not is to see what the temperature is. Cold for the time of year? You're probably in the North. Of course there's a North–South divide.

Anything more complicated than that, though, and I start to lose myself in formless ruminations. There are all sorts of statistical North–South divides concerning (*inter alia*) the number of chips people eat, the number of people living in official poverty, life expectancy, the number of pigeons kept, birth rate, teenage delinquency, geriatric delinquency (very big in Bournemouth), all aspects of human and animal life. But these divides also sever the South East of England from Wales; and the North West from the West Country; and the Midlands from East Anglia. There are divides wherever you look. London alone has enough divides to keep the Adam Smith Institute busy for months. But is there an overwhelming sense that you've crossed some sort of clear, plainly defined Mason-Dixon line once you go Up There?

Well, is there a sense *anywhere* in England, nowadays, that you've moved from one place to another? Let's face it, the English as a nation are incompetent and slovenly beyond words when it comes to defining and preserving their national character, so it's not surprising that any regional distinctiveness within that Englishness is frequently reduced to nothing more than a few tatty monuments and a rump of historically-minded bores who try and hang on to whatever once made their home town special.

What is England, really? If you want to be brutal about it, England is shopping malls, staggeringly thick-witted and insensitive road schemes, lousy architecture, supermarkets, theme pubs and crowds of people wandering around, looking puzzled and disgruntled, dressed in the kind of clothing Poles normally wear. North to South, you find the same chainstores, the same eateries, the same cretinous planning fuck-ups. Only the names of the breweries change, while the road signs sometimes have different numbers on them. In a deeply depressing way, Ted, the fag-smoking lorry driver from chapter one of *The Good Companions*, was ahead of his time when he observed, 'Nothing in it. Been all over, Manchester, Liverpool, Newcastle, Leicester, Coventry, even taken it to London twice. Dozens o' smaller places. All over. Nothing in it. Get sick of it. Same old carry-on every time. Places all alike when you come to know 'em.'

And yet you don't have to be neurotically sensitive to any change in your surroundings to spot that the North *is* different, in all the ways that I've been drivelling on about. The truth is that the North divides itself into countless little autonomous units, all very slightly different from each other – despite the overwhelming sameness of the big English picture – and what happens when a southerner like me goes North is that he realises the frightful, limitless scope of a challenge like that of getting to grips with northernness.

I swilled my mild and bitter. The Inkspots had gone and now, even more amazingly, the loudspeakers were playing Cab Calloway, who was the last person I thought I'd hear in Yorkshire, with the possible exception of Slim Gaillard. The point is, I muttered to myself like any sad old git in a pub in Leeds at nine o'clock at night on his own, would I want to live here? The answer, plainly is *no*, not in Leeds, not Manchester, not anywhere, with the possible exception of Hexham, where I feel I might make a go of it until, probably, the first of October, when I would turn a pale blue and die of hypothermia.

Of course, I wouldn't want to live in Wales, the West Country, Norwich or Southampton, either, so this isn't just anti-North bigotry speaking. In fact, I don't think I could live anywhere except the suburbs of London, not least because if I were to go and live anywhere else, I would never be accepted as *one of them*.

This is a distinction which bugs me. Why is it that northerners can come to London in order to lead richer and more fulfilling lives and be entitled to call themselves Londoners if they want to ('Well, I've been in Crouch End for so long, I feel part of the place now') while at the same time retaining whatever vestiges of northernness they feel like holding on to; whereas a Londoner who moves to, say, Manchester, will never be deemed a Mancunian – nor will his children, nor his children's children? So far as I can see, you'd have to pass through about seven generations before your family was accepted as being even faintly northern. But down here, we welcome northerners with open arms and call them our own dear cockney brothers. I realise that this kind of exclusivity is characteristic of all the provinces, but it rankles when I think of all the Yorkshiremen and women, Lancastrians and Tynesiders who are living here and cheerfully paying our inflated levels of Council Tax and using our execrable public transport and having it, frankly, both ways.

Still. A line must be drawn. It was past nine, now. I looked in my wallet to make sure I still had my ticket to London and finished my beer. Outside, as it says in novels, it was raining. The streets of Leeds were busy with people emerging from the City Varieties Theatre (home to *The Good Old Days*) and the Grand Theatre (home to a Benjamin Britten opera called *Gloriana*). The man in black at the table next to me had subsided and was now cracking off-colour jokes to the two women, who both seemed amazingly tolerant of him. Perhaps they were his sisters. I folded my copy of the *Yorkshire Evening Post*. Time, I thought, for one last curry.

TRAVELS WITH MY BRIEFCASE

Peter Biddlecombe

It is a great truth of modern life that businessmen are today the world's most accomplished travellers. Like Marco Polo, the business traveller has a purpose; he is a man with a mission. Not for him a simple trawl through tourist hell – his experiences are authentic, driven by career rather than courier. Consequently, the adventurous nature of such trips is never forced – the Hindu Kush, Amazonian jungle or Kalahari hold no fears for those who have faced the Tokyo underground in rush hour.

In *Travels with my Briefcase* Peter Biddlecombe introduces us to the world of the business traveller, stumbling across the humorous and the bizarre in the most unexpected places – like Switzerland – and generally proving that you don't have to be a student, aesthete or one-eyed skate-boarder to experience the thrill and excitement of exploring the world.

'This astonishing book is all highlights, and incident on every page'
Daily Mail

'The funniest, yet most serious, book about contemporary Africa on the market'
Guardian

ABACUS
0 349 10583 9

BEYOND THE PYRAMIDS

Douglas Kennedy

Beyond the Pyramids is a delightful wry chronicle of travels through a country of incongruity – an Egypt encompassing a diversity of cultural influences which often belies its image of 'archaelogical theme park'.

With an acute eye for the unusual, the interesting and the plain absurd, Douglas Kennedy takes us on a continually surprising tour beyond beyond the pyramids, to a place where Bedouin watch American television in an oasis; where monks in the desert are computer-literate; and where an entire community of Cairo's poor have set up home in a cemetery.

'He has a gift for sliding in and out of diverse communities and recording his impressions entertainingly . . . This is the first book of a born traveller'
Guardian

'Douglas Kennedy takes on modern Egypt with a vigour uncommon in travel writing'
The Times

'Kennedy writes with clarity and isn't scared of sticking the knife in, yet his criticisms are underlined with concern, not contempt'
Time Out

ABACUS
0 349 10607 X

Now you can order superb titles directly from Abacus

☐ French Lessons in Africa	Peter Biddlecombe	£7.99
☐ Travels with my Briefcase	Peter Biddlecombe	£7.99
☐ The Lost Continent	Bill Bryson	£6.99
☐ Beyond the Pyramids	Douglas Kennedy	£6.99
☐ Malaria Dreams	Stuart Stevens	£6.99

Please allow for postage and packing: **Free UK delivery**.
Europe; add 25% of retail price; Rest of World; 45% of retail price.

To order any of the above or any other Abacus titles, please call our
credit card orderline or fill in this coupon and send/fax it to:

Abacus, 250 Western Avenue, London, W3 6XZ, UK.
Fax 0181 324 5678   Telephone 0181 324 5517

☐ I enclose a UK bank cheque made payable to Abacus for £ ....

☐ Please charge £.............. to my Access, Visa, Delta, Switch Card No.

☐☐☐☐☐☐☐☐☐☐☐☐☐☐☐☐☐☐☐

Expiry Date ☐☐☐☐   Switch Issue No.   ☐☐

NAME (Block letters please) ....

ADDRESS ....

....

....

Postcode ....Telephone ....

Signature ....

Please allow 28 days for delivery within the UK. Offer subject to price and availability.

Please do not send any further mailings from companies carefully selected by Abacus ☐